Reviewed by M. Perce
American Historical ⟨...⟩ y,
1978), 173.

IRELAND IN THE AGE OF THE TUDORS

IRELAND IN THE AGE OF THE TUDORS

THE DESTRUCTION OF HIBERNO-NORMAN CIVILIZATION

R. DUDLEY EDWARDS

CROOM HELM LONDON

BARNES & NOBLE BOOKS NEW YORK
(a division of Harper & Row Publishers, Inc.)

© 1977 R. Dudley Edwards

Croom Helm Ltd, 2—10 St John's Road, London SW11

ISBN 0-85664-454-2

Published in the USA 1977 by
Harper & Row Publishers, Inc.
Barnes & Noble Import Division

ISBN 0-06-491903-X

Printed and bound in Great Britain by
REDWOOD BURN LIMITED
Trowbridge & Esher

CONTENTS

ABBREVIATIONS

Anal.Hib.	Analecta Hibernica
Arch.Hib.	Archivium Hibernicum
Bull.Inst.Hist.Res.	Bulletin of the Institute of Historical Research
Cal.S.P.Ire.	Calendar of State Papers relating to Ireland
Cal.S.P.Sp.	Calendar of State Papers relating to Spain
Cork Hist.Soc.Jn.	Journal of the Cork Historical and Archaeological Society
EHR	English Historical Review
HMC	Historical Manuscripts Commission
IHS	Irish Historical Studies
IMC	Irish Manuscripts Commission
Journ.R.S.A.I.	Journal of the Royal Society of Antiquaries of Ireland
L. & P.Hen.VIII	Letters and Papers, foreign and domestic, of the reign of Henry VIII
NLI	National Library of Ireland
PRO	Public Record Office, London
Proc.Ir.Cath.Hist.Comm.	Proceedings of the Irish Catholic Historical Committee
PROI	Public Record Office of Ireland
PRONI	Public Record Office of Northern Ireland
R.I.A. Proc.	Proceedings of the Royal Irish Academy
S.P.Hen.VIII	State Papers, Henry VIII
Statutes (1786)	The Statutes at large, passed in the Parliaments held in Ireland...

TO RUTH

1. Places mentioned in the text

O'Doherty

MacSweeney

MacSweeney

O'Donnell

MacDonnell
McQuillan
O'gormley

O'Cahan

O'Neill
Clanaboy
McCann
McCartan
O'Hanlon

Earldom
of
Ulster
McGuinness

O'NEILL

O'Donnelly

Barret

Burke

O'Dowd

O'Connor

O'Hara McKeon Maguire

MacDonagh

O'Reilly

MacMahon

Plunket

Preston

O'Malley

O'Gara MacDermot

O'Farrell

Costello O'Connor
Don

Nangle
Barnewall

St.Laurence

O'Flaherty

O'Kelly

Bermingham
O'Connor

Bermingham
Blake

Burke

O'Madden

O'Carroll

O'Molloy
Dempsey

O'Dunn

Earldom
of
Kildare
Fitzgerald

O'More

O'Toole

O'Byrne

O'Hanrahan

O'Brien

MacNamara

O'Kennedy McGilpatrick

Butler
of
Ormond

MacMurrogh

MacMahon

Burke

Fitzmaurice

Fitzgerald

MacGibbon
Earldom Roche
of Desmond

Fitzgerald

Power

Mac Carthy
Mor

O'Sullivan

O'Sullivan

Mac-
Carthy

Barry

O'Driscoll

W.Bromage

Miles 50   100   Km   80   160

2. Families

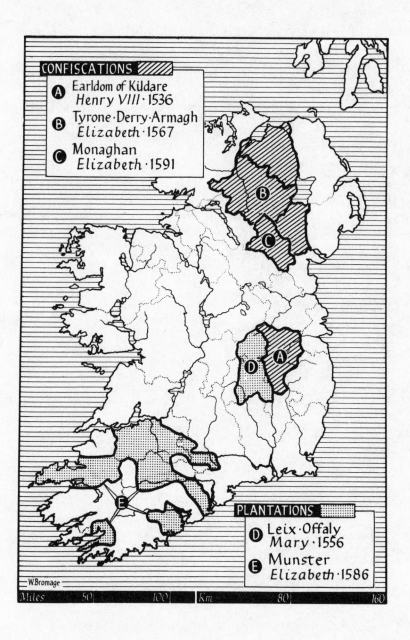

CONFISCATIONS

A Earldom of Kildare
Henry VIII · 1536

B Tyrone · Derry · Armagh
Elizabeth · 1567

C Monaghan
Elizabeth · 1591

PLANTATIONS

D Leix · Offaly
Mary · 1556

E Munster
Elizabeth · 1586

W.Bromage

Miles 50 100 Km 80 160

3. Tudor Plantations and Confiscations

PREFACE

This book is the product of forty years studying Irish history. The period under examination is a watershed, marking the virtual end of the Middle Ages in Ireland and in many ways the beginning of modern history. We can clearly see the beginning, in this period, of the modern state in Ireland.

The approach is necessarily a narrative one and the main stress is on political aspects. When the author wrote *Church and State in Tudor Ireland* he was beginning to realize that a sound understanding of politics was the essential basis for any analysis of Irish history. After completing the *New History of Ireland* he felt more sure of this. Almost inevitably this has coloured his approach to the present volume.

The author is indebted to many institutions and to many people in his efforts to become better acquainted with sixteenth-century Ireland. He is particularly indebted to the Public Record Offices of Ireland, of Northern Ireland, of England, and of Scotland; to the House of Lords Record Office; the Historical Manuscripts Commission, including the National Register of Archives; and to the Irish Manuscripts Commission. Among many libraries, he is most grateful to University College Dublin, Trinity College Dublin, the National Library of Ireland, the Royal Irish Academy, and Maynooth College Library; to the British Museum, the University of London, the Bodleian Library, Oxford, Cambridge University Library, and the Institute of Historical Research; to the Library of Congress, the Folger-Shakespeare Library, Washington, the Newberry Library, Chicago, and the Henry E. Huntington Library, San Marino, California. To the many custodians in these institutions, both past and present, the author expresses his sincere thanks.

The author wishes to record his indebtedness particularly to those who have materially clarified our knowledge of office-holders in Ireland, most of whom are listed in the second edition of the Royal Historical Society's *Handbook of British Chronology* (1961). In this connection it is to be noted that the office of Viceroy, or Chief Governor, in the period covered by this book was held by a variety of titles. The Lieutenant, sometimes the King's Lieutenant or the Lord Lieutenant, was accorded the most extensive powers, perhaps qualified by the need to consult others. The Deputy, or Lord Deputy, the most usual title, had more restrictive instructions involving consultations with the

Council. The Justices, or Lords Justices, usually held temporary offices in the absence of the Lieutenant or Deputy, sometimes after election by the Council in Ireland on a Viceroy's decease.

The author is greatly conscious of the co-operation of University College Dublin which, in association with his teaching of archival studies, has facilitated the establishment of the archives section of the Department of Modern Irish History at 82 St Stephen's Green. The writing of the present book has been a direct outcome of archival thinking and teaching there, in which the author's work has largely depended upon the effective co-operation and determination of Miss Deirdre McMahon, who has special responsibility for historical collections. The advice of other colleagues in this archives section, including Miss Kerry Holland and Miss Orla Whelan, has been particularly important. No Acknowledgements would be complete without the inclusion of the author's indebtedness to his wife, to his children and grandchildren, to his son-in-law John Mattock and to John Collis, to his academic colleagues and friends, and to his students, who have done so much, and suffered so much, in the creation of this book.

Dublin,
August 1974   R. DUDLEY EDWARDS

INTRODUCTION

The Kingdom of Ireland

When the Anglo-Normans reached Ireland, they became involved in the great inter-provincial struggles between several dynasties who were ambitious to extend their kingdoms and, if possible, to establish a central monarchy. Historians now realize that, in fact, no settled kingdom of Ireland existed until in 1541 an Irish parliament recognized Henry VIII as king of Ireland.[1] In the pre-Norman period, it was customary to concede to some outstanding provincial king the title of *high king*. In particular, reverence for the historic centre of Tara, at which religious festivals were held by kings in the pre-Christian period, often led to the proclamation of the king who presided at these ceremonies as High King of Ireland. But it is important to remember that kingship in Ireland before the Normans was not associated with ownership of land. The king was the leader of his people on all public occasions. The association of kingship with ownership of the land does not emerge until after the Anglo-Norman invasion when kings of England claimed, with papal sanction, to be lords of Ireland.[2]

The Church and Royal Patronage

The political rivalry of the kings was a phenomenon of Irish society as far back as the pre-Christian period. Since Ireland had not become part of the Roman Empire, it did not provide the organizational system to which the Christian Church had become adjusted in much of western Europe, including much of the neighbouring island of Britain. The Church accordingly developed in Ireland under the patronage of the kings. This association inevitably presented major problems if the Church's spiritual ethos was not to be subordinated to political expedient. Irish rulers had been traditionally regarded as conquering heroes descended from the pre-Christian Gaelic gods, and so there emerged a cult of great saints in Ireland, such as Patrick, Columcille, and Brigid, around whom numerous religious establishments coagulated and whose prestige became the subject of the political rivalries of the kings.[3] From the seventh century, the isolation of the Irish Christian community from the Roman world began to be broken, and archaic traditions in ecclesiastical matters were modified through the impact of western European monastic leaders and some of the

Roman pontiffs.[4]

Vikings and Normans

The Viking impact elsewhere in western Europe was no more pronounced
than in Ireland. Irish rural society suffered an upheaval as Viking fleets
appeared on Irish coasts and penetrated through the rivers and inland
lakes to the great and wealthy monastic centres of the Christian
communities. Once the Northmen had settled and organized port towns,
there developed an urban society which the rural kings sought to
dominate – sometimes successfully. By the eleventh century, the
Vikings had been largely contained and even christianized, though they
preferred to establish their church contacts with Canterbury, which was
by then under the reforming influence of the Cistercian order and the
reformed papacy. In the conflicts between rival Irish provincial rulers
in the eleventh and twelfth centuries, the Viking fleets of Dublin and
the western isles of Scotland and the influence of the church reform
movement played a decisive part in the emergence of the O'Connor
kings of Connacht – Turlough and Rory successively – who claimed
the high kingship. On the eve of the arrival of the Anglo-Normans, it
appeared that the O'Connor threat from the west which had successfully
dominated the north might overwhelm the eastern and southern
provincial kingdoms. These latter, under English influence, had adopted
a more prosperous style of life in which the traders of Bristol played
such a dominant part that they secured the city of Dublin from Henry
II in 1172 after his successful invasion of Ireland.

The Anglo-Norman invasion was regarded by the Irish Christian
clergy as a consequence of God's displeasure with the Irish people for
becoming involved in the slave trade.[5] The clergy had reason to believe
that the papacy favoured the enterprise of Henry II in Ireland, but the
reference to slavery reinforces the evidence that in the east and south
society was becoming more affluent through the increased employment
of a servile element in society. When Rory O'Connor, the high king
and king of Connacht, submitted to Henry II, as recorded in the agreement made at Windsor in 1175 between his representatives and those
of Henry II, he accepted the Angevin monarch as Lord of Ireland,
ruler of the Hiberno-Scandinavian towns and of the Norman lordships
of Meath and of Leinster. He accepted a situation in which he became,
as the sworn client of Henry II, king of Connacht, high king among the
Irish kings elsewhere, and the responsible authority for the return to
the lands conquered by the Anglo-Normans of the inhabitants who had
fled from them. The servile element in Irish society against which the

clergy had spoken out was to continue under Anglo-Norman auspices.[6]

Gaelic Society

The organization of Gaelic society had been based upon a structure whereby the ruling class, with the assistance of the professional occupations, maintained their authority in their own territories by the acceptance of a legal principle under which they were regarded as sacred, the rest of the population being virtually servile in status.[7] In this relatively primitive society, in which prosperity depended on cattle, the rivalries between neighbouring kings and peoples largely consisted in successive cattle raids which were limited in their destructiveness until a more professional military ethos emerged with the ninth-century Scandinavian invasions. On a higher level of civilization, ecclesiastical communities in their turn became involved in the destruction and society became more militarily orientated. This trend was exacerbated after twelfth-century Norman lords commenced carving out their virtually independent jurisdictions over which the king of England, although nominally overlord of Ireland, had little real power. It was in this environment that by the thirteenth century a Hiberno-Norman society had developed in the east and south, and in a more limited way in the west and north. The influence of the English king, exercised through a primitive central bureaucracy established at Dublin, was never as strong in these latter areas as in the former, where it proved effective in developing a system very comparable to that which existed in the other parts of the Angevin empire.[8]

Conflicts of Power

The weakness of the Irish situation in medieval times was largely due to the conflicting interests of royal power, feudal individualism, and Gaelic regional resistance to the extension of Norman influence. It has been customary to visualize a Gaelic resurgence after the late thirteenth century, but it is important to avoid the error of seeing this as a simple struggle of Irish nationalism against English domination. The first phase of the Anglo-Norman conquest was hardly different to what operated in the Scandinavian period when Gaelic and Viking forces quarrelled, combined, and quarrelled again, with no permanent divisions on a racial basis. Just as the Hebridean lords became involved in conflicts in Ireland and Scotland before the English invaded, so the new Anglo-Norman lordships became involved in rivalries and alliances with their neighbouring Gaelic kings. The collapse of the Angevin empire in the early thirteenth century had its repercussions in these islands. English bureaucracy sustained a serious reverse which weakened the central monarchy during the long minority of Henry III (1216–27). The subsequent attempt to reorganize a more militaristic system under Edward I (1272–1307) weakened the central government in Ireland, as it did elsewhere under the less effective rule of his successor, Edward II (1307–27).[9]

Dilemma of Central Government

The loss of Scotland, which had been conquered under Edward I, accentuated the fears of his son's administrators that Ireland too might become independent, perhaps under a Hiberno-Norman lord like Richard de Burgh, earl of Ulster, lord of Connacht, related by marriage to the new Scottish Bruce dynasty with its many Anglo-French connections. Thus the central government in Dublin alternated in policy between weakening the Anglo-Norman lords and giving way unduly to them when they faced new and threatening Gaelic dynasties throughout the country — occasionally even in the east. By the end of the fourteenth century it is clear that English influence in Ireland was substantially shaken and central government, in an attempt to arrest decay, was reduced to linking itself with the outstanding Norman provincial families.[10] In the early fifteenth century it seemed that the more lively and effective Gaelic lordships would overwhelm their Norman neighbours. The latter, however, successfully withstood these challenges by resisting any attempt by the English government to reassert itself during the renewed rivalry in France of the Hundred Years War. The English monarchy in the moment of victory lost to the forces of regional power. The Wars of the Roses witnessed the eclipse of monarchy at a time when there was yet again a danger of Ireland's following the example of Scotland.

The Papacy

It must not be forgotten that in a special way Ireland was involved with the claims of the pope as a quasi-imperial superior for the English king in his Irish lordship. In many ways, not confined to matters ecclesiastical, the Roman authority either intervened or was expected to do so. Bishops often played as decisive a role as important public officials in situations of political conflict between central and local forces. The Holy See, the first great centralizing power in western Europe since the Roman Empire, was naturally concerned to maintain good relations with the king's Dublin administration as well as with local Gaelic kings and Anglo-Norman lords. Inevitably there were occasions of dispute

regarding succession to the bishoprics and to the abbacies of the great
monastic houses. And while the papacy tended to favour the reforming
policy of the English kings, through which a greater degree of property
was made available for church purposes, it was obliged to resist attempts
to use Rome to strengthen the weakening influence of the monarchy.
Here as elsewhere politics so dominated the situation that the history
of Ireland cannot be placed in its proper historical context until the
political changes have first been considered in detail. Thus the papacy
in medieval Ireland exerted a much more general influence throughout
the whole country than did the English monarchy, except within the
Pale.[11]

Decline of Anglo-Irish Lordship

In 1333, the death of the Brown Earl of Ulster brought about a
situation in which the conflict of central and local interests weakened
the Norman influence and contributed to the expansion of Gaelic lordships. The title of earl of Ulster devolved on descendants of Edward III
in consequence of the marriage of his son Lionel, duke of Clarence, to
the heiress of the de Burgh titles in Connacht, Meath, and Ulster. As a
result of this, the de Burgh territory was fractured into a number of
minor political jurisdictions and the Norman influence in Ulster was
driven east of the Bann. The collateral male de Burghs rejected the
territorial pretensions of the Plantagenets and established virtually
independent lordships in Connacht. To maintain their autonomy, two
collateral lines adopted a hibernicized form of the name – coming to
be known respectively as Upper and Lower MacWilliam. This change in
Connacht, however, was more superficial than real. The Norman
military organization of society was maintained efficiently throughout
the medieval period and the ecclesiastical benefices under Norman
control continued to be more lucrative than those within the Gaelic
spheres of influence.[12] The tenuous administrative connections of
Dublin were also maintained by appointing as royal sheriffs in the west
and north prominent *de facto* landed proprietors, despite their
usurpation of the lands claimed by Clarence and his successors. Concurrently Gaelic lordships became organized around families displacing
the older Gaelic lines as well as the Normans – filling out after the fall
of the earldom of Ulster.[13] Thus the O'Donnells in north-west Ulster
rose to new prominence in place of the O'Gormleys and other outstanding lineages of the early twelfth century.[14] This new political
situation necessitated the provision of genealogies to justify the new
Gaelic lines. Thus, from soon after the Anglo-Norman invasions and

the consequent dispersion of many of the older political groups, a newer historiography is to be seen in the annals and other professional writings designed to further the interests of the new rulers and the professional learned men who kept their records. Once again, political development dictated historic change.[15]

The extent of the economic weakening of the Anglo-Irish lordship is clear from the Statutes of Kilkenny of 1366. This legislation, aiming at the aggressive Gaelic infiltrations, reveals clearly the basic fears of Anglo-Norman civilization.[16] The king's government was obliged to accept such new Norman military leaders as John Bermingham, earl of Louth, for his share in defeating the Bruce invaders.[17] In the same way, earldoms were given to Fitzgeralds and Butlers, whose families had played but a minor role previously, despite what subsequent family historians said to the contrary. This capitulation by the central government coincided with clear testimony that the medieval lordship of the English kings could no longer, as in the past, be compelled to meet the financial demands of the Dublin administration. Again the political changes determined the new patterns in society. In the military history of medieval Ireland, it devolved on the new lordships to defend and protect their peoples with expanded military forces, the maintenance of which permanently restricted the local financial grants to central government.

Gaelic Military Forces

Similarly, the military forces employed in the Gaelic lordships substantially altered the older social and economic organization. Theoretically in Gaelic law, kings exercised no rights of landownership beyond the customary tributes of the fruits of the earth and of the products of the craftsmen. Such tributes, while in theory being still claimed (as is clear from the seventeenth-century recession of O'Neill's rights — *Ceart Ui Neill*), proved in practice less important than the establishment of mercenary troops on sword land, a name applied to territories allocated on their conquest by the Irish kings to their mercenary soldiers. Thus MacSweeney families were established in what is today known as Co. Donegal and there and elsewhere military professional landowners became an additional new phenomenon which the historians honoured by elaborately devising romantic and mythical pedigrees.[18]

Dame Alice Kyteler

The history of medieval Ireland is particularly exposed to anachronistic interpretation in questions connected with religion and nationalism. It is because of the importance of these issues through the centuries that historians in every generation have been up against this difficulty. The primacy of politics is therefore a valuable basis on which to attempt to work out the conflicts of forces and the factors of change. In the realm of law, there was the emergence in the high Middle Ages of the renewed study of Roman law in the West, and it is possible to study here how in Ireland, as elsewhere, political considerations predominated. The western European conflicts between the Empire and the papacy are reflected, as European monarchies in their turn became infected with the Roman imperial tradition. In these circumstances we can see in Ireland the utilization of one law or another to secure the objects of conflicting administrators and rulers.[19] Perhaps a good example of this is afforded by the Kilkenny witchcraft trials of 1325. Dame Alice Kyteler was one of a group of whom several others were flogged or burnt after being accused of witchcraft by Bishop Richard Ledred, an English friar promoted to Ossory. In an age in which the Holy Inquisition was used against heresy and atheism, the bishop, an enthusiastic reformer, found himself frustrated in the investigation of sorcery allegations against Kyteler, who was charged with the death of several others. Ledred became involved in the conflicts in Anglo-Norman Ireland between the rival factions under Edward II. Kyteler was protected from the bishop by royal officials, who in parliament challenged Ledred as an ignorant foreigner, attempting in the Island of Saints to resort to unheard-of ecclesiastical weapons in order to establish his absolute authority in the face of the law of the land. The bishop, thrown into prison when the temporal law was employed against him, never succeeded against Dame Alice. If he did satisfy his own convictions in the processes against her human and animal accomplices, he ultimately found further activities paralysed by the alliance against him of ecclesiastical and royal authorities, against whom he was unable to prevail, even with the Holy See. While the Kyteler case was almost unique in medieval Ireland, it serves to illustrate the way in which the law could be exploited by politics.[20]

The Remonstrance

Concurrently, the court of Pope John XXII was asked to entertain the Remonstrance of the Irish against Anglo-Norman misgovernment and misrule. This document, a product of the age in which Edward II attempted to use the papacy against the Scots and the Irish, alleged numerous instances when royal administrators and feudal military men violated the elementary principles of justice. In its most simple form, the question in Ireland as in Scotland was whether the Holy See should impose extreme sanctions on rebels against the king's authority or whether the king's misgovernment should not be papally condemned. The successful establishment of the Bruce dynasty in Scotland after Bannockburn (1314) probably made it easier for the pope not to regard rebellion in either country against Edward II as heresy. If the papacy successfully avoided this embarrassment, it did not prevent numerous minor English ecclesiastical authorities from denouncing rebels in the strongest terms, thereby providing useful ammunition for subsequent anti-English propagandists in Scotland as in Ireland. There is, however, a much deeper question here. In both Scotland and Ireland, the survival of an older Gaelic tradition maintained the supremacy of political organizations, reinforced by the supernatural and psychological sanctions of the bardic poets. Even against Christianity, these powers still prevailed. Before the church reforms of the twelfth century, the written word might prevail with the Christian community and the canon of the Church come more into line with that in the great Western centres of religion. But a supernatural Gaelic power had become so much attached to the chief books and other reliquaries, that many of them — with their church custodians — were involved in conflicts with the Anglo-Normans. In 1177 such a conflict had occurred in Co. Down with John de Courcy, and resulted in the bringing to Dublin of the ecclesiastical crozier traditionally known as the Bacall Iosa. In such mixed situations, it is to be remembered that the reformers could prevail only by resorting to coercive sanctions which ultimately might react against themselves. In the Gaelic areas, the warrior claims of rulers and dynasties were still being proclaimed, while in the English areas the rule of the king was being enforced by the use of court records and proclamations which created the mentality of a police state. It is a recognized fact that dependence upon the written word weakens the recollection of people accustomed to rely on memory. The heroism of the Gaelic warriors survived the record of an English court order stigmatizing them as felons and rebels, so that those deeds which brought them ignominy in an English sphere, perpetuated the glory of their martial prowess among the Irish. The Remonstrance of John XXII stands as a record of the hatred engendered as the king's power weakened in Ireland. The proceedings against Dame Alice Kyteler set a limit to the extent to which the king's law in Ireland and the pope's could be used together against local interests, Irish as well as Anglo-Norman. In both cases, however unjustified, the officers of the law were brought into contempt for political as well as humanitarian reasons.[21]

Weakness of the English colony

By the fifteenth century it can be said that such conflicting forces had resulted in a stalemate situation in Ireland. The absence of adequate statistical information denies us more than the simplest generalization about the progressive decline of the English colony. Parliamentary enactments make it clear enough that a constant stream of emigrants left Ireland for England and that these were largely from among the king's loyal subjects. Contemporary evidence from sources emanating from England is not quite so precise. In the fifteenth century the increasing English legislation, central and local, against foreigners, is rarely specific as to the origins of the Irish included in that category. To an English record-maker, an Irishman was assumed to mean a resident in Ireland or an immigrant from that country. The subtleties of distinction between loyal subjects and other Irish were rarely recorded. In papal records and university lists, more specific information is sometimes available. It is probable therefore that the Gaelic resurgence was accentuated by a population rise seeping into the English sphere of influence in those areas from whence the migration to England was greatest. Relevant to this was the protest of Chief Justice Topcliffe in the early sixteenth century, that if the papacy were permitted, within walled towns like Wexford, to provide Irish nominees to the exclusion of English local interests, there was no future hope for a civilized way of life in Ireland.[22]

In fact, the Chief Justice had good reason to feel concerned. The Irish upsurge in many instances was possible only through the violent destruction of inadequately manned English centres. The evidence at the beginning of the sixteenth century points to the breakdown of any type of religious activity in places like Tuam and Clonmacnoise.[23] In the weakening of English influence, the occupation of stone churches could have a strategic significance, so that these were often deserted after being repeatedly burnt by opposing forces. The long-term effect of the failure of English government in Ireland contributed to this as the great Anglo-Irish dynasties continued to maintain their military forces by quartering them on the people. Parallel developments, of course, also existed widely in western Europe where no adequate security forces existed to give the civilized elements a sense of stability. So far as Ireland was concerned, the situation was just that much worse, as only by imposing permanently the quartering of their troops on the

English Pale were the Anglo-Norman warrior lords in a position to undertake the king's government. When contemporaries referred to them as being more Irish than the Irish themselves, it is because of their adoption of the Irish security system, 'spend me and defend me'.

Nationalism

Irish historians have tended to see the emergence of nationalism even as early as the Middle Ages. It is not unreasonable to regard as corroborative evidence suggesting that nationalism, perhaps only in a cultural way, clearly existed in Ireland from a very early period, to judge by the common tendency to dismiss the descendants of the invaders, though native-born, as foreigners. When the development of nationalism elsewhere in western Europe is under consideration, the student is most happy in concentrating on the history of the great dynasties who transmitted a political tradition down the centuries before the French Revolution. There is of course nothing comparable to this in Ireland. There survive myths and legends about pre-Norman heroes, kings, and saints, but only occasionally do post-Norman personalities like the Great Earl of Kildare gain a permanent place in folklore. The historians of the leading families, Norman as well as Irish, increasingly interested themselves in the fortunes of their great houses from the late Middle Ages, but were never successful in permanently convincing the Irish people generally that their future fortunes were bound up with those of any particular dynasty.[24] Perhaps this is the chief reason why Hiberno-Norman civilization was unable to stand up to the stresses of the sixteenth century.

Notes

1. W. L. Warren, 'The Interpretation of twelfth century Irish history', *Historical Studies* VII (1969); A. J. Otway-Ruthven, *A History of Medieval Ireland* (1968).
2. F. J. Byrne, *Irish Kings and High-Kings* (1973).
3. Kathleen Hughes, *The Church in Early Irish Society* (1966); *Early Christian Ireland: an introduction to the sources* (1972); J. F. Kenney, *The Sources for the Early History of Ireland* (New York, 1929). F. O' Briain, 'The Expansion of Irish Christianity to 1200: an historiographical survey', *IHS* III (1943), 241, IV (1944), 131.
4. D. A. Binchy, 'The Passing of the old order', in *Proc. International Congress of Celtic Studies, Dublin 1959* ed. B. Ó Cuív (1962).
5. J. F. O'Doherty, 'The Anglo-Norman invasion, 1167–71', *IHS* I (1938–39), 154–7.
6. E. Curtis, 'Rental of the manor of Lisronagh, 1333, and notes on "betagh" tenure in medieval Ireland', *R.I.A. Proc.* XLIII (1935–37).

7. F. J. Byrne, 'Senchas : the nature of Gaelic historical tradition', *Historical Studies* IX (1974).

8. H. G. Richardson and G. O. Sayles, *The Administration of Ireland, 1172–1377* (IMC, 1963).

9. G. J. Hand, *English Law in Ireland, 1290–1324* (Cambridge, 1967); J. F. Lydon, *The Lordship of Ireland in the Middle Ages* (Dublin, 1972).

10. E. Curtis, *Richard II in Ireland, 1394–95, and Submissions of the Irish Chiefs* (Oxford, 1927); A. Tuck, 'Anglo-Irish relations, 1382–1393', *R.I.A. Proc.* LXIX (1970).

11. R. D. Edwards, 'The kings of England and papal provisions in fifteenth century Ireland', *Medieval Studies presented to Aubrey Gwynn S. J.* (Dublin, 1961); M. P. Sheehy, *Pontificia Hibernica : medieval papal chancery documents concerning Ireland, 640–1261,* 2 vols. (Dublin, 1962–65).

12. K. W. Nicholls, 'Rectory, vicarage and parish in the western Irish dioceses', *Journ. R.S.A.I.* CI (1971), 53–84.

13. D. B. Quinn, 'Anglo-Irish local government, 1485–1534', *IHS* I (1938–39), 354–81.

14. K. W. Nicholls, *Gaelic and Gaelicised Ireland in the Middle Ages* (Dublin, 1972), ch. 7.

15. Byrne, art. cit.

16. H. G. Richardson and G. O. Sayles, *The Irish Parliament in the Middle Ages* (Philadelphia,1952), 92ff.

17. Otway-Ruthven, op. cit., 239ff.

18. G. A. Hayes-McCoy, *Scots Mercenary Forces in Ireland* (1937), 24ff.

19. Hand, op.cit.

20. *Proceedings against Dame Alice Kyteler for sorcery*, ed. T. Wright (Camden Soc., 1843).

21. R. Frame, 'The Justiciar and the murder of the MacMurroughs in 1282', *IHS* XVIII (1972), 223–30.

22. F. E. Ball, *The Judges in Ireland, 1221–1921*, I (New York, 1927), 112–13.

23. For a different view see B. Bradshaw, *The Dissolution of the Religious Orders in Ireland under Henry VIII* (Cambridge, 1974), Introduction. Fr Bradshaw follows here the views of Prof. F. X. Martin in his article 'The Observant movement in Ireland', *Proc. Irish Cath.Hist.Comm.* (1960).

24. Poets like Tadhg Dall O h-Uiginn (edited by Eleanor Knott for the Irish Texts Society, 1920) might praise a patron like O'Donnell as rightful king of Ireland, a view not acceptable elsewhere.

1   PROLOGUE 1450–1513

The Anglo-Irish Colony c. 1450

In the mid-fifteenth century, western Europe saw many great lords
placing themselves in military opposition to centralizing dynastic rulers.
This was particularly marked in France and in England, where the very
future of the dynasties seemed threatened. The Hundred Years War had
created a state of chaos and after that war between these two countries
came to an end, continuing rivalries were exploited by the rulers of each
against the other.[1]

In England, under the Lancastrians, the impetus of government was
slowing down. The defeats in France and the weakening of the English
power in Ireland so affected the prestige of the monarchy that it seems
as if the Wars of the Roses would have broken out in any case without
the additional impulse of the king's insufficiency. In an age when martial
men were still regarded with general admiration, the inadequacy of
Henry VI (1422–61) inevitably affected his prestige and left him
dominated by more positive personalities.[2]

In the decaying realms of the king, in Ireland as in France, the
necessity for a military viceroy seemed obvious to the communities
which still looked to Henry VI. In Ireland the persistence of this
admiration for war leaders seems almost pathetic, as one after another of
the outstanding characters fail to resolve the problems of state.[3]

Since the time of Richard II (1377–99), an effort had been made to
strengthen the power of the king by linking it with the great political
rulers in the provinces. A new phenomenon was to emerge in the course
of the fifteenth century, as the powerful Anglo-Irish magnates became
weakened and tended to be replaced by new effective Gaelic lordships
whose significance in the preceding centuries had been minimal. Only
on the eve of the Tudor period, however, did the English community in
Ireland become conscious that it was in danger of total extinction.
This state of alarm led persistently throughout the Lancastrian period to
appeals to the king to send over some conquering hero as a leader;
requests which increasingly proclaimed the weakness of a beleaguered
community ever more vulnerable to invading Irish chieftains. The
financial embarrassment of the king's government right through this
period accentuated the difficulties. The custom arose of financing
military expeditions by putting the unappropriated Irish revenue

entirely at the viceroy's disposal. Whatever force was made available to him in England was ultimately added to the colony's subsistence problems as each representative of the king in turn accumulated debts resulting from the failure of the English exchequer to pay him. By the middle of the century it was clear that the drainage from the English community had increased as each successive military governor was sent over to liberate them.[4]

Richard, Duke of York

The career of Richard, duke of York, who took up residence as royal viceroy in July 1449, can well illustrate these difficulties. As the descendant of former earls of Ulster and lords of Connacht and of lordships in Meath and Leinster, York's interest in Ireland was obvious. As a former king's representative in France and because of his readiness to undertake protective military movements in Ireland he was a particularly attractive choice. Yet having recruited a substantial English following, he found himself heavily encumbered with debt and in September 1450 returned to England, alleging that the loss of Ireland might result if he remained there without adequate resources. Admittedly York was prepared to entrust his powers to James Butler, 4th earl of Ormond, whose capacity to raise forces and deploy them proved effective in defending the troubled English communities, in 1451–52. The Wars of the Roses, however, soon involved York, and his personal claim to the throne occupied by the Lancastrians added an additional political dimension in Ireland. In the initial stages the duke's dynastic ambitions apparently gained little support from his fellow magnates. After defeats in the field, his withdrawal to Ireland in 1459 provoked a constitutional crisis in which, to secure him from the London government, the legislative and judicial immunity of Ireland was recognized by the parliament he summoned there. In taking this step, York not merely secured recognition as a quasi-monarch, but also created a stronger sense of autonomy in the English sphere there, which but for its substantial shrinkage might have led, by the end of the century, to an Ireland as independent as Burgundy. The temptation to emulate York was successively to affect Fitzgeralds of Desmond and of Kildare, and perhaps even Butlers of Ormond and Burkes of Connacht. The reality of the danger was only too obvious to Edward IV, whose accession to the crown of the Lancastrians so quickly followed the defeat and death of his father York in December 1460. If, in the succeeding quarter-century, Yorkist instability precluded success in settling the Irish question, it cannot be said that this failure was due to lack of effort on the part of the king and of his successors. In fact it can be argued that the main interest of this era, until the Tudors were safely settled in England, centred round the control of the king's government in Ireland in a parallel series of Wars of the Ròses between the king for the time being and the most outstanding Anglo-Irish lords who threatened him.[5]

Desmond and Worcester

An early instance of Anglo-Irish quasi-independence is provided by the career of Thomas, 7th earl of Desmond, appointed as deputy by Edward IV for the middle years of the 1460s. His attainder and execution in 1468 by his English successor, John Tiptoft, earl of Worcester (viceroy 1467–70), quickly led to the development of legends as to their cause. However, Desmond had obviously become a menace to the declining English interest. He secured his military position in the Irish manner by quartering his soldiers among the English colonists, and allied himself with the most dangerous of the Irish chieftains who threatened the English interest. Yet he failed to control the independent Irish lords in the south and west, so that Worcester's decision to act with the savagery typical of the English civil war seemed to be the only solution. The repercussions which drew the Desmond Fitzgeralds from their allegiance were certainly not expected by Worcester. The devastation, by Desmond's relatives, of the English regions round Dublin could, after a time, be contained, but political alienation persisted in Munster for more than a century, involving successive generations of Fitzgeralds in intrigues with the Tudors' greatest rivals and enemies – such as the Burgundians, the Hapsburgs, and the Valois.[6]

The Ascendancy of Kildare

Worcester's execution by the Lancastrians in October 1470 did not deter Edward IV from further efforts. The Irish Council, having used the excuse of a viceregal vacancy, had in the summer elected as Justiciar Thomas, earl of Kildare, thereby providing the other Fitzgerald family with the opportunity to secure their pre-eminence in the Dublin area – a position which they maintained until 1534. In 1473 Edward IV countered by appointing commissioners, Sir Gilbert Debenham and James Norris, to treat with the Irish parliament, in answer to a petition to send over a sufficient force of archers financed from England and to secure the return of the absentees. The commissioners apparently satisfied themselves that the defence of the Pale from Irish invaders justified the approval of Kildare's plan for a local defence force. Thus in

1474 there was established the Guild of St George, a military order controlled by Kildare in association with a dozen of the leading gentry of the Pale. In the absence of adequate English finance, the depleted Irish revenues were expected to support what many viewed as a quasi-royal guard for Kildare, a situation which so alarmed Bishop William Sherwood of Meath that he secured parliamentary annulment of the experiment during his occupation of the viceregal office in the mid-1470s.[7]

Indeed Sherwood's temporary replacement of Kildare rather highlighted the paralysis of English power in this renewed rivalry of the Wars of the Roses. So politically impotent was the king that he could not secure the archbishopric of Armagh for his nominee, Edmund Connesburgh, who, faced with the debts of his predecessor to Florentine bankers, was unable to secure the release of the papal bulls of appointment. Again the Yorkist king was obliged to compromise and accept the Italian Octavian del Palatio for the Irish primacy. It is small wonder that he was unable to support Sherwood.[8]

Attempts to Restrain Kildare

The death of Kildare (March 1478) and the election as Justiciar of his son Gerald, 8th earl of Kildare ('the Great'), provided the king with a further opportunity to intervene. Young Kildare was directed under Privy Seal to hold no parliament. The royal authority was entrusted to Henry, Lord Grey, who found himself boycotted on arrival at Dublin. The Constable of the Castle, Prior James Keating of Kilmainham, denied him access. The Chancellor, Roland, Lord Portlester, withheld the Great Seal. A parliament summoned to Trim was prorogued to Drogheda, the sheriffs of Dublin and Louth returning no writs. While Grey at Drogheda held a parliament, imposed a subsidy and an Act of Resumption, Kildare met his parliament at Naas, legislating against Grey and denying the authority which would have displaced him under a mere English Privy Seal. Frustrated, Grey in 1479 returned to England, where Edward IV went through the gestures of sovereignty in the presence of Irish notables, including Kildare and Sherwood. Kildare's return as deputy set the tone of Edward's settlement. Sherwood became Chancellor and Portlester Treasurer. Particular acts of Grey's parliament were approved, while others were remitted for parliamentary sanction by Kildare. Henceforth the Council should act by majority.[9]

If all was lost but honour, the king still preserved the control of at least one of the higher offices. There was also acceptance of his right to summon by writ individuals from Ireland. A continued liability to pay

Kildare a salary was imposed on the English exchequer and the Guild
of St George returned to protect the Great Earl in his quasi-
sovereignty.[10]

One nominal power reserved by Edward IV was again renewed after
his death in 1483 and the brief interlude of Edward V by the last of
the Yorkist kings, Richard III. This was the reservation of the office of
Lieutenant of the King in Ireland to successive children of the monarch,
from whom the deputy derived his office. Richard III appointed his
young son, Edward, prince of Wales, and sent one William Lacy to
convey to Kildare the royal intention of resuming power. Lacy probably
had few illusions, having previously been involved in the abortive
activities of Lord Grey. Kildare was confirmed in office for a year and
invited to visit the king in England. Other great offices were renewed at
the king's pleasure. Kildare temporized, preferring negotiation by his
own nominee, the king's sergeant, John Estrete. Once more the dilemma
of the Irish situation came before the king's Council. Kildare demanded
£1,000 in payment if he were to continue to protect the liege people
from the marauding Irish. Again, the king stalled, the deputy once more
agreeing to visit court.[11]

Kildare now undertook to support yet a further diplomatic mission,
that, in 1484, of Thomas Barrett, bishop of Annadown, whom the king,
unable to support in his diocese, employed for such purposes as winning
over uncertain allies in Ireland. In particular, Barrett was to assure
Desmond of the king's attachment, of his horror at the monstrous
execution of his father, and of his readiness to accept the loyalty of his
southern Irish lieges. Apart from Barrett, of whose mission we know no
more, Kildare was expected to use his good offices with his brother-in-
law, O'Neill of Tir Eoghain, to secure the restoration of the king's
property as earl of Ulster, to attempt to influence O'Donnell in some
undisclosed way, and to secure the exclusion of unwanted papal nominees
to church benefices by enforcing the statutes of Praemunire. Undoubtedly
Kildare made nominal acquiescence; perhaps he even established good
relations with the earl of Lincoln, the new Lieutenant under whom he
had held office since the death in 1484 of the prince of Wales, and
Richard III's heir presumptive.[12]

In summer 1485, Henry Tudor, earl of Richmond and last of the
Lancastrians, successfully invaded the realm and defeated and killed the
king at Bosworth. The power of Kildare was now to be involved in even
greater enterprises in the renewed Wars of the Roses.[13]

Kildare and Ormond

The legendary rivalry of the noble houses of Ormond and Kildare in Ireland was nourished on those occasions when that rivalry became real. If the earls of Ormond were absentees, their capacity to intervene in Ireland was very real. Extending his system of dynastic alliances, Kildare gave a sister in marriage to Piers Rua Butler, the outstanding personality of the Polestown branch of the Ormond family. The arrival in Ireland of a Yorkist pretender, Lambert Simnel, allegedly Edward, earl of Warwick, resulted in his coronation in Dublin as an English king, 'Edward VI'. This abortive enterprise ended in disaster in 1487 at the battle of Stoke, when Henry VII defeated Simnel's army from Ireland (including a Burgundian mercenary force of 2,000). Kildare's involvement in this débâcle would suggest that he had doubted the continued favour of the Tudors, but in fact, his attempted intervention in the English dynastic war was but an unsuccessful effort to cast himself as kingmaker, if not king.[14]

Perkin Warbeck

Though Kildare's intervention in the succession rivalries for the English throne was not successful, it did not terminate such activities in Ireland. In 1491 another pretender, Perkin Warbeck, alleging that he was Richard, the younger brother of Edward V, found support in Cork and from Maurice Fitzgerald, 9th earl of Desmond. The city of Cork at this time played a prominent part in the politics of south Munster, its mayor on at least one occasion acclaiming James fitz Thomas, son of the victim of Worcester, as earl of Desmond. Mayor John Walter became closely identified with the southern movement supporting Warbeck. While Henry VII suspected Kildare's involvement, the earl himself denied it and it appears that he avoided public association with the movement. It was otherwise, however, with Desmond, who managed to involve Scotland, where James IV received the pretender and married him to a near kinswoman, Lady Catherine Gordon. The threat to the Tudors now came also from Scotland's continental allies and particularly from France and Burgundy. Ultimately the insecure Henry VII reinforced himself not merely with a papal bull but by an alliance with Spain, thus involving himself as a satellite in the imperialist expansion of Ferdinand of Aragon and Isabella of Castile.

Poynings's Law

More immediately, the Irish risk dictated the dismissal of Kildare. Once again it became evident that no alternative to the Irish viceroy was possible. In quick succession Henry put forward Walter fitz Simons, archbishop of Dublin, and Robert Preston, Lord Gormanstown. Finally and reluctantly a more expensive approach was undertaken with the dispatch, in 1494, of a military leader, Sir Edward Poynings, as viceroy, together with an English Chancellor and an English financial expert. Speedily this trio implemented the plan for the revived English administration. The Kildare alliance would be destroyed in the field, the parliamentary affirmations of Irish independence abrogated, and the military system of quartering mercenaries on the agricultural community, known as coign and livery, replaced by a financial subsidy. Within two years the plan miscarried. Henry was obliged to go back to accepting Kildare, who ruled unchallenged thereafter to the end of the reign and for the first four years of Henry VIII.[15]

The Poynings episode had a more lasting effect on Irish history than was apparent to contemporaries, if only because of Poynings's Law. At a parliament in Drogheda, as part of the reform programme, it was provided that never again could the king's authority be employed legislatively without previous sanction from England. Before even a parliament could be summoned the Lieutenant should certify to the king and Council there the reasons for its meeting and the measures to be proposed. The licence to hold parliament in Ireland had to be issued under the Great Seal of England. When the Irish parliament met, only the measures approved in England by the king and Council, however much amended from the Bills as proposed by the Lieutenant, could be considered. The Irish parliament was precluded from altering the drafts. Its functions thus confined to acceptance or refusal, it became virtually a registration medium for the legislative proposals of the king and Council in England.[16]

Henry VII and Kildare

Three particular observations need to be made here. The king's Lieutenant was his infant son, Henry, duke of York, who succeeded his father in 1509 as Henry VIII. It is not clear whether Henry VII intended to terminate Irish parliaments altogether. No provision was made to permit their being held by a deputy of the Lieutenant. Certainly no decision was made under Poynings, as the preamble of that law provided that a future parliament would deal with the resumption of royal grants. In fact, Poynings's parliament in its forty-nine statutes was very similar in character to the parliaments of the preceding fifty years, legislating for matters small as well as great, involving as far as possible the Anglo-Irish community as a whole. Never again after Poynings, however, did parliament function in Ireland as before. Thereafter there was a separation of power, the Great Council proclaiming the policy of the executive and the courts of the Chancery, the Exchequer, the King's Bench, and Common Bench coming back once more into the public eye. For this reason Poynings's Law, as it came to be called, is constitutionally important enough to justify Professor Otway-Ruthven in regarding it as marking the end of medieval Ireland. It has to be remembered, however, that for the rest it is mainly a signpost for that Tudor programme which commenced operation fully only after 1534. The second and third points about Poynings are military and financial.[17]

In his weakness, Henry had involved himself with the absentee claims of Thomas Butler, 7th earl of Ormond, whose attempts to regain for the earldom the influence which had passed to collaterals virtually provoked a Butler-Fitzgerald alliance in Ireland. The spearhead of the Ormond movement was Sir James Ormond, natural son of the 6th earl by an O'Brien of Thomond, who was ultimately killed by Piers Rua Butler after he had involved Poynings in a direct confrontation with Kildare which culminated in the latter's attainder and deportation to England. The legend that Ireland was Yorkist in sympathy should not prevent our seeing that the policy of the first Tudor in Ireland was to secure recognition of himself as successor to the York inheritance in Connacht, Ulster, Meath, and Leinster, by his marriage to Edward IV's heiress Elizabeth. By treating Kildare as a traitor, Poynings inevitably involved himself with Kildare's allies in the Ulster earldom, with O'Donnell, O'Neill, and particularly with O'Hanlon and MacMahon. It was these last two who terminated the Poynings military expedition to the north. It was they who helped to save Poynings's face by swearing to the innocence of Kildare when Henry faced facts by making the man whom all Ireland could not rule ruler of all Ireland. Thus the third significant aspect of the Poynings episode, the financial reform, was placed in cold storage.[18]

Other Statutes

Apart from 'Poynings's Law', there were a few outstanding measures among the remaining forty-eight statutes. Henry's control of the chief offices of state was reasserted by providing that they be held at pleasure and not for life. Utopian principles for legal uniformity extended to Ireland legislative enactments of public consequence 'late made' in England; these were subsequently claimed by an obsequious judiciary as extending back to include the earliest public acts of the English parliaments. Land grants in the name of the king issued since the days of Edward II were confiscated in an Act of Resumption which, in fact, had not been visualized in the first parliamentary programme of Poynings. The royal army was to be supported by a reformed system of coign and livery.[19]

Restoration of Kildare

Before the end of 1496 Henry had capitulated to Irish realities by restoring Kildare. The Poynings experiment had been too costly. It could only be maintained by constant financial outlays from England which were unlikely to be recoverable. While the Poynings group had succeeded in uncovering a greater area of potential revenue, while parliament had accepted that this revenue might become a reality by passing the Act of Resumption, the king was not prepared to add to his liabilities by undertaking to pay for Poynings once it was clear that he was unable to conquer the country. The alternative was the one man whose career had shown him capable of maintaining a rough system of Irish justice and Irish order.[20]

In the royal presence, having become a royal relative through his second marriage, to Elizabeth St John, Kildare agreed to certain conditions involving the abandonment of his ambition to be a kingmaker for England. No other pretenders to Henry's throne would receive countenance; parliament would not again be used as an instrument of treasonable faction. Kildare would accept the constitutional changes enacted by Poynings. Nor would anyone else in Ireland be permitted to support rivals to the Tudors. Despite the claims of kinship, Desmond would be compelled to accept the new regime and to abandon Warbeck and others like him.[21]

For the rest, the king was content that Kildare should exercise his authority. Papal provisions would not be tolerated, warfare was to be seriously discouraged, and indeed the deputy was to concern himself where possible in extending the royal power. Inevitably it meant a reversion to Kildare's Irish system of quartering an army on the populace, though the limitations of this were halfheartedly defined. Was the Guild of St George revived? Perhaps the name was tactfully abandoned, but Kildare was permitted to maintain a kind of semi-royal guard. His position was strengthened with the attempt to give him a monopoly of gun-powders and by discouraging defence forces from going beyond the use of bows and arrows — tacitly ignoring the Palesmen's addiction to Irish spears and darts.[22]

Operation of Poynings's Law

Anxiety to maintain parliamentary control is seen in the frequent operation of Poynings's Law with regard to the holding of parliaments and approving the drafts of statutes. It was not always possible to secure complete control by England. The protection of vested interests was commonly achieved by the addition of exemptions from confiscatory measures (or provisos, as they were called) for individual claimants and title-holders. But in general Henry could be satisfied that his Irish deputy, if not interfered with by him, would not permit Irish interference in English affairs. There might even appear to be some gains through the matrimonial alliance. The children of the second countess of Kildare, while inevitably hibernicized, were encouraged from time to time to risk exposure to English ways by visiting the court. Thus a limited policy of anglicization was favoured, though even Poynings had accepted that the proscription of the Irish language and of Irish fashions was ridiculous.[23]

The Battle of Knockdoe

After 1496, Kildare's power in Ireland extended vastly. His protégé Piers Rua Butler was gradually built up at the expense of the absentee Ormonds. Henry may have intended to maintain Sir James Ormond, but Piers Rua defeated and killed him in 1498. Thereafter, an uneasy peace between the absentee and native Butlers enabled Kildare to extend himself into Carlow. For the rest a system of alliances was gradually built up throughout the whole country, under which Kildare was able to impose a system of taxation on Anglo-Irish and Irish alike. Inevitably this involved him in constant expeditions around the country to enforce his authority and restrict the devastations of property which occurred as a result of transient martial rivalries. Perhaps the most notable military event was the battle of Knockdoe in 1504, in which Kildare defeated MacWilliam of Clanricarde. The forces involved on both sides virtually comprised the resources of the outstanding political entities from Dublin to Lough Foyle and from the Shannon to Sligo.[24]

To Henry VII it was subsequently reported that the battle was undertaken against his enemies. Perhaps the king believed this, for the Great Earl was subsequently invested with the Order of the Garter. It is not easy to ascertain the causes for the struggle beyond the fact that Ulick Burke of Clanricarde, Kildare's son-in-law, appears to have threatened the balance of power in the west. He had allied with O'Brien of Thomond and with MacNamara. He had imposed himself on Galway

city. He had intimidated MacWilliam Iochtar and thereby alienated
O'Donnell. He had taken castles from O'Kelly, who complained to
Kildare. The battle was largely fought by the Scots mercenary troops,
the galloglass, employed generally at this time in Irish warfare.
Kildare saw fit to treat it as a major event and brought an overwhelming
force from the Pale, from the north, and from the midlands. The
battalions of the Pale were led under Kildare by Lords Gormanston,
Howth, Trimleston, and Dunsany. From the north came contingents
from the Great O'Neill, from Magennis, O'Reilly, O'Hanlon, and
MacMahon. From the north-west came O'Donnell, Lower MacWilliam,
O'Conner Roe, and O'Kelly. After the battle, says the sixteenth-century
chronicler of St Laurence of Howth, Lord Gormanston turned to
Kildare and urged that they should now destroy their Irish allies. But
the battle, in accordance with contemporary custom, terminated the war.
Kildare had seen to it that no one would challenge his claim to rule all
Ireland.[25]

The battle was noteworthy to subsequent commentators as being the
first major occasion when guns were employed in Ireland. It is true that
there are a few references to guns at an early period and that Kildare had
earlier demolished a castle or two. He also employed at his Dublin
house of Thomascourt a group of gunners to display his powers. It is,
however, unlikely that gunfire played more than a minor part in the
battle of Knockdoe. The earl continued to be interested in its use,
however. Ironically, he met his death from a gunshot wound in 1513,
on an expedition in which he was opposed by O'More of Laois. Thus
despite the good intentions of the king and of Poynings, no monopoly
of guns could be preserved for the king's forces.[26]

Papal Influence in Ireland

A Dutch friar who visited Ireland in the pontificate of Alexander VI
(1492–1503) was struck by the desolation and the savagery of the
land. As a papal collector he was particularly outraged by the extortion
of Maguire, who controlled the entrance to St Patrick's Purgatory and
imposed excessive charges on pilgrims who were shut in overnight in a
smoke-filled cavern. Not surprisingly, Alexander VI attempted to act
the reformer by condemning the superstitious activity which caused his
collector to be outrageously fleeced. In early sixteenth-century Ireland,
however, the power of the pope did not extend that far. Perhaps it was
more effective in Dublin where the same Renaissance pontiff imposed
an interdict after warring factions had pursued and killed one another in
the cloisters of Christ Church in 1498. The same pope, with a fine sense

of the fitness of public penances to be expected from the citizens of a
city a thousand miles from Rome, condemned the mayor of Dublin in
perpetuity to walk barefoot annually in procession on a great church
feast-day.[27]

Death of Kildare

At the end of the reign of Henry VII, the Ireland of the Great Earl of
Kildare was probably more peaceful and more desolate than it had been
in two generations. The prosperity of the Fitzgeralds undoubtedly
brought to the citizens of Dublin an increasing amount of trade and a
greater feeling of affluence. How far were the liege people of Henry
satisfied with their lot? How secure were they from the Wicklow chiefs?
The death of the earl of Kildare in 1513 was to result in a recurrence
of the uncertainties that had marked the beginning of his career. It was
an uneasy successor who endeavoured to preserve the family supremacy
in the succeeding twenty-one years.[28]

Notes

1. *New Cambridge Modern History*, I, *The Renaissance* (1957), ed. G. R. Potter.
2. Maurice Keen, *England in the Later Middle Ages* (1973), section V, ch. 17.
3. E. Curtis, *A History of Medieval Ireland* (2nd ed., 1938), 295ff.
4. ibid., chs. 15, 16.
5. A. J. Otway-Ruthven, *A History of Medieval Ireland* (1968), 377.
6. Art Cosgrove in T. W. Moody and F. X. Martin edd., *The Course of Irish History* (Cork, 1967), 158ff.
7. D. B. Quinn, 'Guide to English financial records for Irish history, 1461– 1558, with illustrative extracts, 1461–1509', *Anal. Hib.* X (1941), 39–40.
8. *Statute Rolls of the Parliament of Ireland, 1st to the 12th years of the Reign of King Edward IV*, ed. H. F. Berry (later Twiss) (Dublin, 1914).
9. *Statute Rolls of the Parliament of Ireland, 12th and 13th to the 21st and 22nd years of the Reign of King Edward IV*, ed. J. F. Morrissey (Dublin, 1939).
10. H. G. Richardson and G. O. Sayles, *The Irish Parliament in the Middle Ages* (Philadelphia, 1952), 264ff.
11. Otway-Ruthven, op. cit., 400ff.
12. ibid., 401–2.
13. S. B. Chrimes, *Henry VII* (1972), 257ff.
14. Agnes Conway, *Henry VII's relations with Ireland and Scotland* (Cambridge, 1932), ch. 3.
15. Donough Bryan, *Gerald Fitzgerald, the Great Earl of Kildare* (Dublin, 1933), 181–209.
16. D. B. Quinn, 'The early interpretation of Poynings' Law, 1494–1534', *IHS* II (1941), 241; III (1942), 106.
17. Otway-Ruthven, op. cit., 408.
18. Bryan, loc.cit.
19. Conway, op. cit., ch. 7.

20. ibid.
21. Bryan, loc.cit.
22. R. Dudley Edwards, *A New History of Ireland* (Dublin, 1972), 60ff.
23. Bryan, loc.cit.
24. G. A. Hayes-McCoy, *Irish Battles* (1969), 48ff.
25. K. W. Nicholls, *Gaelic and Gaelicised Ireland in the Middle Ages* (Dublin, 1972) 148–9.
26. Hayes-McCoy, loc.cit.
27. A. Gwynn, *The Medieval Province of Armagh* (Dundalk, 1946), 172ff.
28. P. Wilson, *The Beginnings of Modern Ireland* (Dublin, 1912), 81ff.

2 REFORMATION DIPLOMACY

Garret Og, 9th Earl of Kildare

Through Henry VIII, Ireland became involved in contemporary European rivalries — particularly with the Hapsburg-Valois confrontation which made a reality of the Reformation challenge to the Catholic rulers.[1]

Garret Og, 9th earl of Kildare, succeeded without much difficulty to his father's possessions and titles. A talented man, partly anglicized through the influence of an English stepmother, Elizabeth, the dowager countess, two English wives, Elizabeth Zouche and Elizabeth Grey (another royal cousin), and long residence in England, he lacked the charismatic quality of his father and never showed himself capable of rising triumphantly above the great challenges confronting him. He probably inherited less of his father's personality than did his sister Margaret, whose forcefulness proved a tremendous asset in the rise of her husband, Piers Rua, who ultimately became earl of Ossory and Ormond. In fairness to Garret Og, the problems which faced him were much more complicated and difficult to solve than those which had confronted his father: by the end of his twenty years on the Irish stage, the Ireland of the Great Earl of Kildare had passed away.[2]

In the first five years after the Great Earl's death, his successor encountered few difficulties. He continued his father's policy of keeping order by leading devastating marches against his enemies, whose territories he systematically destroyed. On the whole, however, his expeditions were concentrated on his more threatening enemies in the neighbourhood of the Pale. Against these he could be savage, as when he crucified Archdeacon Kavanagh for murdering Bishop Doran of Leighlin. For the rest, Kildare became involved in the old rivalries with the Butlers and thanks to the determination of his sister Margaret, the conflict was maintained with relentless vehemence on both sides until the House of Kildare had collapsed. Perhaps his first mistake was made after 1516 when he sided with the absentee Butlers against Piers Rua. His greatest problem, however, emerged in 1518 when the negotiations between Desmond and the French first came to light and Henry VIII felt driven to attempt the reconquest of Ireland by appointing the earl of Surrey as Lieutenant in 1520.[3]

Henry VIII and Ireland

The general plan in 1518 was to secure Henry VIII's dominions from his enemies by holding Ireland down with an effective military force. If possible, Desmond was to be cajoled into submitting. Moreover, the papal power was to be exploited by extending to Ireland the legatine authority of Cardinal Wolsey in an attempt to end the stream of benefice-seekers from the independent parts of the country, who acted as agents for those involved in intrigues with the continental powers.[4] The scheme, reminiscent of the late fifteenth-century enterprises, at first proved a great success. Surrey, the first visiting Lieutenant since Edward IV's time, greatly impressed Dublin and the loyal Anglo-Irish. Outstanding lords like O'Donnell and O'Neill came to negotiate with him. He made an impressive appearance in the south-east of Ireland.

Kildare and the Butlers

After six months, however, the usual second phase of intervention commenced. Frustrations, diseases, and unexpected minor setbacks reduced the Lieutenant's support and on being refused additional supplies from England (justified as essential to maintain the king's power in the Pale), Surrey felt rebuffed. Henry thereupon lectured him in a magniloquent statement, in which he put conciliation before conquest and refused to lend financial support to the expedition. Surrey followed this by requesting his recall. Although the king reluctantly consented to this, there was a delay to determine how the Irish government should be maintained after the Lieutenant's departure. Ironically, because of the opening of hostilities between England and France, the very matter which had created anxiety in 1518 as a result of Desmond's intrigues with Francis I of France, Henry was distracted from Ireland. So far as keeping Munster quiet was concerned, Surrey favoured the employment of Piers Rua Butler, who was by now claiming to be earl of Ormond. Henry temporized, reluctant to over-encourage the Irish Butlers against the English side of the family, but eventually he agreed and in 1522 Surrey was replaced by Piers Rua with an understanding that Kildare would reside in England. In 1523, at the instigation of Piers Rua, Kildare was requested to return to impose some sort of order on the Leinster Fitzgeralds. However, as James, 10th earl of Desmond, continued his father's negotiations with France, the Irish situation proved too much for the new deputy and in 1524 it was necessary to replace him with Kildare in a new compromise arrangement, with Piers Rua as Treasurer.

No compromise could work. Kildare seemed unable to rule without exploiting the situation to the detriment of the Butlers, who from this time systematically intrigued in England against him.[5] In the succeeding five years, Kildare was nominally maintained as deputy, subject to continual investigation in England of complaints against him. His power in Ireland was now much more restricted and the strength of his enemies steadily coalesced in a determined effort to end the tradition that only one man, the earl of Kildare, could rule all Ireland. When, on being sent to England, Kildare delegated his power to his cousin, Sir Thomas Fitzgerald, the Irish Council revoked his authority and appointed Lord Delvin instead. In the following year, however, 1528, Delvin was kidnapped by O'Connor of Offaly, an old reliable kinsman and ally of Kildare. In this situation yet another solution was attempted in England. The king, possibly under the influence of Wolsey, reappointed Piers Rua as a temporary measure and then created a new situation by resurrecting the lieutenancy for his illegitimate son, the duke of Richmond.[6]

Attempts to Undermine Kildare

Richmond's appointment (August 1529) coincided with a new phase in royal policy generally.[7] Wolsey, having failed to win papal approval for the royal divorce, fell from favour. For a time, the king acted as his own chief minister and was led to another solution in Ireland. (This may have resulted from the threat implicit in Charles V's displeasure at the insult to his cousin, the Princess Mary, who had been passed over by the rejection of her mother.) A triumvirate was entrusted with power; it consisted of Archbishop John Allen of Dublin, Prior John Rawson of Kilmainham, and Chief Justice Patrick Bermingham. These could be relied upon to be hostile to Kildare and favourable to the Butlers. Their authority was to be reinforced by the dispatch as deputy of Sir William Skeffington, an efficient military character, later known in Ireland as 'the Gunner'. Skeffington loomed larger in the public eye than did the triumvirate. Their authority was terminated in his favour and Kildare was permitted to return to Ireland in his private capacity — without any political authority. Once again the arrangement was purely temporary. By 1532 Kildare had successfully undermined Skeffington's authority and Henry, preoccupied with destroying papal authority in England, restored Kildare with yet a further compromise, now entrusting the treasurership to Lord James Butler, son of Piers Rua (who had now become earl of Ossory).

Before the end of 1532, in an expedition against Birr Castle, Kildare sustained a shot in the thigh from which he never recovered. During the following two years, from the autumn of 1532 to the spring of 1534, it became more and more apparent that he had ceased to be master of the situation. The Wicklow Irish raided the capital. The collateral Geraldines surpassed themselves in their lawlessness. The deputy's opponents regrouped to displace him, and complaints to England reached a crescendo. A new minister, Thomas Cromwell, gradually emerging as the king's favourite adviser, supported the anti-Kildare alliance. In the summer of 1533, John Allen was appointed Master of the Rolls. It appeared likely that a new bureaucratic arrangement would be made, but the king balked at taking the decisive step of embarking on a full-scale military enterprise under Norfolk or Skeffington. Inevitably distracted from Ireland in the process of working out the constitutional changes required to inaugurate the Reformation, Henry for the moment left the initiative to the Kildare faction.[8]

Rebellion of Silken Thomas

When Kildare was summoned to attend the Council in England and explain the Irish disorder, his son, Silken Thomas, was in February 1534 temporarily appointed head of the government. Thomas's decision, four months later, to go into rebellion may have been precipitated by the rumoured execution of his father, but it cannot be attributed solely to his own impulsive nature. On the last day of May 1534, as part of a plan to restore Skeffington and extirpate the papal authority in Ireland, the king had agreed with the Butlers to give them Palatine powers in four countries. The action of Silken Thomas in defying the king and raising the standard of revolt must have sprung from the conviction of a dominating element of the Kildare Fitzgeralds that only by open warfare could they preserve their Ireland against Henry. In appealing to Charles V for support, they were doing no more than had been done in 1529 by Desmond and for that matter by O'Brien of Thomond.[9] But the dispatch in summer 1534 of an ecclesiastical agent to the papacy to secure crusader rights for the Irish movement against Henry VIII involved Kildare (as Silken Thomas had become on his father's death in autumn 1534), in the international papal plans against the king.

Although the Kildare revolt was a disaster, while it lasted it secured the benevolent neutrality of the Pale. Subsequently the government was able to treat the Pale area as having been involved and this proved an effective and intimidating weapon in rendering the parliament of 1536 complaisant. There does not appear to have been much of a religious movement against the king. After the capture by Skeffington

of Maynooth Castle, among those executed was John Travers, chancellor
of St Patrick's Cathedral, Dublin. The name of Travers appears in the
Catholic martyrologies of the next generation as one who suffered for
having written against the Royal Supremacy. While there is some doubt
about the matter, he does appear to have been the only ecclesiastic
executed for complicity in the rising.[10] Therefore the defeat of Kildare
hardly went beyond the family's own connections.

The O'Connors of Offaly maintained a sporadic type of warfare for
some years. Kildare's stepbrother and successor, Gerald, the 11th earl,
was eventually smuggled out of the country in 1540. A number of
independent Irish lords, from MacCarthy in the south to O'Donnell in
the north, combined to safeguard the young Kildare against the king
and O'Neill was sufficiently committed to the enterprise to fight
against Leonard Grey, Skeffington's successor as viceroy, until the
disastrous defeat at Bellahoe in 1539. The Butlers succeeded in keeping
their sphere of influence totally independent of Kildare. For the rest, it
can be said that the militant movement on behalf of the papacy was a
failure. The antipathy to Henry's changes took another form.

Death of Skeffington

The destruction of Maynooth and the collapse of the Geraldines appears
to have so intimidated the Anglo-Irish that difficulties in parliament
were minimal. The proposed legislation was considered in England in
the summer of 1535. It was then realized that Poynings's Law would
make it difficult to negotiate contentious matters and accordingly a
Bill was approved to suspend it for all public measures during that
parliament.[11] The death of Skeffington on 31 December 1535
necessitated the postponing of parliament until Grey had been formally
empowered to act. Military activities were still in progress in the
midlands and even as far afield as Limerick, but the parliament duly
met at the beginning of May and quickly approved about a dozen
measures before postponement became necessary.

Parliamentary Problems

Recognition of the king's marriage with Anne Boleyn was being
enacted in Ireland about the time she fell from grace in England and
accordingly it was necessary to seek sanction for legislation to annul
this second marriage. There were, of course, other difficulties to be
resolved. The dissolution of a number of monasteries in the Pale had
been decided on and formed part of the plan of reconquest which had
visualized the conversion of houses in outlying districts into military

fortifications.[12] The monasteries were, however, sufficiently influential to resist expropriation and delaying measures were resorted to which seriously impeded further progress. Constitutionally the Irish parliament lagged behind English developments, so that there appears to have been three houses in the Irish parliament until legislation was introduced abolishing the Convocation House of the Lower Clergy as an essential element in the Irish parliament.[13] Clerical resistance to the ecclesiastical changes concentrated on this technical matter.

Legislation of Reformation Parliament

The first measure enacted had included the attainder of the Fitzgeralds of Kildare and certain named adherents — whose properties were declared forfeit to the Crown.[14] There was also an act providing for the forfeiture of the property of absentee owners, including the earl of Shrewsbury and the English Butlers, as well as English religious houses having daughter houses in Ireland.[15] The royal alliance with the Irish Butlers was ratified by a measure recognizing the legitimacy of Piers Rua as his father's heir.[16] The royal supremacy and the denial of the pope were declared statutory — consequential upon measures to the same effect already enacted in England.[17] An act of Subsidy gave a modest revenue to the Crown for ten years.[18] Appeals to the court of Rome were prohibited.[19] To describe the king as a heretic or call in question the Boleyn marriage was made treasonable.[20] Proceeds from the papal taxation of church benefices known as first fruits were transferred to the Crown,[21] and the royal manor of Leixlip was resumed.[22] By July 1536 matters appeared to have settled down in Dublin. A new English Under-Treasurer, William Brabazon, was active in surveying the enhanced royal properties. George Browne, appointed by the king to the vacant archbishopric of Dublin, was taking stock of his new position and preparing to continue the oversight of the friars which he had carried out in England by authority of Thomas Cromwell, whom Henry had created viceregent of the clergy. But there was friction too as Allen, the Master of the Rolls, Browne, and Brabazon were jealous of one another's authority and all of them resented the rough manners of Lord Leonard Grey, the Lord Deputy.

Opposition within Pale

During the autumn of 1536 and throughout the early part of 1537, the new administration in Dublin found itself involved in a conspiracy of obstruction by notable Palesmen. The threat to hold everyone as accessories to the rebellion had been actually carried into the preambles of some of the statutes. The government found itself unable to negotiate leases of escheated property unless guarantees were forthcoming that immunity from treason trials would be guaranteed by an Act of Oblivion.[23] The devastation of the Pale had already shown the government the impossibility of securing more than a very limited subsidy from the laity. The clergy in diocesan benefices as well as the religious houses before their dissolution were obliged to take on a major part of the financial burden.

Appointment of Commissioners

English ignorance of conditions in Ireland was not wholly responsible for the persistent belief among the royal advisers in England that a vast revenue existed in Ireland if only it could be effectively organized. Dissatisfied with the slowness of the Dublin administration, Henry dispatched at the end of July 1537 four commissioners led by Sir Anthony St Leger to take over from the deputy and Council, survey the escheated lands, reassemble parliament, and put pressure on the houses into passing the approved measures. As part of their work the commissioners convoked grand juries within the Butler sphere of influence who were encouraged to comment on the lawlessness of the gentry and the dissoluteness of the clergy. While the Butlers must have lost in prestige after the execution of their cousin Anne Boleyn, Piers Rua and his son James were still important and essential to the strengthening of the royal power in Ireland; the leaders of the ecclesiastical reforms, Archbishop George Browne and Bishop Edward Staples of Meath, were subjected to royal reproof for their arrogance and their obstructiveness.[24] The reformers had thus to tread warily.

Commissioners' Sessions

The later stage of this parliament is of interest for a number of reasons. Sessions were held in connection with the military expeditions at Kilkenny, at Cashel, and at Limerick, although an act of the reign of Edward IV confined meetings to Dublin and Drogheda. The decision to dissolve religious houses had the result of reducing the number of Lords Spiritual in the Upper House, the mitred abbots disappearing with the surrender of their monasteries. When the commissioners arrived, they were fortified with royal letters to the Lords and Commons making it perfectly plain that the king regarded opposition or obstruction as disloyal and, in the case of officials, likely to result in punishment.[25] Nevertheless, it still was not possible to secure enactment for the whole programme. In all, twenty-eight Bills were considered and twenty-six were passed. The government was unable to secure measures defining the qualifications of officials and compelling residence in the border areas. Nor apparently was the Bill imposing more drastic fines for previously utilizing papal dispensations and grants proceeded with, as the more moderate provisions of an earlier English Faculties Act were passed. The commissioners, presumably with royal consent, withdrew a Customs Bill and modified the 5 per cent property tax so that it applied only to the clergy.

The main body of the measures enacted divided naturally into two parts, of which the more important were the fifteen on the statute roll (chs. 17–31). Five minor Bills had been passed in the second session from July to September 1536, before the commissioners arrived: they were responsible for the sessions of October-December 1537. Their first measure, chapter 17, nullified the Anne Boleyn marriage and bastardized her daughter, Elizabeth. Understandably, when the statutes were printed in 1572, this measure was omitted, as it would have reflected on the reigning queen. By the nineteenth act the Irish parliament was reduced to two Houses – customary in England for more than a century.[26] It may be assumed that the representatives of the diocesan clergy, the proctors in the Convocation House, ceased to be regarded as an estate of parliament from the arrival of the commissioners. Thus by a revolutionary measure, claimed as a Declaratory Act, the Irish parliament was brought into line with that of England. In a later age it became customary for a Convocation of the Clergy to be held concurrently with the meeting of parliament. As in England, Convocation usually met in a House of Peers and in a House of Diocesan Representatives.

When the legislation of Henry VIII was repealed in the reign of Mary, what happened to the proctors? We have no definite information on this subject, but it is not unreasonable to infer that the third house in the Irish parliament was not restored, as Queen Mary, like all the other Tudors, believed in establishing uniformity in government practice. It must be stressed, however, that without any contemporary journals or diaries, and with only the statutes printed subsequently to draw upon, this is a mere hypothesis.

With regard to the other acts passed in these final sessions, chapter 18 imposed first fruits on superiors of religious houses.[27] Chapter 22 made it treasonable to marry Irishmen who had failed to take the Oath of Succession to the king and his descendants and successors by Jane Seymour.[28] Chapter 21 revoked a grant of religious lands at Duleek originally intended for a government official.[29] Chapter 23 practically abolished papal jurisdiction in Ireland:[30] the Oath of Supremacy was imposed on all office-holders. Chapter 24 restored the liberty of Wexford county, already the king's county by a previous act.[31] Under chapter 25 a tax of one-twentieth was imposed on the clergy, following the English act for first fruits and tenths.[32] Chapter 26 compelled everyone (on pain of fines graded according to social rank) to speak English and dress in the English fashion.[33] The 27th legalized the dissolution of thirteen monasteries.[34] The 28th made it illegal to export wool.[35] The 29th imposed an English act restricting clerical dues on proving wills, but provided a more generous scale of these than in England.[36] Chapter 30 was a Faculties Act[37] and chapter 31 a definition of the Poynings's Law suspension.[38] It was made a felony to test the Suspension Act in the courts.

It appears that this legislation was secured only through the passing of a first Pardons Act (ch. 20), early in the first session of the Commissioners. Since chapter 29 opened with a reference to being subsequently passed,[39] it appears that there was a prorogation on 20 October 1537. Presumably by that date the greater part of the government's legislation had been enacted. A second Pardons Act[40] (ch. 35) validated irregularities, as the earlier measure had not taken cognisance of earlier legislation which made it essential to recite, in the case of murder, the offence pardoned. The manner in which suspension of Poynings's Law was defined implies that legal critics of government were prepared to test in the courts the legality of any legislation which did not provide for the king's honour, the increase of the revenue, and also the common weal. This litigious attitude necessitated extreme care in passing the legislation. The first Pardons Act would probably not have been amended if the government were to secure the abrogation of the Queen Anne Boleyn Succession Act, since this act had made it treasonable to deny the lawfulness of that marriage, and immunity from prosecution had to be conceded.

The final series of measures, eleven in all, were more concerned with the common weal. Chapter 32 revived the liberty of Wexford town, extinguished by Lord Shrewsbury's loss of his liberty under the Absentee Act.[41] Chapter 33 legalized the commissioners' leases.[42] Chapter 34 imposed a time limitation protecting those prosecuted under the recent laws.[43] Chapters 36[44] and 37[45] attempted to make navigable the rivers Barrow and Boyne. Chapter 38 secured the king's title to the parsonage of Dungarvan.[46] Chapter 40 attempted to protect church tithes in corn.[47] Chapter 41 clarified payment time for the subsidy.[48] Two acts empowered the commissioners to legislate temporarily, chapter

39[49] citing Bills not finalized in parliament and chapter 42[50] embody-
ing the orders regarding Bills for residence in the Marches, for clerical
absentees, and grey merchants (non-guild members). Apparently, just
before Christmas, the commissioners, as they informed Cromwell on
2 January 1538, came upon an act of 1477[51] declaring parliament void
if all its representative members were not resident in their constituencies
and if they did not therein have a real property qualification. Moreover,
legislation passed after the second adjournment was invalid. It was
therefore decided to dissolve.

Reaction to Religious Policy

After the termination of parliament, the commissioners completed their
activities in surveying the confiscated properties. The dissolution of the
monasteries sanctioned by statute was part of this process. There appears
to have been some public anxiety still in Dublin and in the Pale. The
intrigues of the administrators extended even to adverse reports on
individual commissioners. The prelates of Dublin and Meath busied
themselves in implementing the new ecclesiastical policy. It soon
became apparent, however, that public opinion was apathetic about
the king's claims in religion and the archbishop of Dublin in particular
felt discouraged by the reaction to his measures.[52] For this he blamed
Lord Leonard Grey more than anyone else. He considered the deputy's
treatment of him reacted adversely on those he hoped to intimidate in
enforcing the royal supremacy. In all this the king's orders were obeyed
wherever the archbishop was strong enough to enforce them with the
assistance of the secular officials recently appointed. However, apart
from these Englishmen, there did not appear to be any administrative
support except occasional assistance from the Butlers, Piers Rua, and
his son Lord James.

Recall and Execution of Grey

Early in 1538 the Lord Deputy was involved in further military
expeditions which took him into the midlands, to Limerick, and as
far as Galway. There appears to have been a renewed fear of foreign
interference, from the papacy and even from Spain. The nervousness of
the commissioners in terminating parliament reflects a certain anxiety
that the king's power in Ireland depended on popular acquiescence. It
is clear enough that this was wholly contrary to the notions of Henry
VIII and Cromwell. It had been assumed that the Reformation
legislation enacted in England would automatically operate in Ireland
once the invading forces of Skeffington and Lord Leonard Grey were

sufficiently in control. After the end of parliament, however, it is clear
that the deputy was anxious to compromise. He secured submissions
from prominent Irish chiefs, and restrained the more offensive and
outrageous actions of the ecclesiastics who, by destroying venerated
shrines, alienated pious people who might well revolt against what to
them were public enormities. In April 1540 the Lord Deputy was
recalled and in consequence of official criticisms from Ireland, he was
put on trial and executed in July 1541.

The case against Grey seems flimsy to the modern student. His
capacity to outrage the sensibilities of high officials, lay and clerical, is
quite obvious, but the statement that he organized a conspiracy of
independent Irish lords to combine with foreign forces poses another
question. There is no doubt but that Henry VIII and Cromwell were
nervous in the prevailing foreign and domestic climate. The English
popular uprising of 1536 known as the Pilgrimage of Grace had been
easily outmanoeuvred, but it left the king anxious to reaffirm conservative traditions. The realization that Cromwell's policy of alliance
with the German Protestant princes had been at least partly a failure
led in 1539 to the enactment by the English parliament of the Statute
of Six Articles, which, in its anti-Lutheran provisions, sought to reaffirm the doctrinal orthodoxy of the English Church. With the
ascendancy of Cromwell weakening before his fall, the necessity for
self-protection in Ireland for Browne, Brabazon, Allen, and Butler
led to emphasis on Grey's enormities, and assertions that the deputy
was re-establishing the Kildare supremacy in his own person. As brother
of Elizabeth Grey, countess of Kildare, Grey was particularly
vulnerable to allegations that could appear credible to the suspicious
and fearful king. While the deputy had defeated O'Neill at Bellahoe, it
was not at all clear that the Geraldine League had been dispersed. It
was easy to blame him when the young 11th earl of Kildare escaped
from the country, and to regard him as an accessory before the fact.
That they found Grey guilty of conspiring at Galway with foreign
intriguers friendly to Cardinal Pole shows how far the king's judges
would go to bring down those who displeased him. It may be inferred
that Grey's actions in Ireland were so terrifying that the official group
who denounced him feared destruction at his hands. In the case of
the Butlers this would appear to be a fact. As regards the others it
must remain a hypothesis.[53]

Apart from the war, Lord Leonard's greatest achievement was to
conciliate independent Irish and Anglo-Irish chiefs. His success
emerged when St Leger, the next deputy, took over and completed his

policy. Again it necessitated diplomatic methods in effecting ecclesiastical changes. The execution of Cromwell in 1540 facilitated this.

Grey's temporary replacement by Sir William Brereton, the Marshal of the Army, appeared to indicate that military matters were still paramount. The whole situation was, of course, very confused: the decision to proceed against Grey for treason was probably taken by Cromwell in the belief that his bureaucratic arrangements for the government of Ireland under the Lord Lieutenant were in danger of being destroyed. It is also possible that he may have felt ready to ally with Ormond, who would be likely to co-operate with the English officials. Whatever the circumstances, it can be concluded that Grey's concept of a chief governor was too regal-like to be acceptable under the new regime and that the only effective way of recalling him was that to which Cromwell resorted, only a few months before his own disgrace and death.

St Leger's Policy

After Cromwell, it was probably the king who took the decision to return St Leger to Ireland as Grey's successor. Revenue commissioners were associated with him to continue the type of financial activity inaugurated in 1537. As Lord Deputy, St Leger was successively involved in the working-out of a policy of appeasement, the holding of a parliament, and the adjustment of Ireland to a new European situation, when Henry VIII and France again became involved in war.

The policy of appeasement might be said to have become essential after Cromwell's death. His fall inevitably threatened the administrative bureaucracy with which he had become associated. In particular, the religious policy of the Reformation was necessarily halted. Ecclesiastical reformers had resented Grey's preference for nominal conformity and had sought the active persecution of adherents of Rome, and the admonition of unenthusiastic officials, both spiritual and lay. Under St Leger, at least for some time, even Archbishop Browne appears to have acquiesced in nominal conformity. There was of course the additional difficulty that the king seemed to be under the influence of an anti-Protestant group led by Stephen Gardiner, so that such married ecclesiastics as — allegedly — Browne, were fearful lest the penalties of the English Statute of Six Articles be applied to them. In this way Archbishop Browne became a pioneer in the elaboration of a political doctrine that became more and more significant in sixteenth-century Ireland.[54] Where it would appear that measures providing for religious uniformity with England were likely to affect adversely the English (and particularly the new English) element in the community, to the advantage of the independent Irish beyond the reach of the king's writ, for most purposes it became essential to apply in practice a different standard in Ireland to that demanded in England. It was the working-out of this policy which ultimately subordinated religion to politics and set limits to the success of the Reformation in Ireland.

In fairness to Archbishop Browne, who appears to have been guided mainly by what he conceived to be the wish of his prince, it is unlikely that he saw in this policy anything beyond an acceptance of reality which justified the state in conniving at the failure of loyal subjects to observe its religious regulations in every particular. Certainly he could not in 1540 have foreseen that the acceptance of this policy by the Catholic Queen Mary in the next decade would save him from being burnt at the stake like Archbishop Cranmer.

Declaratory Act

Perhaps the most significant event in the lord deputyship of St Leger was the holding of a parliament in which Henry VIII, his heirs and successors, were recognized as kings of Ireland. The decision to pass this declaratory act arose from the belief, widely held in the Pale, that the title of Lord of Ireland, under which the English king had ruled there, was derived from papal grants and in particular from 'Laudabiliter', the alleged papal brief of Adrian IV in favour of Henry II. Henry VIII, although accepting the advice from Ireland in favour of a declaratory act, was dominated by a reluctance to accept a measure which might in any particular appear to concede to the king of England, at the instance of the Irish parliament, any authority which he did not already claim. So deeply ingrained was this attitude that even after the measure had been passed, he insisted upon the enactment of a second version incorporating certain corrections representing more specifically the royal position as he saw it. In the event, it was the first version which came to be printed some thirty years later: since the destruction of the Statute Rolls in the Irish Record Office in 1922 his Majesty's corrections no longer remain on record.[55]

With the passage of this act (33 Henry VIII Session 1 ch. 1), in a certain sense, a new era begins in Irish history — that of the kingdom of Ireland. The contrast here is with the English lordship which began under Henry II and with the United Kingdom of Great Britain and Ireland which was created in 1800. Administratively, however, the date is of less significance than 1534, when the continuity of English administration commenced: this lasted down to the Union with Britain.

The Parliament of 1541

Apart from the declaratory act, only a small proportion of the legislation of this parliament demands attention. *Ex post facto* ratification of the statutes of the 1536–37 parliament was necessary because of the legal issues which had led to its unexpectedly unplanned dissolution. In 1541 therefore, in the second session, by chapter 1 of the subsequently printed statutes,[56] provision was made for meetings of parliament and for adjournments, and a definition was made of the qualifications for knights of the shires and representatives of the boroughs. By chapter 2, provision was made for the election of Lords Justices when the viceregal office was vacant.[57] By chapter 4, grants of land from the king were given legislative recognition.[58] By chapter 5 the dissolution of the remaining religious houses, and particularly of the priory of Kilmainham, was approved.[59]

In 1542 the county of Meath was divided into two, the county of Westmeath being created (34 Henry VIII Session 1 ch. 1).[60] Two other measures, not subsequently printed, require attention. With minor adjustments the Subsidy Act of the preceding parliament was continued for ten years as from the autumn of 1546, making it less necessary to summon any parliament before the reign of Queen Mary (34 Henry VIII Session 2 ch. 1 unprinted). By 35 Henry VIII ch. 1 unprinted, the earldom of Ormond was confirmed to James Butler, in succession to his father Peter (Piers Rua).

The remaining measures were concerned with general questions like the control of grey merchants.[61] There were also measures to bring Ireland into line with England as regards marriage (33 Henry VIII Session 1 ch. 6)[62] and consanguinity[63] (33 Henry VIII Session 1 ch. 4); for criminal matters such as robbing one's master[64] (33 Henry VIII Session 1 ch. 5) and for civil matters such as the right of plaintiffs to amend pleadings[65] (33 Henry VIII Session 1 ch. 3); as regards distraining on lands (33 Henry VIII Session 1 ch. 7)[66] and recovering goods taken by distress (33 Henry VIII Session 1 ch. 10 unprinted); regarding servants' wages (33 Henry VIII Session 1 ch. 9);[67] against vagabonds (33 Henry VIII Session 1 ch. 15);[68] and for joint tenants (33 Henry VIII Session 1 ch. 10).[69] Ecclesiastical affairs which were the subject of legislation included the act for tithes (33 Henry VIII Session 1 ch. 12)[70] and the act for erecting vicarages (33 Henry VIII Session 1 ch. 14).[71] Of general interest were the provision for recovery in avoiding leases (33 Henry VIII Session 1 ch. 11)[72] and the act for attournments (33 Henry VIII Session 1 ch. 13).[73] The Act of Capacities provided for qualifications for office (33 Henry VIII Session 1 ch. 8).[74]

In the second session of 33 Henry VIII, apart from the re-enacted act establishing the kingdom of Ireland (ch. 1 unprinted), a measure was passed regarding mispleadings (ch. 3 printed).[75] In the following year the remaining measures protected persons in service from being kept in custody in court (34 Henry VIII Session 1 ch. 2),[76] and re-affirmed the royal provisions for the manor and castle of Dungarvan (34 Henry VIII Session 2 ch. 1).[77] Finally, in a measure unprinted before the twentieth century, provision was made to subsidize the construction of walls for the borough of Navan (34 Henry VIII Session 2 ch. 3).

St Leger and the Irish Chiefs

Following the tradition of the preceding parliament, the Lord Deputy utilized the meetings of the present one to impress the general community in Limerick and Trim, as well as in Dublin. In the surviving records it was noted that eminent Irish lords were associated in the ratification of the legislation. For these, in at least one instance, James, earl of Ormond, acted as interpreter. At Limerick, O'Brien of Thomond was stated to have given his consent by proxy.[78] It was the inauguration of the policy of conciliation: from this St Leger proceeded on a fairly systematic plan to secure by legal instrument submissions and re-grants for both lay and spiritual lords.

It had been said by Grey's critics that unlike St Leger's agreements, his had rarely included legal sanctions, but on the whole the procedure was comparable, although St Leger stipulated for forfeitures in the event of subsequent rebellion. Provisions tended to differ between chieftains nearer to Dublin and those further afield.

Surrender and Re-grant

Perhaps the main difference between the Grey and St Leger agreements may be summarized by saying that with St Leger it became formal policy to accept surrenders and approve re-grants. The result of this policy was to convert into English landowners the independent Irish and Anglo-Irish lords who had previously ruled over territories according to various types of Irish custom, under which they did not enjoy the rights of tenants-in-chief under the Crown. Under English law the tenant-in-chief under the Crown exercised absolute ownership over the estate. By Irish law the land was usually held by a family group among whom the existing adults had a usufruct (enjoyment of the fruits of the land) but no absolute ownership, which, in accordance with the English law of real property, could be transmitted on death to a man's heir by the rules of primogeniture. It was only gradually that these distinctions emerged. Not until the reign of James I was the Irish system subjected to analysis: it was then rejected by Sir John Davies as being 'void for uncertainty'.[79] Although this uncertainty would deter no modern lawyer specializing in company law, it was unacceptable to Tudor administrators. The surrenders under Henry VIII were primarily aimed at converting ruling lords into persons who held an ascertainable position within the understanding of contemporary English law, and whose power and property would pass to an heir. The Irish chiefs, under Grey, agreed to accept the overlordship of a king who demanded the observance of his fashions, the payment of his tributes, and the renunciation of any rivals, particularly the pope. The chiefs who surrendered to St Leger accepted not merely Grey's policy but in addition surrendered all personal ruling claims as against the Crown and received back in exchange a grant of their territories by feudal law — giving to them and their heirs an absolute property unknown to Irish law and custom. An Irish chief transmitted his regal authority to his successor, elected from his kin by the preponderating influences within his own territory — not necessarily in accordance with the rules of primogeniture. In consequence conflicts often arose about succession. In modern English real property law down to the early twentieth century, the medieval principle associating land ownership with public office tended to be forgotten. In Irish society in the sixteenth century the family community held its landed property in perpetuity. This was not necessarily connected with office. Elective offices did of course result in the enjoyment of landed rights customarily reserved for a chief. In many instances, for his *Tanaiste* or successor designate, similar provision was made. The chief, however, did not have the right in law to disturb existing families from their lands. Under the influence of feudalism the doctrine of conquest came to be accepted so that chiefs allocated what came to be called 'sword-land' to their fighting-friends, whether kinsmen, allies, or mercenary leaders. In this way a great part of Ireland had for most purposes a new system of land ownership. It was this system which was now to be extended over whole territories. It involved the principle of forfeiture at law on breach of the conditions. In accordance with immemorial tradition, the rights of a family in land might continue to exist in an attenuated form where through conquest, the greater part of the territory was enjoyed by newcomers. This *de facto* situation was now to be replaced by the English system which barred the recognition of anyone except those whose title was recognized in law and whose property was more particularly and exclusively delimited than had been customary in the Irish traditional system. From the standpoint of capitalistic economics the new system was infinitely more preferable as it made possible the transfer of properties by buying and selling, and the building-up of a highly profitable economy.

St Leger and the Episcopacy

The St Leger agreements with the spiritual lords were no different than those with their lay contemporaries. Again the contrast with what had occurred in Grey's time deserves consideration. On a number of occasions Grey had secured submissions from bishops and other clergy in the course of his military expeditions into the semi-independent areas of Ireland. From these clergy he claimed to have secured the admission of the king's title over the Church and the renunciation of the pope. Thus in Limerick and in Galway, in the course of his expedition in 1538, as he subsequently reported to the king, he exacted the Oath of Supremacy from the resident bishops. Under St Leger, on the other hand, the same formalized approach which had marked the submissions of the independent chiefs became customary. A benefice-holder possessing bulls of appointment from the pope, surrendered and received a re-grant. Occasionally, conflicting royal and papal title-bearers involved the Dublin administration in taking a decision, which usually depended on local politics. Thus it was that Roland de Burgo, papally provided to Clonfert, secured state support against the royal nominee Richard Nangle, who had failed to gain local reinforcement and who had to be contented with acting as a suffragan bishop under George Browne in Dublin. It has been argued that to surrender the papal bulls was to do no more than had been done in the king of England's sphere of influence since the passage of the statutes of Provisors and Praemunire of the late Middle Ages. There is no doubt, however, that prelates like Roland de Burgo were perfectly well aware that the royal supremacy was something new, even if the king himself liked to argue otherwise. Certainly they would have agreed that strict obedience to the king involved no further connection with the pope.[80]

Papal Mission to the North of Ireland

The agreements achieved by St Leger appeared generally to implement the decisions of the 1541 parliament and certainly justified the claims in 1542 that Ireland was enjoying an unwonted peace. As if to give point to this, the papal intervention in the north of Ireland by Jesuit agents proved a fiasco. The leading Irish lords made it clear that they could not be received publicly and ultimately they withdrew to Scotland.[81]

St Leger's policy therefore was not merely successful in securing the pacification of Ireland. It was able to reinforce the king's determination to render his dominions independent of any foreign interference. The papal expedition to the north had followed an appeal from northern lords, transmitted by the bishop of Derry, who had represented the situation as necessitating immediate papal action if everything were not to be lost. The papal reaction had been twofold. Nominees had been provided to such bishoprics as appeared to be likely to accept provisors and reject the king's men and, through the French and Scottish sovereigns, a Jesuit mission was introduced. On the whole, wherever a papal appointee was in a position to represent himself as being concerned exclusively with spiritual matters, his chances of local acceptance were good.[82] The Jesuit missionaries, however, were in a different category. Despite the emphasis in their credentials on their spiritual functions, it was obvious to Irish rulers like Conn O'Neill (recently ennobled as earl of Tyrone after the renunciation of his title of O'Neill) that the papal emissaries were involved in the political enterprise against the schismatic Henry.

Success of St Leger

By 1543 St Leger was in a position to pride himself on the docility of the leaders of a transformed Ireland. Among the many who had submitted, there were some who had visited England and been invested with earldoms and other royal titles. Among these, in addition to the earl of Tyrone, was Upper MacWilliam who had become earl of Clanricarde and O'Brien who had become earl of Thomond, together with recipients of lesser titles, like MacGiolla Padraig who became Viscount Upper Ossory. St Leger could also congratulate himself on settlements with such former difficult persons as O'Donnell and James fitz John Fitzgerald, 13th earl of Desmond. It could of course be said that Ireland had been pacified before. Chiefs had submitted on a national scale to Richard II and to Richard, duke of York, and the pacifications had proved to be temporary. It is clear that St Leger was aware of this; he was careful not to overstate his claims as Grey was alleged to have done. In particular, he did not assume that the promised tributes would be paid immediately, even though he could claim that the chances of increased revenue were good.

St Leger's Critics

The deputy had every reason to be careful. His predecessor's critics
were still active. At an early date Robert Cowley reported to London on
a viceregal verbal indiscretion in which he implied that Henry VII's
title had been questionable until he married Queen Elizabeth. St Leger
took this seriously enough to get the rest of the Council to support him
against Cowley's allegation in a signed statement to London. Cowley
had been closely connected with the interests of Ormond, and, like
Grey, St Leger began to resent Ormond's growing strength. At the 1541
parliament, Ormond assumed the role of interpreter at the public
receptions of the Irish-speaking lords. His own immediate neighbours
were under constant pressure to accept his patronage. There is evidence
too that the English members of the administration, notably Sir John
Allen and Brabazon, had reservations on the Lord Deputy's conciliation
policy. Even if Cowley's action was untimely, a more aggressive policy
would have been more pleasing. The conciliatory policy restricted public
expenditure, but provided few opportunities for further confiscation
and loot. Brabazon in particular, with his financial responsibilities,
stood to gain by an abandonment of the conciliatory policy, in view of
the prevailing belief that direct control of a greater area would secure
the property of a larger number of dissolvable religious houses. To
Allen, the Lord Deputy's claims that conciliation would soon provide a
steadily flowing revenue from the Irish lords was nonsense.[83]

Effective action in bringing down another viceroy could only follow
from further political changes in England. Cromwell's downfall had
enabled the Norfolk interest to influence the king in his fifth marriage
– to Katharine Howard. Her disgrace almost inevitably had its
repercussions on the Howards. The sixth marriage, to Katharine Parr, in
1543 perceptibly weakened Norfolk, although he was not brought to
the foot of the scaffold until the king was on his death-bed. Even at
that late stage Norfolk's rivals could not dictate major political changes.

Meanwhile, in Ireland, St Leger's involvement in providing military
support for the king's enterprises against France and Scotland enabled
him to show his strength. The newly reconciled Irish were induced to
participate in the siege of Boulogne in 1544. Their contributions,
though small in number, came from a wide spectrum, though not from
the independent lords in the Ormond sphere of influence. Their
participation in the French war apparently introduced an unexpected
ferocity, distinguished prisoners losing their heads rather than their
ransoms – much to the amusement, allegedly, of the English king. In
retaliation, the French ensured that their Irish prisoners would provide

no future genealogical material for recording Irish historians: they were castrated.

The Gowran Letter

The Scots enterprise of 1544 led St Leger to entrust Ormond with the generalship of the Irish forces. In this case the strategy involved co-operation with the exiled Lennox and with Donal Dubh MacDonnell, Lord of the Isles. They failed to take Dumbarton Castle, the supposedly favourable garrison proving recalcitrant. Before Ormond, on Lennox's advice, retired to Ireland, a letter arrived at Gowran anonymously accusing St Leger of deliberately throwing Ormond into a situation out of which it was hoped he would not escape alive. Subsequently it emerged that the Gowran letter was from Walter Cowley, son of the disgraced Robert and holder of the office of Solicitor-General in Ireland.

St Leger and Ormond

The conclusion of military activities probably strengthened the position of St Leger at court. In Ireland, however, Ormond took the initiative by alleging that the Lord Deputy had made illegal exaction on his freeholders. Concurrently the supporters of the aggressive policy felt strong enough to show a certain favour towards Ormond. Evidence emerged of threatening statements made by St Leger against the earl. The Lord Deputy, not content with reasonably favourable statements about him being formally represented to England, insisted that he would prefer to serve the king elsewhere and would confront his opponent before the Council in England.[84]

Attempts to Remove St Leger

St Leger's opponents were sufficiently strong to secure an order from England that Brabazon should act as head of the executive in his absence. During the discussions in England St Leger had the advantage that testimonies of his success in pacifying Ireland were submitted on behalf of most of the leading Anglo-Irish and Irish lords. The latter in particular paid tribute to the fairness of his dealings and to the fact that he had not availed himself of opportunities to make private profit at their expense. His regime, they said, in contrast to preceding viceroys, had endeared them to the king's government in Ireland and to the king. Although Brabazon dutifully procured testimony on behalf of Ormond, the investigations of the allegations proved disastrous for the allies. Allen and Cowley were sent to the Fleet: the latter, perhaps through fear of the rack, confessed to the authorship of the Gowran letter and sought to incriminate Allen, who quickly disowned him. They were both deprived of their offices as Chancellor and Solicitor-General respectively. Brabazon appears successfully to have stayed in the background. Ormond and St Leger were formally reconciled at the meeting with the Council, and the Lord Deputy returned to Ireland — vindicated. Ormond died of poisoning after a feast in London in October 1546, in circumstances which do not appear to have been investigated.[85]

Comparison of Grey and St Leger

Attempts to compare and contrast the fortunes and fates of Grey and St Leger as viceroys under Henry VIII yield conclusions of some consequence. Henry VIII's reign in England commenced with a greater degree of stability than had been possible under his predecessor. As he became more involved in international affairs, the problems of his father's reign recurred. These he attempted to meet, drastically, by consolidating his position within his own dominions and by widening his horizons at home. The breach with Rome complicated relations with the Empire but not with France. The papacy's lack of support in England enabled the king to strengthen himself and gain greater security by winning a substantial party to his cause. Through the dissolution of the monasteries, he was able to offer investments on easy terms to many rising families.

In Ireland there was less success. The papacy had been a good friend to the interests of the king of England in Ireland. As the English power receded, however, in the late fifteenth and early sixteenth centuries, the papacy was prepared to co-operate with the new independent Irish lordships in appointments of Irishmen to benefices hitherto monopolized by Englishmen. While in England the provision of Italian ecclesiastics to lucrative benefices caused envy and resentment against the papacy and support for the royal policy of gaining greater control over the Church, it was otherwise in Ireland. Thus there was more loyalty to the Holy See in Ireland, although not enough to maintain a papal crusade against the king.

The destruction of the Kildare Geraldine interest created an imbalance in Ireland until the culmination of the Tudor conquest. In Henry VIII's reign this imbalance recurred in the successive viceroyalties of Grey and St Leger. Under Henry VII the projected conquest had been abandoned after Poynings, and Kildare was allowed to wield power which, although subject to some restrictions, involved no financial outlay from England. For more than two generations the Geraldines maintained a balance and after their destruction England was again obliged to choose between continued financial outgoing or a Geraldine-like policy of conciliation and goodwill. The rise of the Polestown branch of the Butlers to the earldom of Ormond provoked a problem for successive English deputies that led them to attempt a renewed balance of forces on the Geraldine model. In Grey's case reversion to this policy proved fatal, because of the precarious international situation in which the exiled Geraldines seemed linked both to the deputy and to the king's enemies abroad. (Adoption of the Geraldine policy appeared to prove Grey's guilt as their accessory.) In St Leger's case matters developed differently: the Kildare menace had receded internationally while the Ormond influence at home appeared more sinister to the king. Under Grey the forces of south-west Ireland and of Desmond in particular proved dangerously unreliable because of the international situation. Under St Leger difficulties arose as Desmond and Ormond moved closer together, through alliance and intermarriage. A Butler-dominated Munster and south Leinster seemed likely to emerge, which would be so extensive as to threaten the deputy and perhaps become too powerful for the liking of the king's government in England. It was in these circumstances, as Henry became more dependent on a small group of English counsellors, that the disappearance of Ormond from the political scene was an advantage. The fact that no effort was made to investigate his poisoning would suggest an awareness of potential embarrassment.

With the return of St Leger it must not be concluded that the challenge to his policy was at an end. Rather it was that the government had an opportunity to extend its influence during the minority of Thomas, 10th earl of Ormond. Simultaneously, St Leger could breathe more easily during the uneasy armistice between English conciliar rivals which lasted till the death of the king. With the advent of the aggressive Protestant policy under Edward VI St Leger was confronted with the recurrence of the crises which had failed to topple him in 1546. Even if the Irish equivalent of the Wars of the Roses was at an end, the rivalry of aggressive and conciliatory English policies was not.

Notes

1. James Hogan, *Ireland in the European System* (1920).
2. R. Dudley Edwards, *A New History of Ireland* (Dublin, 1972), 63ff.

3. D. B. Quinn, 'Henry VIII and Ireland 1509–34', *IHS* XII (1960–61), 318–44.
4. Wolsey's Irish material can be found in State Papers, Ireland, Henry VIII (PRO, London).
5. Quinn, loc.cit.
6. D. B. Quinn, 'Tudor Rule in Ireland 1485–1547', Univ. of London Ph.D. thesis (1934).
7. D. B. Quinn, 'Henry Fitzroy, Duke of Richmond and his connexion with Ireland 1529–30', *Bull.Inst.Hist.Res.* XII (1935), 175–7.
8. Quinn, 'Henry VIII and Ireland'.
9. *Cal.S.P. Sp.* (1534–35), 131. James, 11th earl of Desmond was accepted by the emperor as his ally against Henry VIII.
10. See R. D. Edwards, 'Venerable John Travers and the rebellion of Silken Thomas', *Studies* XXIII (1934), 697.
11. See R. D. Edwards, 'The Irish Reformation Parliament of Henry VIII 1536–7', *Historical Studies* VI (1968), 81–4.
12. *L. & P., Hen.VIII*, VII, 1211.
13. *S.P. Hen. VIII*, II, 404–7, Grey to Cromwell.
14. 28 Hen.VIII c.1. *Statutes* (1786 ed.), I, 66.
15. 28 Hen.VIII c.3. *Statutes*, I, 84.
16. This chapter was not published until the present century. The first edition of the Irish statutes was published under the patronage of Sir Henry Sidney when the Butlers were out of power. E. Curtis did not know of the original. *Cal.Ormond deeds*, III, 206.
17. 28 Hen.VIII c.5. *Statutes*, 90.
18. 28 Hen.VIII c.26. *Statutes*, 174.
19. 28 Hen.VIII c.6. *Statutes*, 91.
20. 28 Hen.VIII c.7. *Statutes*, 93.
21. 28 Hen.VIII c.8. *Statutes*, 96.
22. See B. Bradshaw, *The Dissolution of Religious Orders in Ireland*, 254.
23. Edwards, 'Reformation Parliament', 73.
24. ibid., 75.
25. *S.P. Hen.VIII*, II, 422–6.
26. 28 Hen.VIII c.12. *Statutes*, 102.
27. 28 Hen.VIII c.26. *Statutes*, 171.
28. 28 Hen.VIII c.28. *Statutes*, 174.
29. Unprinted.
30. 28 Hen.VIII c.13. *Statutes*, 104.
31. Unprinted.
32. 28 Hen.VIII c.14. *Statutes*, 110.
33. 28 Hen.VIII c.15. *Statutes*, 119.
34. 28 Hen.VIII c.16. *Statutes*, 127.
35. 28 Hen.VIII c.17. *Statutes*, 132.
36. 28 Hen.VIII c.18. *Statutes*, 135.
37. 28 Hen.VIII c.19. *Statutes*, 142.
38. 28 Hen.VIII c.20. *Statutes*, 157.
39. D. B. Quinn, 'Parliaments and Great Councils in Ireland, 1461–1586', *IHS* III (1942), 75, n.11.
40. Unprinted.
41. Unprinted.
42. 28 Hen.VIII c.25. *Statutes*, 169.
43. 28 Hen. VIII c.21. *Statutes*, 160.
44. 28 Hen.VIII c.22. *Statutes*, 161.
45. The Boyne act was unprinted.

46. 28 Hen.VIII c.23. *Statutes*, 168.
47. 28 Hen.VIII c.24. *Statutes*, 168.
48. Unprinted.
49. Unprinted.
50. Unprinted.
51. This 1477 act was unprinted. It is given in full in *S. P. Hen. VIII*, II, Part III, 534–5.
52. R. D. Edwards, *Church and State in Tudor Ireland* (Dublin, 1935), 47ff.
53. R. Bagwell, *Ireland under the Tudors* I (1885), 243.
54. Edwards, *Church and State*, 76ff.
55. D. B. Quinn, 'Bills and statutes of Irish parliaments of Henry VII and Henry VIII', *Anal.Hib* X (1941).
56. 33 Hen.VIII s.2.c.1. *Statutes*, 205.
57. 33 Hen.VIII s.2.c.2. *Statutes*, 207.
58. 33 Hen.VIII s.2.c.4. *Statutes*, 211.
59. 33 Hen.VIII s.2.c.5. *Statutes*, 213.
60. 34 Hen.VIII c.1. *Statutes*, 232.
61. 33 Hen.VIII s.1.c.2. *Statutes*, 178.
62. 33 Hen.VIII s.1.c.6. *Statutes*, 181.
63. 33 Hen.VIII s.1.c.4. *Statutes*, 179.
64. 33 Hen.VIII s.1.c.5. *Statutes*, 180.
65. 33 Hen.VIII s.1.c.3. *Statutes*, 179.
66. 33 Hen.VIII s.1.c.7. *Statutes*, 183.
67. 33 Hen.VIII s.1.c.9. *Statutes*, 185.
68. 33 Hen.VIII s.1.c.15. *Statutes*, 195.
69. 33 Hen.VIII s.1.c.10. *Statutes*, 186.
70. 33 Hen.VIII s.1.c.12. *Statutes*, 189.
71. 33 Hen.VIII s.1.c.14. *Statutes*, 193.
72. 33 Hen.VIII s.1.c.11. *Statutes*, 188.
73. 33 Hen.VIII s.1.c.13. *Statutes*, 192.
74. 33 Hen.VIII s.1.c.8. *Statutes*, 184.
75. 33 Hen.VIII s.2.c.3. *Statutes*, 209.
76. 34 Hen.VIII c.2. *Statutes*, 235.
77. 34 Hen.VIII s.2.c.1. *Statutes*, 237.
78. Bagwell, op.cit., I, 257–8.
79. Sir John Davies, *Le primer report des cases et matters en ley resolues et adiuges en les courts de roy en Ireland* (1615; Edinburgh, 1907).
80. Edwards, *Church and State*, 92ff, 101ff.
81. ibid., 117ff.
82. ibid.
83. Bagwell, op.cit., I, 282ff.
84. ibid., 282–5.
85. ibid.

THE PROTESTANT CHALLENGE

Accession of Edward VI

With the accession of Edward VI, an aggressive Protestant group tended to dominate policy, particularly in relation to Ireland. That same mentality, which in relations with Scotland tried by violence to secure a matrimonial arrangement between Edward VI and Mary queen of Scots, was in the ascendant in taking decisions against the St Leger policy of conciliation of Ireland.[1]

Brabazon's Policy

It appears that once again the English bureaucrats in Ireland took the initiative. In particular, Brabazon, who as Lord Justice had resorted to a major military attack on Brian O'Connor, chief of Offaly, while St Leger was under fire before the Privy Council in London, now reinforced his ideas in massive memoranda against the restored St Leger.[2] The kernel of his viewpoint was that only through an active military policy could English interests in Ireland survive. Conditions in the south and west were notoriously vulnerable to an invasion from France or from any other power. The Irish ports were prey to the pirates who lived around the coasts and were virtually cut off from the hinterland by marauding Irish chieftains. The Lord Deputy's policy, like that of the Geraldines, was to prefer the Irish to the English. The Pale had suffered from his exactions and from exposure to irrepressible Irish chiefs who had proved in his absence to be capable of resorting to force against the peaceable inhabitants. In a systematic survey of personnel in Ireland, Brabazon distinguished between the effective military-minded officials and the indolent, corrupt, and inefficient supporters of conciliation. An active policy would necessitate a greater English outlay, but would inevitably result in an increased revenue in Ireland, through confiscation and resettlement.[3]

The government of Protector Somerset, which had seized power in England somewhat irregularly by suppressing the will of Henry VIII, decided to favour a more aggressive line in Ireland. St Leger was retained, but reinforced early in 1548 by a military commander, Sir Edward Bellingham, who was particularly concerned about the fortifications of the southern coast. His initial activities so satisfied his allies in Ireland and his masters in England that in April it was decided to recall St Leger and give his office to Bellingham.[4]

Bellingham's Campaign

Early in the viceroyalty, a quarrel was picked with O'Connor of Offaly.
Bellingham's general aggressiveness so outraged the midland Irish that
even a rival of O'Connor's like his brother Cahir and his traditional
enemy, O'More, combined with him to stage an unsuccessful resistance.
After a devastating campaign, the deputy captured O'Connor's fort at
Daingean and reconstructed it as an outlying garrison point for the Pale.
For the rest, he kept his eye on the strategic points throughout the
country and secured regular and effective communications which
enabled him to enforce his policy, albeit in a rough and ready manner.[5]

In the religious sphere, the Protestant changes approved in England
were introduced wherever the deputy's power was effective. There was
some reluctance to read the new royal injunctions in English at Mass in
St Patrick's Cathedral in 1548. Hearing of this, Bellingham admonished
Fitzwilliam, the treasurer of the cathedral, and warned him that there
would be no toleration for any obstruction to 'that godly and true
order. . . . . .set forth in the Church'.[6]

Return of St Leger

Though Bellingham for the moment succeeded in intimidating opposition
in Ireland, and though the government was content to debase the coinage
to provide an adequate income for the increased costs, matters soon
took a different turn. The restiveness of the Irish generally became so
apparent that there was a risk that an invasion from France might be
followed by a national uprising against England. So in 1550 St Leger
returned.[7]

Religious Changes

The Order of Communion introduced in English into the Latin Mass
provoked the first positive hostile reactions in the Pale to the changes in
religion. Edward Staples, bishop of Meath, complained bitterly of the
effects of the first Protestant changes in his diocese. Towards the end of
1548, his sermons, insisting that the Mass was a commemoration and
not a sacrifice, resulted in a general reaction of hostility among the local
gentry. Intimidated, the bishop sought refuge in Dublin, apparently
intending to remain where his security would be more certain.[8]

With the fall of Somerset in 1551 the end finally came for the policy
of moderation: his successor, John Dudley, earl of Warwick, increased
the emphasis on the religious policy.[9]

Sir James Croft

The reason for St Leger's return did not satisfy the more aggressive element in England. Accordingly, it was decided to reinforce him with a more militaristic associate, with special responsibility for fortifications in the south where the dangers of a French invasion were considered to be greatest. Sir James Croft (or Crofts), the designated expert, was directed to pay special attention to the ports from Waterford to Kinsale and Baltimore. In fact, after inspecting the fortifications at the different ports, Croft favoured the establishment at Baltimore of a semi-military plantation, as he felt that it was essential for security reasons to settle a number of new English families there. While this policy was not acted on in Baltimore, he continued to plan for English settlements in other places.[10]

Intrigues against St Leger

Once St Leger appeared to have restored order and quietened the Irish lords who had become restless under the temporary Lords Justices, Sir Francis Bryan (16 December 1549 – 2 February 1550) and Sir William Brereton (2 February – 10 September 1550), the intrigues commenced against his conciliatory policy. Under Brabazon there had been a considerable amount of nervousness in the north where, in February 1550, French diplomatic agents were negotiating agreements with the independent Irish chiefs O'Donnell and O'Doherty, as well as with the earl of Tyrone. Concurrently, the papal archbishop of Armagh, Robert Wauchop, visited his diocese, but found a reluctance on the part of the northern chiefs to identify themselves publicly with him. While it is probable that the archbishop's activities were confined to his spiritual functions, the fact that he operated under the aegis of the Franco-Scottish alliance inevitably influenced those who regarded associates of the French as committed to their foreign policy. In less than a month the northern visitors withdrew and peace was made between England and France. The circumstances may have influenced Tyrone and his Irish allies to transmit some of their French correspondence through the king's archbishop of Armagh, George Dowdall, to the Dublin government. It seemed likely, therefore, that if these matters were not too closely investigated, the situation would quieten down in the north.[11]

Policy of Conciliation

During the summer of 1550, the conciliatory policy was pursued. The papal bishop of Dromore was permitted to surrender his bulls and gain royal recognition for the same diocese. Sir John Mason, the English ambassador in France, was sending fresh warnings regarding George Paris, an Irish exile there, who had allegedly been intriguing in the south and west of Ireland. It was decided by the English Council to send conciliatory letters to the leading Irish lords to strengthen the hand of St Leger.[12] By the autumn of 1550, but for one factor, the political situation seemed to have stabilized: that factor was religion.

Problems Facing St Leger

Before the end of the year St Leger was involved in securing compliance with the government's changes in the liturgy of the Mass. These involved the replacement of the stone altars in the churches by wooden tables, and the prohibition of public celebration of the Mass except as provided in the Order of Communion. In consequence the Lord Deputy found himself involved in discussions with Primate Dowdall, who was not prepared to celebrate communion in accordance with the new liturgy. St Leger, who favoured nominal conformity, was not anxious to coerce the primate too much, particularly as he regarded him as a reliable element of resistance both to papal authority and to the French.[13]

The situation was complicated by the fact that English proclamations, in ordering the abandonment of popish rituals, identified the proscribed liturgy with the pope. But most of the public missals in use in England would have substituted the king for the pope. Dowdall had subscribed to the royal supremacy under Henry VIII, and was therefore valuable to St Leger, as he was likely to influence many loyalists among the Anglo-Irish of the Pale, who had a comparably conservative outlook on the recent religious changes.[14]

St Leger was thus involved in a more difficult religious controversy than any which had existed since Cromwell's death. His predecessor, Bellingham, had identified himself fully with the Protestant policy of Somerset, to the extent of participating in a new attack on images in churches and in the devastation of religious houses in those independent Irish areas penetrated on his military expeditions. The destruction at Clonmacnoise in this reign was recorded by the annalists much as the earlier destruction of the Vikings had been recorded. St Leger's policy was to safeguard the primate from persecution by conniving at his withdrawal from Dublin into his own diocese. At the same time he made much of the necessity of facing the language problem. An Irish translation of the Book of Common Prayer was not to emerge for another generation, but St Leger must be credited with attempting to procure a Latin version when he could not arrange for one in Irish and where an English version would have been meaningless. While there does not appear to have been any more than an informal arrangement permitting the continued use of a Latin communion service, it is undeniable that the viceroy was seeking to quieten the public by restricting the area of controversy. His efforts, however, were the subject of criticism and complaint.[15]

Dowdall and Browne

Archbishop Browne of Dublin had apparently lapsed into a conservative attitude before Henry VIII's death. Before the first changes were promulgated in Dublin, he was alleged to have criticized a Scottish preacher who challenged the orthodox views on the Blessed Sacrament. Towards the end of the reign Browne was again to be criticized by John Bale, bishop designate of Ossory and an enthusiastic reformer of the second generation, for obstructing the most recent English changes sanctioned in the second Prayerbook. However, between 1547 and 1553, Browne had conformed to the first Prayerbook, probably under the influence of Lord Deputy Bellingham, who took seriously the duty of enforcing the first Act of Uniformity. After St Leger's return in 1550, Browne complained that he was obstructed in carrying out the Protestant policy by the viceroy, whose personal attitude he represented, perhaps unintentionally, as being publicly opposed to the government's new regulations. St Leger, anxious to keep the peace between the archbishops of Armagh and Dublin, found himself on the side of the former in a controversy which ended only with the flight from Ireland of Dowdall and the transfer after July 1551 to Browne of the primatial title, after a petition to Warwick. Browne was of no help to the deputy: he continued to criticize him publicly. However, it was not to be the archbishop whose challenge of St Leger would prove successful. Andrew Brereton, an English adventurer planted by Bellingham, upset first the earl of Tyrone and then the deputy.[16]

Andrew Brereton

In November 1550, Brereton, who held a lease at Lecale from Bellingham, had become the subject of a complaint by Tyrone for having executed out of hand two of his brothers-in-law, who had come into that area to distrain for Tyrone's rents. The earl had taken the matter to Dublin and in the inquiry which followed, Brereton had called him a traitor and accused him of intrigues with the French — on the authority of someone described by St Leger as a wood-kern. The deputy believed that Brereton's methods of dealing with the Irish would inevitably set Ulster

afire. He was directed to leave Lecale, but permitted to return to
England. There his contacts were sufficiently good to influence the
Council in April 1551, now that the French danger was over, to withdraw St Leger and restore to Brereton his northern position. Gradually,
the methods which Somerset had employed against the Scots were
becoming normal in dealing with the Irish.[17]

Croft Lord Deputy

In June 1551, Sir James Croft, having displayed enthusiasm and effec-
tiveness in fortifying the coast, replaced St Leger as Lord Deputy.
Unlike Bellingham, he was not a convinced coercionist. He tended, in
fact, to pursue the moderate methods of St Leger. On 17 August,
however, the king himself assured his Irish deputy that the pacification
of Ireland's chiefs would be achieved not by their voluntary submissions,
but by the exercise of the royal power. Concurrently, Archbishop
Browne accused St Leger to Warwick of treasonable practices.[18]

Browne and St Leger

In a long letter the archbishop rehearsed a number of incidents, which
in fact implied no more than that St Leger was hostile on the religious
issue to the advanced policy of Warwick. He insinuated rather than
directly alleged that the former deputy's behaviour had been treasonable.[19] It may seem easy to regard the archbishop's accusations as
malicious and unjustifiable, but he displayed a great fear of St Leger
and of his vindictiveness. Browne had previously dispatched to the
Council of London some doctrinal works advocating transubstantiation,
which St Leger had given him when he was deputy. St Leger had subsequently, Browne believed, been informed of this and had told a third
party that he was determined to make Browne suffer for it.

It should also be remembered that, to the Protestant party, the upholders of the older rite were no better than papists and might well be
involved with foreign powers against England's Protestant government.
Moreover, after the recall of St Leger, about the end of July 1551,
Archbishop Dowdall had withdrawn from Ireland — inevitably creating
the suspicion at Dublin that he was involved with the Catholic powers.
And while the Dublin archbishop used this excuse to secure government
acquiescence in the transfer of the primacy from Armagh to himself, his
belief in the existence of a critical situation could well have been
genuine.

Unfortunately for Browne, he secured no support in Dublin against
St Leger — except possibly from Bishop Lancaster of Kildare. In

particular, Sir John Allen, the former Chancellor, testified in St Leger's
favour, although indicating clearly his preference for the archbishop over
the former deputy. Once again the matter of viceregal behaviour was the
subject of investigation by the English government: on this occasion
Lord Deputy Croft was directed to carry through the investigation in
Dublin. Allen's answers certainly corroborated other evidence that St
Leger's conciliatory attitude made him regard the advocacy of the
Reformation with distaste. However, Allen denied that St Leger had
said to him that religion would mar all and he denied having said to
Browne that the deputy had said anything like it. No doubt the former
chancellor was not anxious to find himself back in prison — where he
had been on a previous occasion when he had been involved in unsus-
tainable charges against St Leger. It may be concluded then that the
charge of treason was not sustained — though it appears that Browne
did not earn the reproofs which had been experienced by St Leger's
former adversaries. There is the additional implication that London
tardily came to the conclusion in the summer of 1552 that the
question of religion required to be handled more moderately in Ireland
than elsewhere.[20]

The European Situation

The international situation with France and Scotland had still been
critical in the autumn of 1551 when Lord Deputy Croft was successfully resisted by north of Ireland Scots, against whom he had proceeded: it became more favourable in the following spring. In April
1552 Warwick, who had become duke of Northumberland late in the
preceding year, successfully negotiated a peace with France. By
returning the captured Boulogne, the English negotiators secured a
substantial subsidy and arranged to obviate future Irish difficulties by
pardoning and restoring the exiled Gerald of Kildare. The good
relations subsequently maintained between France and England seem
to have proceeded on the basis of each power supporting one religion
at home and a different one abroad. For Northumberland, the continuation of a policy of a radical Protestant nature became increasingly
necessary as the king's health declined and the danger of his being
succeeded by his Catholic half-sister Mary loomed larger. Abandonment
by the French of Irish alliances could therefore be an advantage. And
there even appears to have been an understanding that Scotland would
also not be used as a springboard against England. Within less than a
year, Northumberland was to secure French acquiescence in his plan to
transfer the English realms from the Tudors to the Dudleys, on the

death of the king.[21]

Meanwhile, in Ireland, Lord Deputy Croft occupied himself with strengthening internal as well as maritime fortifications, urging the government to reinforce him with better bishops and better coin.[22]

Plantation Project

As early as Bellingham's day, a policy of plantation of Leix-Offaly had been under consideration. Under orders from London, primarily as a protective measure, the fortification policy was now to be made permanent after systematically surveying the lands of the O'Mores, the O'Connors, and their allies. Early in 1552 Edward Walsh, a Waterford citizen, elaborated a plan to establish a large-scale colonization scheme in the east midlands. His project exemplified the continued hostility of the Anglo-Irish to any ideas of anglicizing the natives. He urged the reversion to what he regarded as the older colonial methods in Ireland, favouring settlement in depth by massive grants of small areas to loyalists from England or Ireland. Walsh's policy did not commend itself to a needy government whose financial necessities led it to maintain a policy of plantation rents. But it increasingly influenced the administrative ideas which for nearly a hundred and fifty years were to dominate English statesmen in their planning for Ireland. Another contemporary scheme was that suggested by a group of English and Anglo-Irish land speculators, who offered their services in return for a grant of the lands of O'More and his allies. This scheme also proved unacceptable, probably because it seemed likely to lead to the setting-up of a new palatinate jurisdiction in Ireland. Ultimately, a plantation scheme was devised in which some of the newer adventurers participated. The government's involvement was minimal. The new settlers were selected in large part on the understanding that they would be available for military service when needed. In return for the leases of confiscated monastic and native properties, they would pay a reasonable rent. These were the initial stages of what developed in the next reign into the statutory establishment of King's County and Queen's County, replacing the hitherto independent lordships of Offaly and Leix. In the short term, however, the government was to be disillusioned by the failure of the scheme to increase revenue.[23]

The plantation policy almost inevitably created general instability among the Irish of the east midlands. Cormac O'Connor of Offaly arrived in Paris, anxious to align himself with the forces planning to invade Ireland and defeat the encroaching English. He is notable because hitherto such attempts to secure foreign aid had originated in the west from O'Brien, in the south from Desmond, and in the north from O'Donnell: they had hardly involved any of the independent lordships nearer to the Pale. Because of their association with the Fitzgeralds of Kildare, the O'Connors probably had some knowledge of their continental connections. At this juncture they were to be disappointed with their initiative. Henri II of France, having successfully disposed of the English threat, was anxious to avoid marginal issues and keep the way clear for the next great movement against the Hapsburgs. Like George Paris, Cormac O'Connor was obliged to accept fair speeches in the hope that a better day might come for his Irish plans. Meanwhile, the government of Edward VI in Ireland was adding to Edward's difficulties by the pursuit of its religious policy.[24]

Deficiencies of Episcopacy

It has been pointed out that Lord Deputy Croft, in addition to his military concerns, was anxious to secure better bishops and better coin. He was finding the religious policy of the English government as negative as had St Leger. Instructed to set forth the Word of God, Croft found himself frustrated by the failure of the bishops and of other church ministers. Although there was now available an edition for Ireland of the Book of Common Prayer, Croft seems to have had no more support than had his predecessors. The precision of his statements to the lords of the Council in England make it clear that the Reformation had come to a halt. He insisted that he required either the appointment to existing vacancies of dependable English bishops or the assistance of a spiritual adviser of episcopal rank upon whom he could rely and to whom he would pay whatever fee the English Council suggested. The implication is clear – that the Lord Deputy could not rely for such services on Archbishop Browne, Bishop Staples, or any other nominal Protestant already in the Irish Council. Twelve months later his viewpoint is apparently corroborated by the episcopal consecrations of Bale and Goodacre – two of the few suitable English nominees whom the government secured from England. It is a reasonable inference that Croft's alternative, a special spiritual adviser, was never provided. For the remainder of his stay in Ireland the deputy, a genuine supporter of the Reformation, was obliged to confine himself to despoiling the churches and retrieving their valuables – many of these being assigned to the royal mint recently established in Ireland.[25]

Debasement of Currency

The debasement of the currency was a feature of government activity in
England from the later days of Henry VIII. The extension of this policy
to Ireland had the direst consequences: the public lost faith in the
coinage. That such a result was inevitable would have been appreciated
in the nineteenth century, but during the 1540s it had little influence
on government thinking. There is evidence that Northumberland had
more advanced economic ideas than had his predecessors in government,
as indicated by his utilization in English financial negotiations of Sir
Thomas Gresham (the enunciator of Gresham's Law: 'bad money drives
out good'). But the thinking did not extend to Ireland sufficiently soon
to suit Croft. The reaction of both the merchants in Dublin and the
military forces was to judge coinage by its purchasing power if not from
its intrinsic value. Croft was obliged to report that his efforts to teach
modern economics had proved a failure and that commercial users
were not prepared to believe that coins should be taken at their face
value. His reiteration of the need for the government to abandon its
policy of relying on the debased coin did not at first secure acceptance. Instead he was expected to treat his hearers to an edifying lecture
which would persuade them to regard the Reformation as antecedent
to more material reforms. It has been said of Northumberland that,
while he pushed the Reformation, he was more concerned with its
revenue potential than with the actual work of converting the people
to Protestantism. Such a criticism at this juncture had some validity.
Croft was recommended to press on wherever possible with the policy
of destroying monasteries and images and securing their valuables for
the state. Of course, this could be considered a mere continuation of
Protector Somerset's policy by Northumberland. It was under Somerset,
for example, that St Patrick's Cathedral in Dublin had been partially
destroyed, its dean being directed to transmit to Thomas Agard in control
of the mint a thousand ounces of plate, for which he was to be given
twenty pounds. The reiteration to Croft of that type of advice may
not have resulted in much additional metal for the mint. It did, however, provide the deputy with adequate justification for leasing religious
properties wherever he settled a garrison or an adventurer. It also
explains in part why the annalists in the next century emphasized the
extent of the sales of church metals by government despoilers.[26]

Success of Croft

Eventually, Croft was successful in gaining approval for a new policy
regarding the coinage, though once again the interests of Northumberland

and the Council took precedence over the interests of the Dublin
government. Croft was directed to postpone a revaluation until after the
dispatch of a further consignment of coin to Ireland to meet the most
urgent demands. Moreover, disappointment was expressed at Dublin's
failure to increase the revenue. This serves to remind us that the
aggressive policy was based primarily on the belief that there would be
a substantial tribute from Ireland in the short run. There was more than
a hint that officials in Ireland were more concerned with their profits
than with those of the government. Although, unlike others, the deputy
displayed no tendency to make whipping boys of colleagues when his
own efficiency was called into question, he seems to have endeavoured
to shield Brabazon, whose accounts suggest a long-term administrative
failure.[27] In the long run St Leger, who was to succeed Croft before the
end of the reign, was blamed for being at least partly responsible for the
financial failure of the Treasurer.

The successive deputies seemed to have maintained an accord regarding policy. On 8 May 1552 Sir Thomas Cusack – for long a friend to
St Leger – reported at length to Northumberland on Croft's success in
stabilizing the Irish lordships generally. It was particularly satisfactory
that in Munster the earl of Desmond had become reconciled to the new
order, even if his Protestantism was no more than nominal and the old
rites were persisted in throughout his territory. MacCarthy Mor had
submitted and there was no longer any fear that any Irish group would
support an invader. Cusack reported equally optimistically on the west,
where good relations now existed between Clanricarde and MacWilliam
Iochtar. In the north there was for the moment peace and Cusack was
sanguine that the deputy's measures would contain the Scots as well as
the O'Neills. The dangers from O'Donnell had receded. It was only in
the north midlands that Cusack saw any possibility of trouble. While
O'Reilly was now loyal, the minor chiefs east of the Shannon were
restive. However, Cusack believed that their mutual antipathies should
keep them from bothering the English government.[28]

With hindsight, the historian can easily qualify the Chancellor's
optimism. A major problem arose from a series of challenges to the
hereditary principle, in the south, west, and north. The government was
of course committed to maintaining the heirs designated at law for
their new peerages. The difficulties in the south were resolvable. In
Clare they were to prove a major problem necessitating the creation of
further peerages. In the west the consequences of the matrimonial
adventures of Clanricarde assumed Tudor-like proportions which were
not resolved until the end of the century. But in the north the baron of

Dungannon, heir of Tyrone, was to become such a liability through his vulnerability to the military genius of his rival Shane O'Neill, that for twenty years government prestige in the international sphere was seriously affected.[29]

There were also problems looming for Protestantism. Despite the loyal protestations of the earls, Catholicism still flourished in the south-west and north, except in a few walled towns. While the exigencies of the English situation necessitated the introduction of the more radical second Prayerbook, Northumberland can have had no illusions about the lack of success of the first Prayerbook in Ireland.[30] For now, however, his greatest preoccupation was with the Irish financial situation.

Brabazon as Treasurer

On 29 May 1552, dissatisfaction was registered at the non-emergence of the promised increase in Irish revenue. Over the preceding few years the Treasurer's accounts had been the subject of unresolved investigations. The sixteenth-century accounting system was virtually an open invitation to any enterprising treasurer to exploit his position. Sir William Brabazon succeeded in building up a fortune from which his descendants, the earls of Meath, were to profit. His own ambitions may be deduced from his attempt to marry the widow of the executed Silken Thomas. His utilization of his powers as receiver of the properties of the dissolved religious houses enabled him to acquire widespread territory in the north of the modern County Wicklow, subsequently in Athlone and later in Mellifont. Brabazon died in July 1552, leaving to his co-Treasurer, Andrew Wyse, an alleged debt to the Exchequer of £12,000. These uncertainties were subsequently to lead to Wyse's imprisonment and to allegations that St Leger was an accessory to embezzlement.

John Bale

More immediately, by the end of the year, Ireland had to experience another transient administration, this time presided over by Sir Thomas Cusack and Gerald Aylmer. The withdrawal of Croft — in the first instance for consultation — was ultimately to lead to the return of St Leger. In the meantime a decision had been made by Northumberland regarding the vacant bishoprics. Hugh Goodacre was designated to Armagh and the celebrated John Bale to Ossory. Though the primacy was to be maintained in Dublin, a northern archbishop was still con-sidered essential, but the Irish Protestants experienced the humiliation of Cashel, the southern archbishopric, remaining unfilled. Some effort, therefore, was being made to keep Ireland in line with Northumberland's more Protestant policy for England, but the vagueness and uncertainty of the whole situation emerged clearly on 2 February 1553 at the consecration of the new bishops. Archbishop Browne displayed no knowledge of the ordinal for the consecration of bishops which had been issued more than a year previously. Perhaps he might have been absolved for displaying no knowledge of the second Prayerbook — only recently proclaimed in England — but he scandalized at least one of the bishops elect, John Bale, by his obvious reluctance to accept the revised Liturgy as applicable in Ireland. The ebullient Bale, whose autobiographical extravagances were to be published surreptitiously in the reign of Queen Mary, insisted on the newer rite being employed — declaring that he would tolerate none other once he arrived at his see of Ossory. One can hardly accept the uncorroborated statements of Bale against any opponent — whatever he said about his few friends. Certainly Sir Thomas Cusack and his fellow Lord Justice permitted the use of the new Prayerbook. But it is unlikely that Bale exaggerated in claiming that the viceregal authority was necessary to overcome the fears expressed by opponents of the newer Protestantism, who foresaw a riot in the capital city.[31]

Again, in his own diocese at Kilkenny, the testimony of Bale — however entertaining — would hardly be sufficient to sustain a case in a modern court of law against officials of Church and state who obstructed and frustrated his efforts to enforce the second Prayerbook. We do not, however, have to dismiss as imaginative the bishop's descriptions of the reactions to his sermons against the pope and on the idolatry of the Mass. If we are unconvinced by his allegation — for which some corroboration exists — that the early death in Dublin of Archbishop Goodacre was due to his being poisoned by Armagh popish clergy, it is only reasonable to infer that Bale himself, in the face of rejoicings at the restoration of Catholic services after the death of Edward VI, disappeared out of his diocese and out of the country, in fear of his life.[32]

Return of St Leger

The return of St Leger did not take place until after the proclamation as queen in July 1553 of the Lady Jane Grey and indeed until after the proclamation some ten days later of her successor, Queen Mary Tudor. Subsequent events were to show that however Catholic was Queen Mary, so far as Ireland was concerned she was still a Tudor.

Notes

1. W. K. Jordan, *Edward VI : the Young King* (1968); J. K. McConica, *English Humanists and Reformation Politics under Henry VIII and Edward VI* (1965); A. G. Dickens, *The English Reformation* (1970); S. T. Bindoff, *Tudor England* (repr. 1969).
2. D. G. White, 'The reign of Edward VI in Ireland', *IHS* XIV (1965), 197–211.
3. ibid.
4. *Handbook of British Chronology* (2nd ed., 1939), 115.
5. White, op. cit.
6. Edwards, *Church and State*, 128.
7. ibid. See also: White, op.cit.; and E. P. Shirley ed., *Original Letters and Papers in illustration of the history of the church in Ireland during the reigns of Edward VI, Mary and Elizabeth* (1851), no. 16.
8. ibid., nos. 5, 7.
9. W. K. Jordan, *Edward VI : the Threshold of Power* (1970), ch. 2.
10. White, op. cit.; also P. Wilson, *The Beginnings of Modern Ireland* (Dublin, 1912), ch. 6.
11. Edwards, *Church and State*, 150ff.
12. ibid.
13. Shirley, *Original Letters*, no. 23.
14. White, op. cit.
15. Shirley, *Original Letters*, nos. 23, 26.
16. White, op.cit.; Wilson, op.cit., 408.
17. R. Bagwell, *Ireland under the Tudors* I, 353ff.
18. *Cal.S.P.Ireland 1509–73*, 115.
19. Shirley, *Original Letters*, no. 23.
20. Edwards, *Church and State*, 119ff.
21. White, op.cit.
22. Shirley, *Original Letters*, no. 25.
23. White, op.cit.
24. ibid.; also Wilson, op.cit., 408.
25. White, op.cit.
26. D. B. Quinn, 'Tudor Rule in Ireland'.
27. White, op.cit., 207–8.
28. Wilson, op.cit., 342ff.
29. ibid.
30. Edwards, *Church and State*, 141ff.
31. ibid.
32. White, op.cit.

4 THE CATHOLIC REACTION

Mary Tudor's Policy

Continuity in methods of governing Ireland links the short reigns between the death of Henry VIII and the accession of Elizabeth I. It is important not to make too much of the Catholic reaction. Its primary significance was in the sphere of foreign affairs rather than in religion. Mary the Catholic was as much a believer in coercion and force as her brother Edward the Protestant. The disastrous consequences of her foreign policy were apparent subsequently, by contrast with the more successful methods of her younger sister. The relative insignificance of England comes out clearly under Mary, whose decision to abandon the French alliance for a Spanish one rapidly subordinated her government to the position of a satellite of the Hapsburgs. Just as under Edward VI, the government's sense of urgency created an impatience with conciliation as a policy. The continuation of the plantation policy provoked such a widespread unrest among the Irish chiefs that nothing but Mary's early decease would have prevented their general alliance with France and Scotland. It is in this context that one must see the dramatic alterations in public observance that took place in Ireland after the death of Edward VI.[1]

The religious changes introduced by the queen in England, though gradual, precipitated Protestant riots and early in 1554 a rebellion led by Sir Thomas Wyatt. The successful crushing of this rebellion, in which Sir Thomas Radcliffe (Viscount Fitzwalter and subsequently Irish Lord Deputy) took a leading part, resulted in the decision to proceed more drastically against the opposition and even against Lady Jane Grey, who was a possible focus for further trouble. Thereafter Queen Mary used her power as sovereign to strengthen the Catholic position. But she was careful to involve parliament in the restoration of papal authority in England. The Spanish alliance and the subsequent Spanish marriage were also causes of popular dissatisfaction. While the queen was determined to proceed with her policy, she endeavoured to maintain a diplomatic attitude and it was in these circumstances that St Leger's return to Ireland was proceeded with. The queen's difficulties in Ireland were twofold: first, most of the leading members of the Dublin administration were convinced Protestants and second, most of them believed that the Irish were conspiring with the Scots and the

French. A cautious policy, favouring moderation, was therefore the safest.[2]

Religious Policy in Ireland

The surviving documentation suggests that the main interest in the first two years was concentrated on the religious question. The absence of much documentation in the archives of the Secretary for State hints that Mary's short reign created in retrospect too many embarrassments for the statesmen who survived her. But if government policy in Ireland was mainly concerned with moderation, the religious issues were in fact those most likely to require attention and conservative public opinion made it relatively easy to abrogate Protestantism without any undue demonstrations of hostility. Probably only Bishop Bale in Ossory experienced a demonstration of riotous Catholicism and he himself is our source for the evidence that elsewhere the Protestant bishops were prepared to compromise with Mary. In these circumstances a different policy was adopted in Ireland. In England heresy or matrimony constituted the usual grounds for depriving a bishop; in Ireland no bishop was deprived for heresy.[3]

Financial Situation in Ireland

The financial situation which Mary inherited did not make it easy to maintain a policy of expansion. There still existed under Edward VI a belief that substantial mineral wealth existed in Ireland, but even before the king's death the mining experiment undertaken to provide the raw material for the royal mint at Dublin had proved disastrous. Accordingly, St Leger was directed in his official instructions — which concentrated as much on financial aspects as had his instructions from the queen's father — to close down the mining enterprise and dismiss the Germans who had been imported to locate the precious metals. So serious was the crisis that a royal warrant was issued to borrow 6,000 pounds from the executors of Justice Luttrell. St Leger was deprived of one source on which government had leaned heavily during the reign of Edward VI. So far from sanctioning the continued spoliation of the monasteries, under Mary it became official policy to restore monastic houses wherever possible: this inevitably increased public liabilities. In practice very little was accomplished in this direction apart from a few spectacular restorations such as that of the Knights of St John at Kilmainham, for which a new English prior, Oswald Massingberd, was provided. Nor could the queen demur when the earl of Desmond requested immunity from rent demands for monastic houses granted to him, which he declared he had restored to their orders. The queen was careful to protect the royal prerogative against Gaelic lords who sought direct provision from the pope. But the scarcity of money was serious and the Dublin exchequer continued its barrage of financial demands on England. In the event a go-slow policy was virtually dictated, though circumstances such as the restoration of the Fitzgerald estates to Kildare under Edward VI pointed ominously towards an early resumption of plantation projects. These were necessary if only to reimburse the royal grantees who were now obliged to make way for restored religious and restored Geraldines. Perhaps one good illustration of the new policy can be seen in the decision to re-establish St Patrick's Cathedral in Dublin. The slowness with which this was accomplished and the appearance among the prebendaries to be appointed of the name of George Browne, former archbishop of Dublin, represents a fair example of the complexities of the state's problem.[4]

Episcopal Appointments

In the first months of her reign the queen accordingly contented herself with appointing ecclesiastics to vacancies created by the Protestant flight from Ireland or by the failure of the preceding regime to fill them. Thus to Ossory went John Thonery and to Cashel went Roland Baron, while to Armagh and the primacy returned Dowdall. But the queen was careful, no doubt under St Leger's tutoring, to hasten slowly and accordingly we find on 20 November 1553 that the commission for the discharge of the duties of justice of the peace in the county of Dublin included George Browne, who was not to be deprived of his archbishopric for another year.[5]

It was in March 1554 that the first steps against married clergy were taken. Thomas Lancaster was deprived of the bishopric of Kildare, which went to Thomas Leverous. In the previous reign Sir James Croft had been ready to promote this former tutor (who had spirited young Kildare out of the country) because he considered him the most outstanding exponent of religion gracing the pulpit — whether his sermons were in English or Irish. Admittedly Croft was desperately seeking suitable religious ministers to advance the Reformation and therefore presumably prepared to accept a conformist who would so use the Protestant liturgy that it would appear more like a popish Mass. Nevertheless, within two years of Croft's abortive proposal, Mary was constrained to accept Leverous as a Catholic reformer.[6]

No doubt Leverous was unmarried, unlike Staples, removed from Meath in June 1554 under commission from Cardinal Pole to William

Walsh, who subsequently replaced him. It must also have been for
matrimonial reasons that Archbishop Browne had on 10 May been
ordered to London, where subsequently Pole deprived him, forgave him
his matrimony, and rehabilitated him as a priest fit for promotion to
the Dublin prebend of Clonmeathan, in the charter of St Patrick's
Cathedral — issued on 18 February 1555. History is silent on whether
the queen and her Council discussed the advisability of burning
Protestants from Ireland. Perhaps a more tolerant policy was proposed
by King Philip, to whom the queen was married on 25 July 1554, some
four months before Pole's arrival in England. Or perhaps the more
moderate line was dictated from Ireland, where Walsh's legatine
commission under Pole kept him so busy throughout that summer that
he neglected to secure his bulls of appointment from the papacy — an
omission which necessitated on 18 October 1555 his protection by
royal authority to enjoy the temporalities of Meath.[7]

Concurrent with the issue of St Patrick's charter was the appointment
as archbishop of Dublin of Hugh Corren (or Curwen), appointed by the
king and queen as from 23 February 1555. On the preceding day there
had issued from the royal chancery the *congé d'élire* to the Dublin
chapters. It was not until 21 June that Curwen was regularized in
jurisdiction by the pope. During the early months of that year other
Catholic changes took place in Ireland and on 10 March, Cardinal Pole
(at the instance of the king and queen) petitioned the pope to create a
kingdom of Ireland — thus regularizing the schismatic act of Henry
VIII in parliament. On 7 June Pope Paul IV graciously consented to
this in a bull absolving their Majesties from all censures. Subsequently
the king and queen represented the papal action as having conferred on
them all the pope's interests in Ireland, but in the meantime, by
proclamation of 13 June, they publicly banned all writings against the
pope.[8]

Pole and the Tuam Archbishopric

It was not until 1 July 1555 that Pole's legatine authority in Ireland was
formally approved by the pope. And it was under this authority that on
18 September an ecclesiastical inquiry took place on the conflicting
claims to the Tuam archbishopric of Christopher Bodkin and Arthur
O'Frighil. Perhaps this was the most difficult political issue presented
to Pole in Ireland during his brief tenure of the legateship. Bodkin's
prestige at Galway had been so high that he had virtually forced himself
on Henry VIII as archbishop of Tuam. In all the political negotiations
with Galway and with the Clanricardes, Bodkin's goodwill counted

immeasurably under Edward VI as it had under Henry VIII. The decision to recognize O'Frighil was possible only by confirming the temporalities to Bodkin and acknowledging his right to the succession. In Elizabeth's reign, in a powerful plea for Bodkin, David Wolfe, the papal nuncio, assured the pope that Bodkin alone had made possible the reconsecration of Tuam Cathedral after its devastation in the wars, when it had become the horse-stable of contending armies.[9]

Dismissal of St Leger

The end of the year brought the conclusion of the connection with Ireland of Sir Anthony St Leger. During the preceding two years, financial investigations had led to the imprisonment of Andrew Wyse, in London's Fleet prison, charged with the repayment of Brabazon's debt. In the autumn of 1555, Sir William Fitzwilliam accused the Lord Deputy of complicity in the financial muddle and, by implication, of embezzlement. On 18 December the deputy requested permission to visit London to undergo 'his purgation'. In the next generation, Campion and Stanihurst attributed St Leger's recall to the discovery that he had ridiculed transubstantiation in comic verse. It is more likely that counsels for stronger government prevailed in London and that the St Leger who had put Protestantism second to politics was now redundant in Ireland. Early in the new year steps were taken to appoint a new deputy.[10]

Appointment of Fitzwalter

Sir Thomas Radcliffe, Viscount Fitzwalter, was instructed on 28 April 1556 by Philip and Mary to advance the honour of God, the true Catholic faith and religion, and the honour and dignity of the pope, by example and in every other way. At the request of all spiritual ministers he was to be prepared to repress heretics and Lollards. For the rest his instructions were of the formal type given to his predecessors.[11]

Attempts at Financial Reform

Concurrently Sir Henry Sidney was appointed vice-treasurer and receiver-general. On 27 May, the Irish privy council began to clear up the financial mess, with a proclamation to all creditors of the state to put in their claims against their Majesties. Thereafter some attempt was made to assess all charges on government — particularly military charges. An attempt was also made to exclude claims which were regarded as improper. On 3 June a new policy had clearly been decided on — that of getting rid of the Scots by using the resources of the nobility and gentry of Ireland against the northern menace. The Council worked out a detailed system of military contribution from every county and barony within the Pale and it appears that two areas, the midlands and the north, were expected to bear the main cost of the expedition.[12]

The Deputy and the O'Mores

In the midlands swift action was taken against the O'Mores, but the action was not pursued to the point where serious government involvement would arise. Instead, by order of 28 June 1556, the earl of Kildare was made responsible for the maintenance of the fort of Daingean in O'Connor's country of Offaly. It was hoped that some similar arrangement could be made with the earl of Ormond for O'More's country. Before the end of the year plans were worked out to divide O'More's country between the natives and new settlers — the former being confined to the area 'beyond the bog'. At the same time the new deputy turned himself to the problem of the north and on 10 August Sir George Stanley was appointed Marshal of the Army of Ulster with the title of general, being given in commission a group of advisers.[13]

The Deputy in the North-East

In the north-east a plan was devised to defend neighbouring territories from the Scots and ultimately to expel them. Already, in June 1556, a naval expedition under John Baseinge had been sent against the Scottish coast. The expedition was intended to cut off the MacDonnells in Antrim from any reinforcements and then, in an all-out attack, to defeat and expel them. Fitzwalter had a flair for dominating a situation temporarily: he was less successful in following up his first advantage. Against the Scots he had issued a protective order in favour of Tyrone, which was succeeded by an agreement that the earl and the leader of his Scottish mercenaries, another MacDonnell, should field a substantial body of troops for a short period in which it was hoped finally to defeat the Scots. Within a short time, however, it became clear that the initial success could not be maintained. The MacDonnells were again in large numbers infiltrating the Route, MacQuillan's country in north Antrim.

Plantation Schemes for North-East

In autumn 1556 there were rumours that the MacDonnells were intriguing in France. At the same time the idea of an English plantation in the north-east was emerging and on 17 November the queen sent the Lord Deputy plans for his consideration, including a proposal that he

should comment on a scheme for settling north-east Ulster to keep the
Scots out. Early in the new year the deputy responded favourably,
linking the idea of an English settlement with the queen's plans for
advancing Catholicism. It was essential, he said, to secure an English
bishop who could be relied on to impose new standards in church
matters and who would not tolerate the more primitive system prevailing in Gaelic Ulster. More important than sermons, said Fitzwalter,
was an English standard in dignified church buildings and ornaments so
that the natives would be impressed by the contemplation of a permanent structural reform. He hoped it would be possible to set up
church buildings as part of the urban construction that was visualized,
and that within three or four years relatively permanent church
buildings would be erected. In such a situation the new English bishop
could be expected to establish new standards. No longer would the
clergy prove to be the most unreliable element in the community with
the lowest standards in church observance, while they themselves were
no better than mischief-makers and spies for every transient intriguer
and foreign conspirator.[14]

Failure of Deputy in North-East

Unfortunately for Fitzwalter (or Sussex, as he became in 1557), the
northern plan proved wholly illusory: it soon emerged that he lacked
the constructiveness to follow up initial success. What was worse, his
methods succeeded in alienating the tiny Anglo-Irish element in the
north and Primate George Dowdall in particular. Before the end of 1557,
Dowdall had denounced Sussex because his army had been allowed to
burn not only great quantities of crops on the excuse that they might
provision the Scots (causing non-combatants to perish from starvation)
but also church premises and properties.[15] The primate could hardly be
termed a supporter of Gaelic disorder. He was at pains to secure from
the queen permission to use excommunications and other church
sanctions against the wild Irish who refused to obey the law of England.
Dowdall's position was pragmatic: he believed that it was realistic to
preserve areas traditionally regarded as being Anglo-Irish. At
Termonfeckin in County Louth, where he normally resided like his
Anglo-Irish or English predecessors, he proposed to endow a chantry
for the perpetuation of divine service. But he appeared to have lost all
confidence in the new English administrators who showed scant concern
for the well-being of the ordinary people and resented criticism in
Council, considering it disloyal if not traitorous. Perhaps Dowdall was
overwrought by the autumn of 1557 and the early months of 1558,

when he was summoned to England to substantiate his charges. He was possibly unduly apprehensive at the attitude towards him of Sussex's soldiers; to declare that they all spoke of him as a traitor may have followed from some extravagant utterances, to which the primate attributed undue importance. He regarded himself as having lost face by the army's destruction of sacred images in his cathedral church. Sidney, who temporarily occupied the office of Lord Justice during Sussex's absence in England, believed the primate's accusations were unjustified, but went on subconsciously to corroborate Dowdall's views on English sensitivity to criticism by insisting to Sussex that Dowdall's allegations were due to personal spite.

By the end of Mary's reign, Sussex's policy in the north-east had failed to exclude the Scots permanently. They had come back in increasing numbers, under Sorley Bui MacDonnell, and had created a restiveness among the Irish. The deputy's military ineptitude was only too apparent in his failure to protect Tyrone and his son Dungannon from the aggressive group among the O'Neills who gathered around the more colourful Shane and ultimately destroyed the English influence in the centre of Ulster.

Sussex's Parliament

The acts of the Irish parliament held under Sussex are perhaps the most comprehensive statement of government policy. On the statute roll are recorded the titles of Philip and Mary, king and queen of England, Spain, France, and the Two Sicilies, of Jerusalem and Ireland, Defenders of the Faith, archdukes of Austria, dukes of Burgundy, Milan, and Brabant, counts of Hapsburg, Flanders, and the Tyrol. The first act on the statute roll affirmed the legitimacy of the queen and attributed the diseased state of society to the displeasure of Almighty God following the pronouncement of the illegal and unjustifiable divorce between her father and her mother.[16] The pleasure of parliament in participating in the declaration of the lawfulness of the marriage of Henry VIII and Catherine of Aragon extended to the repealing of all acts of parliament and sentences of divorce passed to the contrary.

By the second act the capacity of the queen to be the sovereign as fully as if she were a king was affirmed, stressing her responsibility and obligation to protect her realm and punish all ill-doers — to the frustration of ignorant and malicious persons.[17]

Philip's right and title as king for the duration of his marriage to Queen Mary was affirmed by the third act, which made it high treason to deny his royal authority. It recognized him as governor for the minority of any child of theirs succeeding to the throne, in the event of Mary predeceasing them.[18]

By the fourth act, English measures passed in the reigns of Richard II, Henry IV, and Henry V for the repression of Lollardy and the punishment of heretical preachers and persons were revived and made of full force.[19]

Chapter V repealed all statutes enacted against the apostolic see of Rome since 1529, but safeguarded ecclesiastical property which had been secularized. The measure embodied the papal bull of Paul IV empowering Cardinal Pole to call the people in to the right way and reconcile the realm to the Church. It permitted for twenty years, despite the mortmain acts, the granting of property to the Church, while safeguarding the title of the Crown.[20]

In the Act of Subsidy, the sixth act on the Roll, a ten-year tax of 13s. 4d. was imposed on all tilled plough-lands as from 29 September 1556. This was justified on the grounds of the queen's responsibility as legitimate ruler of Scotland and because the north of Ireland had been invaded and occupied quite improperly by the Irish Scots from the Isles (known as Redshanks), whom she was determined to expel. This had already been effected in part by Lord Deputy Sussex. It was provided that the gentry involved by the government in military hostings should be exempted from the tax.[21]

The policy of plantation was legislatively inaugurated by the seventh act, which affirmed the right of the king and queen to authorize the Lord Deputy to grant estates or leases to English and Irish subjects in the countries (or regions) of Leix, Slewmargy, Offaly, Irry, and Glenmaliry. These of right belonged to the sovereigns, but allegedly had been of late possessed by the O'Mores, O'Connors, O'Dempseys, and other of the Irishry — rebels, subsequently driven out by Sussex. The grants were to be subject to rents and there were to be exemptions for the land claims of the earl of Kildare and certain ecclesiastics, to be mentioned in the next succeeding act.[22]

By the eighth act, in relation to the regions just mentioned, the rights of the king and queen and the heirs and successors of the queen were affirmed, and their conversion into shire grounds declared. It was recited that the O'Mores, O'Dempseys, and O'Connors and others of the Irishry lately inhabiting the above countries, had by their sundry manifest treasons after many pardons granted to them yet often rebelled. Thus Edward VI was provoked to use his power against them and recovered those countries. Since then they had traitorously, contrary to their bounden duties, by force entered the said countries and held them against their Majesties until Lord Deputy Sussex by the sword evicted these Irish enemies out of the countries. As these were not within any shires in which by legal process lands could be passed in grants by the Lord Deputy, they were set up as King's County and Queen's County. The act was not to prejudice the rights of the earl of Kildare or the bishops of Dublin, Kildare, and Leighlin.[23]

The ninth act was part of the expansion plan and authorized the future conversion into shire grounds of waste grounds 'where divers robberies, murders and felonies be daily committed'. The sovereigns, however, were authorized within seven years to abrogate the act or anything arising from it after proclamation under the Great Seal of Ireland.[24]

By the tenth act, not subsequently printed, it was provided that the former archbishop of Dublin's alienations of church property should be revoked, including any lands unlawfully held by wild Irishmen or rebels. It is not clear why this act, alone of the measures of the parliament, did not get into print. It can only be conjectured that if Adam Loftus, George Browne's successor in Sidney's time, when the statutes were being printed, had desired to have the measure included in Hooker's edition, it would not have been omitted. Presumably, with the reversion of policy under Elizabeth, the archbishop was in a position to effect satisfactory compromise with Browne's grantees.[25]

The eleventh act was concerned with the exposition of Poynings's Law. It was recited that ambiguities in the act of Henry VII demanded more precise definition. It was laid down that the sovereign was to certify under the Great Seal of England the approved measures, and there was no reference to the privy council. In Ireland, the chief governor and the Council were empowered to send over supplemental measures after parliament had held its first meeting. It was laid down that any Bill was to be deemed enacted, if passed, by the three estates of parliament. This would seem to imply that the proctors were not restored. There were provisos for safeguarding the validity of all previous acts and of the provisos of this session.[26]

The twelfth act provided for the discharge of the first fruits of ecclesiastical benefices. The state renounced its claim for the payment of first fruits and of the annual tenths formerly paid on grants of manors to ecclesiastical corporations. (Although reference was made to the Irish act for twentieths, it is implied that in fact tenths were levied.) Within five years this act was to be repealed under Elizabeth.[27]

The thirteenth act legislated against the Scots and particularly the Scots mercenaries. Despite the queen's title or claim regarding Scotland,

it was made high treason to bring in or retain Scots men-of-war and
felony to marry any Scot. There were provisos protecting Scots
merchants or mariners in Ireland for commerce and it was provided
that Scots who were made denizens could be exempted. The act
implied that MacDonnell infiltration into Antrim was illegal. It was to
be repealed under James I.[28]

Statute XIV against idle men recited the evil consequences of the
avoidance of labour by rural workers, who preferred to buy and sell
horses to the consequent detriment of husbandry. As from 1 May
following, a fine of 40 shillings was to be imposed on labourers for each
horse bought. Exemptions could operate for millers and carters buying
for personal trade purposes and also, between 1 August and 31 October,
labourers might claim exemption. It is difficult to see how this act
could have been enforced.[29]

The fifteenth act provided that the owners of stolen goods which
had not been recovered might seek equivalent goods from attainted or
escaped felons. Provision was made to render sheriffs liable for claims
under this act.[30]

The sixteenth and final measure attempted to impose prohibition on
the manufacture of whiskey. The recital alleged that the universal
making of whiskey, or *aqua vitae*, among the Irish wasted corn.
Accordingly manufacture was forbidden except by viceregal licence
under the Great Seal. Offenders were liable to imprisonment at the
viceroy's pleasure and a fine of £4 Irish could be imposed for every
breach of the law. Exemptions were permitted for peers, for landowners
of £10 valuation upwards, and for municipal freemen of parliamentary
boroughs who might manufacture for their own use.[31]

Sussex's Viceroyalty

On 10 March 1558, parliament was dissolved at Drogheda by the Lord
Justice in Sussex's absence. Sussex's viceroyalty has been regarded as a
turning-point in Anglo-Irish relations because of his association with
the policy of plantation – highlighted in the parliamentary statutes.
The aggressive expansionist policy which had already received some
favour under Edward VI was thereby publicly established as official
English policy in Ireland, implying abandonment of what W. F. Butler
has termed 'the policy of surrender and re-grant'. Perhaps the whole
matter can be seen more clearly if it is visualized as part of the policy
developed by the Anglo-Spanish alliance, consummated by the royal
marriage. The association of Spain with colonial enterprises in the New
World indubitably contributed to the establishment of King's County

and Queen's County, together with naming their chief towns Philipstown and Maryborough. The statutory confiscation of the lands of the O'Connors of Offaly, of the O'Mores of Leix, and of other Irish midland rulers inaugurated this policy and indeed distracted historians subsequently from the equally significant but more transient aspects of the same policy in the north of Ireland.[32] There is no doubt that it was on Sussex's advice that full royal approval was given to plans for an English settlement around the eastern shores of Lough Neagh. Sussex was advising the appointment of an English bishop in connection with the proposed plantation and his vice-treasurer, Sir Henry Sidney (after whom subsequently Lough Neagh was for a time renamed Lough Sidney), was himself seeking to build up a substantial estate in the Lecale area. This policy, however, became involved in the other statutory expansion policy of driving out the Scots. Despite initial success, Sussex in this was unable to claim any long-term achievement. Even during his own viceroyalty, he was obliged to accept the return of the MacDonnells under Sorley Bui, who ultimately secured recognition for his family from Elizabeth I. In fairness to Sussex, however, it should not be forgotten that the aggressive policy in Ireland had to be substantially modified when the king and queen became involved in a dispute with Paul IV in which the legatine authority of Cardinal Pole was terminated. Almost concurrently the outbreak in June 1557 of war with France (which also involved Scotland) resulted in the loss of Calais, decisively influencing royal policy until the end of the reign.

Papal Dispute

The papal dispute with Philip and Mary was primarily over Spanish policy in Italy. Nevertheless, it had serious repercussions for Philip's English queen and her dominions. It halted the first phase of the Counter-Reformation in England and Ireland so that thereafter the royal authority could not depend upon papal support. Thus it appears that William Walsh, Pole's chief delegate in Ireland in the exercise of his legatine authority, failed to secure papal provision for his see of Meath, to which his joint sovereigns had advanced him. It may be because of these circumstances that the initial instruction to Sussex to repress heresy, which had secured statutory endorsement, was not proceeded with. In fact, official immunity grants were issued to prominent English officials in Ireland because of the war situation with the pope as well as with Scotland and France.[33]

Sidney Replaces Sussex

As with Bellingham under Edward VI, the Sussex policy became a liability once Irish lords were in a position to intrigue with foreign powers. The viceregal policy had attempted to secure the support of Kildare and Ormond as well as of leading lords of the Pale, the midlands, and the north-east. In the war situation the inadequacy of his equipment and the shortage of money and English soldiers inevitably affected Sussex. His value to Mary at the beginning of her reign in defeating Wyatt's rebellion made it almost inevitable that the queen would appeal to him to return to England in the crisis over the loss of Calais in January 1558. In these circumstances, on 18 September 1558, Sidney temporarily replaced Sussex at the head of the queen's government in Ireland, and Dowdall, who had proved so invaluable not ten years earlier in securing the allegiance of the northern chiefs, expressed himself very forcefully against Sussex's behaviour in Ireland.[34] It seemed that the independent Irish were never more likely to secure support from France and Scotland than at this time. Consequently, the queen's Irish advisers considered that it might be in their own interests to be recalled rather than to be driven out, as had happened to the English at Calais.

Death of Mary

When Mary died on 17 November 1558, it could be said that the international situation had proved too critical for the queen's advisers to give much attention to Ireland. Primate Dowdall, while critical of Sussex for his policy of devastation and his ultimate lack of constructiveness, appeared to favour his retention if he could be induced to be more conciliatory towards the independent Irish. For Dowdall had said that a godly Reformation could be achieved only by eradicating the Irish and the Scots and re-peopling the country with English. And even though the primate had then gone on to reject his own opinion as impracticable because of its costs, so that the only solution left was conciliation, the state of panic after the loss of Calais appears to have dictated a decision not to replace Sussex lest a nationwide rebellion break out.[35] Thus the reign of Catholic Mary ended much as had that of her brother — relying upon an aggressive policy to hide the deficiencies of government in Ireland and thus inevitably increasing the estrangement of the people from England.

Notes

1. D. M. Loades, *Two Tudor Conspiracies: Wyatt and Dudley, against Queen Mary* (Cambridge, 1965); D. M. Loades, 'Papers of George Wyatt', Camden Society, 4th Series, V (1968); E. H. Harbison, *Rival Ambassadors at the Court of Queen Mary* (Princeton, 1940); W. Haller, *Foxe's Book of Martyres and the Elect Nation* (1963).
2. P. Wilson, *The Beginnings of Modern Ireland* (Dublin, 1912), ch. 7.
3. Edwards, *Church and State*, ch. 11.
4. Bagwell, *Ireland under the Tudors* I, 391ff.
5. Edwards, *Church and State*, 162−3.
6. ibid.
7. ibid., 164−6.
8. 3 & 4 Phil. & Mar. c.8. *Statutes*, 252.
9. Edwards, *Church and State*, 164.
10. Shirley, *Original Letters*, no. 27.
11. ibid.
12. ibid.
13. Bagwell, *Ireland under the Tudors* I, 399. Also R. Dunlop, 'The Plantation of Leix and Offaly', *EHR* VI (1891), 61−96.
14. Shirley, *Original Letters*, no. 27.
15. ibid., no. 29.
16. 3 & 4 Phil. & Mar. c.13. *Statutes*, 274+6.
17. 3 & 4 Phil. & Mar. c.14. *Statutes*, 274+8.
18. 3 & 4 Phil. & Mar. c.11. *Statutes*, 273.
19. 3 & 4 Phil. & Mar. c.9. *Statutes*, 266.
20. 3 & 4 Phil. & Mar. c.8. *Statutes*, 252.
21. 3 & 4 Phil. & Mar. c.12. *Statutes*, 274+3.
22. 3 & 4 Phil. & Mar. c.1. *Statutes*, 240.
23. 3 & 4 Phil. & Mar. c.2. *Statutes*, 241.
24. 3 & 4 Phil. & Mar. c.3. *Statutes*, 244.
25. 3 & 4 Phil. & Mar. c.10. Unprinted.
26. 3 & 4 Phil. & Mar. c.4. *Statutes*, 246.
27. 3 & 4 Phil. & Mar. c.10. *Statutes*, 266.
28. 3 & 4 Phil. & Mar. c.15. *Statutes*, 274+10.
29. 3 & 4 Phil. & Mar. c.5. *Statutes*, 248.
30. 3 & 4 Phil. & Mar. c.6. *Statutes*, 247.
31. 3 & 4 Phil. & Mar. c.7. *Statutes*, 251.
32. R. Dunlop, *Ireland under the Commonwealth* (Manchester, 1913) preface to vol. I.
33. This could be inferred from policy documents.
34. Shirley, *Original Letters*, nos. 29, 30.
35. ibid.

5 ELIZABETH'S SETTLEMENT

Accession of Elizabeth

The continuity of Tudor policy is well illustrated by Elizabeth I's
decision to maintain in office prominent English members of the Irish
administration, notably Sussex and Sidney. The queen, as she indicated
in her first instructions to the Irish deputy and Council, had been left
by her sister with serious military and financial problems. Inevitably
these problems were approached in the context of the war with
France, in which the Spanish alliance had involved both Tudor queens.
In the negotiations which led in 1559 to the Treaty of Cateau-
Cambrésis, the Spaniards showed little concern for the English desire
to secure the restoration of Calais: this did little to render the
Spaniards more popular at the new queen's court. Elizabeth, however,
was of necessity obliged to maintain the Hapsburg alliance, if only to
enable her to resist the claims to her throne by her cousin Mary queen
of Scots, who on the death of Mary Tudor was recognized (by order of
Henri II of France) together with her husband, the Dauphin François,[1]
as ruler of Scotland, England, and Ireland.

Elizabeth and Philip II

The Anglo-Spanish alliance was equally important to Philip II, who
went to the extent of seeking the hand of the new English queen. Not
merely did he accept her refusal graciously, perhaps regarding it as a
temporary one, but he also implicitly connived at the new religious
settlement, which reaffirmed the state's supremacy over the Church and
re-established the moderate Protestant liturgy based upon an English
translation of the Roman Catholic Latin Missal. Queen Elizabeth was
at pains to make these changes slowly in an effort to reduce opposition
as far as possible. The persecution of Protestantism was immediately
abandoned. The toleration of private Protestant services was encouraged
and the queen's own attitude was made manifest when she withdrew
from public Masses before the Elevation. (The bishops who celebrated at
Mary's funeral and at her own coronation refused to alter the Roman
Catholic rite.) Philip acquiesced in these changes perhaps as an
aberration tolerable in an ally against France until a new pope, in
succession to the irate Paul IV, might be pressed into acknowledging
Elizabeth's succession rights. For the moment he was perforce obliged

to depend upon the advice of his ambassador to Elizabeth, Bishop Quadra, and on the advice of the bishop of Arras, through whom he frequently communicated with England.[2]

Restoration of Sussex

More immediately, as from 13 December 1558, Sir Henry Sidney was appointed Lord Justice, until on 30 August 1559 the decision to restore Sussex as Lord Deputy was implemented by Queen Elizabeth.[3]

The decisions thus taken clearly indicate the belief that the need for continuity in the rule of Ireland dominated court thinking at the beginning of Elizabeth's reign. It was perhaps a safe decision while the war situation continued, but in terms of a reversion to a Protestant policy, it was also a statesmanlike appreciation that those who had negotiated the parliamentary changes for Mary were best equipped to reverse them under her successor. There were, of course, minor changes in the personnel of the Irish Council, as not all Mary's advisers in Ireland could be relied upon to accommodate their religious views to those of Elizabeth. Irish Council changes, however, were at first negligible in number; nor were displaced Protestants necessarily restored to their former offices. The queen's foreign advisers on Ireland were particularly aware of the constitutional difficulties that could arise, as the Irish clergy were generally regarded as being much attached to Rome. Still greater was the potential danger from leading Irish nobles and chiefs, some of whom were in touch with Bishop Quadra by the middle of 1559. Quadra reported to Philip his fears lest positive discouragement should make these resort to France. In the circumstances Elizabeth may have felt that Sussex's former Catholic behaviour would enable the statutory changes towards Protestantism to be brought about imperceptibly.[4]

Sussex had the initial advantage that a more realistic approach to the coinage in England and in Ireland resulted in a decision to improve substantially the quality of minted money. On the other hand, stern admonitions regarding over-expenditure combined with a heavy stress on military duties, involving constant journeyings throughout the country and a reorganization of the system of local participation in viceregal hostings, which foreshadowed future dissatisfaction from the overburdened loyalists.[5]

The Parliament of 1560

On 12 January 1560 parliament met. Its main concern was to secure in Ireland the ratification of the religious changes statutorily sanctioned in

England the preceding year. As under Henry VIII there were, of course, minor adjustments to meet the somewhat different circumstances in the minor kingdom. Sussex appears to have carried out his task with the minimum of difficulty, but as surviving information has been very attenuated, conclusions depend largely on inference from surviving scraps of intelligence.[6]

By the first act,[7] the jurisdiction of the Crown over the state with regard to ecclesiastical matters was restored to its position in the later years of Henry VIII. However, unlike her father, Elizabeth was at pains to avoid offence. Derogatory remarks about the Holy See were avoided. Instead, foreign jurisdictions incompatible with the Crown's claims were declared illegal. As in England, the queen avoided the title of Head of the Church, contenting herself with the virtually synonymous claim to be the only supreme governor in all things ecclesiastical as well as temporal. An oath subscribing to this was incorporated in the statutes and imposed on all officials as well as on university graduates and successors to hereditary estates.

The Protestant liturgy of Edward VI in its revised form was re-introduced with minor alterations so that an English Communion Service adapted from the Roman Mass, but avoiding the terminology of sacrifice, again became the law of the land. Sir Anthony St Leger's compromises providing for the use of a Latin version in those parts where English was not understood, now secured statutory approval and there were incorporated some mild references to the reforming favour for national languages; it was noted that a literary knowledge of Irish was usually too inadequate for there to be any question of its use as an alternative. Such was the Uniformity Act[8] of Queen Elizabeth. With minor adjustments a century later it remained the governing provision regarding public religious service until the disestablishment of the Protestant Episcopalian Church in 1870. The queen's desire to hasten slowly is perhaps indicated by the provision that the changes would not pass into law until the last day of the parliament (1 February), by contrast with her more precipitate sister whose short-lived proceedings were applied from the first day of her parliament.

The third act dealt drastically with the finances of the Counter-Reformation by re-establishing the Crown's titles to tithes, twentieths, and tenths.[9]

A position comparable to that of the papacy in the appointment of bishops was asserted for the Crown by the fourth statute, which abolished the right to elect archbishops and bishops, substituting a procedure for royal appointments by letters patent.[10]

Recognition of Queen Elizabeth's right and title to the imperial Crown of this realm was affirmed by the fifth act,[11] which acknowledged that she was of the blood royal. The Elizabethan approach was less direct than Queen Mary's had been; her legitimacy had been affirmed in the title of an act. Elizabeth's predicament, however, was at least as serious, considering France's attitude to Mary queen of Scots and to the fact that forces existed which favoured a papal pronouncement on Elizabeth's position.

The provisions under the act of Philip and Mary declaring it treasonable to challenge the royal title were continued by the sixth act.[12]

The remaining two acts were subsequently published, unlike a ninth statute protecting the tithe rights of one of the Barnewells. These applied to the Hospital of St John of Jerusalem at Kilmainham and its prior, Sir Oswald Massingberd. By the seventh act the Crown resumed possession of Kilmainham priory and by the eighth act Massingberd, who was allegedly involved in conspiracies against the queen, was outlawed. This latter provision might be regarded as the one statutory measure against a Catholic religious restored under Mary.[13] Actions against others, however, followed refusals to take the Oath of Supremacy; this resulted in the deprivation of two bishops.

Rumours about the proceedings of this parliament far exceed the body of precise information at our disposal. Half a century later, it was insisted that the overwhelming opposition had led to adjournments, if not prorogations, until Elizabeth could consult her Lord Deputy directly. Thereafter it was alleged that the measure only reached the statute roll on the understanding that they would not be invoked against the upholders of the old religion.[14]

Certainly the events of this parliament were very much restricted in time. Actual consideration of legislative proposals must have been minimal. It is possible to infer the attitudes of a few participants. Of Hugh Curwen, archbishop of Dublin, anxious some years later for translation to an English diocese, it was subsequently stated by the Lord Deputy that at least he had been on the royal side in the statutory changes. The inference that the lead against the queen among the bishops was taken by Walsh of Meath, legatine deputy of Pole under Mary, would follow from this and from his subsequent refusal of the oath in February 1560 and deprivation a few days later, even if there were not some secondary corroborative evidence. Perhaps the earl of Desmond could be counted among the queen's opponents in the light of secondary evidence to this effect in contemporary diplomatic circles abroad and because in various conflicts of the next two decades he was out of royal favour.[15] Was the earl of Kildare another opponent? Despite contemporary evidence of his involvement in opposition and indeed in conspiracies against the queen and in favour of Philip II, it is unlikely that Kildare committed himself publicly against the court, no matter how much Sussex suspected him subsequently. For Kildare, who had tasted the bitterness of exile and enjoyed the conflicting experiences of restoration and favour by Edward VI and Mary, caution must have been attractive. Had Kildare publicly allied himself with those who challenged her royal claims over ecclesiastical affairs, it can be assumed that Elizabeth would never have countenanced him as a negotiator with Shane O'Neill, against the wishes of her honoured Lieutenant, Sussex.

Regardless of opposition, the measures appeared on the roll of the parliament which was dissolved on 1 February 1560, and with the exception of the Barnewell statute were afterwards printed. When the Irish Record Commission reviewed the statute rolls in the early nineteenth century, certain minor discrepancies regarding individual statutes were noted in the Shaw Mason collation. With most of the other rolls it perished in 1922, but there is no adequate reason to support the view that they were improperly recorded on the roll. Accordingly the view that the legislation was not passed can be dismissed. Immediately afterwards the Dublin administration acted by tendering the oath to several of the bishops, some of whom, including Curwen and Bodkin, subscribed. On 4 February, Walsh of Meath and Leverous of Kildare were deprived of their bishoprics for refusing to take the oath. The question arises whether there were other refusals of the oath: it has sometimes been assumed that there were not, as there were no further deprivations. It seems a more justifiable inference that government, assuming that there would be refusals by a majority of the remaining bishops, took fright and decided not to face the consequences which would have to follow if the remaining Irish bishops had to be replaced. Even as it was, in the case of the archbishopric of Armagh and perhaps in other cases, the temporalities were being enjoyed by papal nominees in defiance of Elizabeth.[16] It has to be remembered, however, that this is a mere surmise and against it there is evidence that the policy regarding Ireland now favoured a sharp enforcement of the new laws within the queen's sphere of influence while avoiding extremes in the areas controlled by the wild Irish. Circumstances quickly made it manifest that such a policy could only be maintained by strictly subordinating it to political eventualities.

Kildare's Intrigues

In the weeks after the dissolution of parliament the government became aware of the extensiveness of the hostile reaction to the changes. Foreign intrigues apart, the evidences of conspiracies in Ireland were sufficient to lead Sussex, now made Lord Lieutenant (May 1560), to believe that Kildare, Desmond, Shane O'Neill, and others were actively pursuing policies hostile to Dublin Castle and to the viceroy in particular. In consequence of his representations on these matters the queen directed him on 27 May 1560, by diplomacy or otherwise, to secure the earl of Kildare and see to it that he appeared at court. In her instructions to this effect Elizabeth apparently accepted as fact Sussex's allegations that Kildare was involved in a plan to have him removed and to betray all Englishmen in Ireland. The recital by the queen of the evidence of other conspiracies would indicate that in the international situation there was again a measure of panic in Ireland over the chances of a general revolt.[17] We may accept that the queen's reaction was a cooler one, except for her obvious indignation at Kildare's ostentatious attendance at Catholic Masses celebrated without any pretence at privacy. In the event, Kildare was able to satisfy the queen about his allegiance, but the government almost inevitably moderated the operation of its anti-Catholic laws.

Treason and Nonconformity

Perhaps at this point a distinction must be made between treason and nonconformity. In separate acts the Elizabethan settlement provided against the exercise of foreign jurisdiction and outlawed the old religious ceremonies and rites of Catholic Ireland. To connive at or be an accessory to breaches of the Act of Uniformity with regard to public prayer may be termed acts of nonconformity which the government was gradually obliged to tolerate. It was treason, on the other hand, to become involved in active attempts to depose the queen or support those campaigning to depose her. Within a few years these problems became complicated, particularly for those who sought to distinguish between temporal and spiritual allegiance, conceding the first to Elizabeth, including perhaps obedience to the law requiring attendance at established religious services on formal occasions. As regards spiritual allegiance to the papacy, the prohibition of attendance at Protestant services made more embarrassing a situation which became extremely critical when in 1570 Pope Pius V excommunicated Elizabeth and called for her deposition. As it turned out, however, among those in Ireland of the loyal tradition, it was still to prove possible to distinguish between temporal and spiritual loyalty, even though the queen and many of her statesmen were not prepared so to distinguish after Pius V's action. So far as Ireland was concerned, however, the Dublin administration rarely proceeded to extremes over religion in the first decade after the parliament of 1560.[18]

Lack of Clergy

While the queen had favoured a sharp enforcement of the religious changes, she was far too alert about the dangers, national and international, to adhere rigidly to one policy. Perhaps her greatest anxiety is apparent in the decision at the end of May 1560, in the light of Sussex's fears, to have Kildare sent to England for questioning. It seems that Kildare was successful not only in clearing himself of any complicity in conspiracies against England, but also in sustaining an argument that Irish problems must be approached in a different way from that which had been proposed by Sussex and accepted by the queen. In the matter of religion that Protestant policy was being consistently retarded by the failure to secure preachers for Ireland. A few days after the summons to Kildare Matthew Parker, archbishop of Canterbury, was obliged to report that while he could make a few suggestions, he could find no one anxious for appointment to the Irish mission. Nor was Parker's experience unique and in a short while the failure of government to strengthen the small English Protestant group resulted in its members, with rare exceptions, being refused permission to abandon Ireland and to return to England.[19]

David Wolfe

If the queen found herself developing second thoughts on an aggressive Irish policy because of the insufficiency of Protestant personnel, it must have been with mixed feelings that she learned of the Irish activities of the papal nuncio David Wolfe. The presence in Ireland of a papal agent was sufficiently exasperating to lead her — despite her concern about the international situation — to refuse the visit of Martinengo, entrusted by the pope with an invitation to her to be represented at the Council of Trent. But she was sufficiently well informed of the Irish situation to regard Wolfe's presence as necessitating more tactful handling of people like Kildare.[20]

Kildare's Mediation

Accordingly, on 18 September 1561[21] we find Kildare being entrusted with the responsibility of securing an oath of submission from Shane

O'Neill and before the end of the year, despite Sussex's displeasure, arrangements were in train for a visit to London from Shane O'Neill.

Sussex's Position

So far as Sussex was concerned, the changes in royal policy concerning Ireland were exasperating. He did not underestimate the difficulties. For instance, in November 1560 he supported Curwen's request to be allowed to retire to England with the reminder that in both countries he had been the outstandingly reliable ecclesiastic in the controversies over religion. On the other hand, to Sussex the decision to use Kildare to negotiate with O'Neill was virtually an act denying confidence in himself. Apart from his suspicions of Kildare's involvement in an Irish conspiracy there was the basic belief that the Fitzgeralds were more Irish than English, more partial to rebels and enemies than to loyalists and English. Kildare's confidence in his ability to win over Shane O'Neill made Sussex sure of the correctness of his own view-point in linking these questionable Anglo-Irish with the queen's greatest enemy in the north, with whose immediate ancestors Kildare's disloyal predecessors had been dynastically connected from the beginning of the century. Surely the queen, whose own Irish connections were with the Butlers, could not be unaware of the necessity to build up her support in Ireland with the allies of the house of Ormond — more English by far, to Sussex, than were the Fitzgeralds. But in this perhaps the viceroy was less aware than the queen that Ormond's reaction to Irish situations could be as unpredictable for an Englishman as were those of the queen herself.[22]

Down through the centuries in the relations of Dublin and London the necessity to give public countenance to an over-exacting deputy always greatly exercised the leading English statesmen. The fact that Sussex could no longer control the Irish decisions taken in England did not in any way lead to public questioning of his proceedings. If anything, it was to the contrary: a stiff policy with papists was still being formally maintained so that Sussex felt fully justified in holding aggressive forces ready in the north against O'Neill. In these circumstances, on 31 March 1561, O'Neill's decision to postpone his London visit was announced, in consequence of which a more con-ciliatory policy was imposed upon Sussex in his public dealings with O'Neill.[23] The Lord Lieutenant's reaction in finding his viceregal authority thus flouted is usually seen as one of concealed if not openly expressed resentment. As in the case of the challenge to his decision in Mary's reign about the succession to the earldom of Thomond (in 1558, when he decided in favour of Connor O'Brien as 3rd earl of Thomond), so the encouragement of the pretensions of Shane O'Neill contrary to Sussex's own partiality for the baron of Dungannon resulted in a life-long hate relationship between Sussex and Shane. Unfortunately for the viceroy, the weakness of England's position in the north-east became more apparent early in 1561 to all but himself and his supporters. To Sussex the fact that MacDonnell on 28 April was in touch with France and that O'Neill was in touch with Philip II was only proof of the rightfulness of his attitude towards them both, if indeed proof was necessary. To the queen, on the other hand, regardless of her own decision on the papal emissary, which she actually took on 1 May, the negotiations in north-east Ireland necessitated some further thought. Accordingly on 8 June, with royal approval, O'Neill was proclaimed in Dublin as guilty of contumacy and treason, on the grounds of his failures to implement his promises and his associations with rebels and traitors. If in this the queen was conceding yet another chance to the policy of Sussex, his capacity to lose the last trick in the game continued to deprive him of the long-term confidence of his sovereign. As under Mary when Dowdall had called his policy in question as achieving nothing but destruction, his actions were once more dogged with ill-luck so that the psychological success appeared to lie with his opponents and his critics. In the long run such situations usually proved fatal to the Irish plans of strong-minded administrators, as London rarely had the perseverance and the strength to support such viceroys after they had lost face in Ireland.

Sussex's Failure Against O'Neill

Pursuant to the military policy he had practised since Mary's time Sussex proceeded against O'Neill with a formidable hosting in which many of the Anglo-Irish gentry and nobility participated. Not for the first time, the viceroy, failing to come to grips with O'Neill, was reduced to sanctioning cattle-chasing, this time with disastrous results. In an unexpected encounter the viceroy's captains were overwhelmed and defeated, Jacques Wingfield playing a particularly ignominious part which was subsequently unsuccessfully hidden from the queen. Only the coolness and courage of Sir William Fitzwilliam prevented an utter rout. Sussex, who admitted more to Cecil than he did to the queen, attempted a bluff by announcing O'Neill's defeat, specifying his alleged losses, but the true facts reached London almost quicker than they did Dublin and were communicated to Philip II by his ambassador, Quadra. About the same time the tactful discouragements of Irish appeals to the pope as well as to Spain were being spoken of and these ultimately came to the ears of the queen who, not surprisingly, decided to employ Kildare in negotiating with O'Neill in December 1561. Much to the indignation of Sussex and his supporters, Kildare successfully concluded with O'Neill an agreement which brought him to London early in 1562 to visit the queen in defiance of Sussex and on the guarantees of Kildare, Ormond, Desmond, Thomond, and Clanricarde.[24]

Even more mortifying for Sussex was the successful initiation of Pale demands for an inquiry into the Lord Lieutenant's excesses, which with London's resentment at his failure to court-martial Wingfield cannot but have left him convinced that he was out of favour. Sussex, however, was supported quite fully in the London negotiations with O'Neill, though it was obvious that the Irish chief had greatly impressed the queen and had successfully secured some support from Lord Robert Dudley. Thus while Sussex's objections to O'Neill's statements were noted, he seemed powerless against the forces which brought the queen and O'Neill to agreement on 30 April 1562.[25] It must have seemed equally mortifying that the queen, for anti-puritan reasons, reversed decisions to promote certain ecclesiastics in Ireland.[26] In the long run, however, thanks to Cecil, whose successful Scottish policy strengthened Protestantism in the three kingdoms, Sussex was to secure another chance in Ireland which at least won him a reputation for statesmanship which survived after he had finally withdrawn from the Irish scene.

Shane O'Neill in London

It is instructive to study the diplomatic documents of these O'Neill negotiations, not only because of their influence on subsequent events but also because of their revelations as to the viewpoints of the protagonists. On one matter, that of religion, they were significantly silent, all the more so because on 3 April, Bishop Quadra had informed his master that O'Neill's position was invaluable to Spain, as he had refused to communicate according to the Protestant rite in London and everyone knew that he had gone to the sacrament at the Spanish embassy.[27]

In the course of his answers to the London government's questions about his behaviour, O'Neill had successfully maintained a distinction between his confidence in his sovereign and his distrust of her governor. Thus he answered inquiries as to his military actions against chiefs in Ulster by insisting that these were activated by his desire to support her governor despite Sussex's disastrous decision again to bring in the

Redshanks, 'to the great danger of the Crown'. That O'Neill should conclude this answer with a request that the Scots-occupied land should be restored to loyalists like himself ultimately secured him an extended sphere of influence in this area, partly because Sussex had no other response but that Shane's promises should be assessed on the basis of his past actions. In the matter of Shane's claims as the elected captain of his people, and his implicitly hostile reaction to the surrender of his father Conn and the territorial grant to him as earl of Tyrone and to his illegitimate son Matthew as baron of Dungannon, Sussex again stood upon the letter of the law. In the past, in Thomond for example, the deputy's rigidity had been followed by subsequent succession disputes which had been left to his successor to resolve. Now in the case of Tyrone, O'Neill denied the validity of the patent of 1542 to his father Conn as he had no estate in the country other than that which was held by consent of the lord and of the inhabitants only. Legally, to O'Neill, 'by the law of the Pale' letters patent could take no effect without inquisition and as Tyrone was part of no shireground, this had not been done. Again the deputy's response demonstrated the width of the gap between O'Neill and the rigidity of the English statesman. On the one hand, Sussex alleged that the Tyrone freeholders had been consenting parties to the letters patent of Conn and Matthew O'Neill. Sussex, however, also argued that the law of the Pale did not apply 'among the Irishrie'. There, he insisted, the prince's title proceeded from conquest. He appears to have thought to make his argument unanswerable by saying that if the Crown abandoned the patents, the status of the new earls among the Irish would thereby be overthrown.[28]

Yet again, in answer to Shane's recital of the territories and peoples he claimed to rule the responses were quite inadequate. To Shane, beyond Tyrone, subordinate to him were Magennis, MacMahon, Maguire, O'Cahan, O'Hanlon, Macartan, Dufferin, the savages, and many O'Neills. In addition Clandeboy and the Route should be included 'which the Scot engageth'. He claimed ancient rights over O'Reilly, rents from many lesser lords, and, until his father Conn's surrender, O'Neill had enjoyed a black rent of 40 shillings from Louth. To all this Sussex could only respond with a demand for more particulars. Finally, in a direct bid from power to power, the Irish chief declared his competence to serve the queen with 'a more perfection' than his father had been able to accord to Henry VIII. Apart from the obvious reference to his father's impotence in Tyrone on abandoning his chieftainship for an earldom, it was a flaunting by Shane of the same unique position in the north as his ancestor, the

Great Earl of Kildare, had demonstrated to Henry VII when it was alleged against him that all Ireland could not rule him. The lesson was not lost on Elizabeth nor upon her courtiers who, according to Campion, described Shane as 'Oneile the Great, cousin of St. Patrick, friend of Queen Elizabeth, enemy to all the world beside'.[29]

On 30 April 1562 indentures were made at London between Queen Elizabeth and Shane O'Neill. O'Neill took an oath of obedience and promised to reduce to order the lands from Tyrone to the north-eastern sea. He was conceded the government of the countries of O'Cahan, the Route (MacQuillan's country), Clandeboy, and Kilultagh.[30]

O'Neill undertook to induce the captains of these countries to visit the Pale and express their obedience to her Majesty within two months. He would protect them against molestors, but he agreed not to make war unless so empowered by the queen's chief minister in Ireland and her Council.[31]

In controversies against captainships O'Neill's right to arbitrate was asserted. Controversies between O'Neill and other independent lords were referred to the queen's chief minister and the Council of Ireland.[32]

General hostings in Ulster against rebels or enemies of the queen would be supported by O'Neill 'with his nation'. On this service he could levy the *buannacht* (or military cess) due to the queen. He could appoint his own deputy. Outside of Tyrone he was not to take the *buannacht* or levy *coisire*, coign, or livery. O'Neill undertook to support any organization set up for the queen to reform Ulster and to obey any future council established there.[33]

In any dispute between O'Neill and O'Donnell or O'Reilly or Maguire, six arbitrators would adjudicate, including the earls of Kildare and Ormond and four members of the Council of Ireland, of whom two were to be nominated by O'Neill and two by the other party to the dispute.[34]

O'Neill undertook not to attack those of his men who had formerly supported the queen against him, in particular Felim Rua and Henry O'Neill, who were to give him their pledges. Again, provision was made to decide controversies through arbitrators selected from the neighbouring gentry or by commissioners sent to the border by the Irish Council.[35]

O'Neill undertook not to retain fighting men except those born in Tyrone or in the territories committed to his rule. Outside Tyrone he would take no pledges from any countries.[36]

On the queen's behalf her subjects of the Pale would assist no malefactors against O'Neill and, in the redistribution of preys of cattle, commissioners would be made available to go to the border.[37]

On the vexed question of conflicting rights of O'Neill and the baron of Dungannon's son Brian, adjudication would operate. In the meantime O'Neill was accorded the position of captain.[38]

With regard to the English garrison at Armagh, in order to avoid quarrels with the neighbouring people they were to be permitted to be provisioned from the Pale under O'Neill's safeguard.[39]

The four earls, Kildare, Ormond, Thomond, and Clanricarde, would arbitrate on the legality of O'Neill's imprisonment of Calough O'Donnell in accordance with international law and Irish custom. More immediately six pledges would be given to the queen by O'Neill, three from his London retinue and three to be selected by herself from Ulster. One outstanding issue against O'Donnell — O'Neill's claims for the castles of Lifford and Finn — would be the subject of arbitration by two of the earls.[40]

Sussex and Shane O'Neill

Sussex's feelings at this juncture must have been similar to those of Sir Edward Poynings after Elizabeth's grandfather returned Kildare to Ireland to replace him in 1496. The fact that Sussex and O'Neill were by this time temperamentally incapable of seeing one another's point of view can only have been too evident to the queen and her London advisers. It seems that Lord Robert Dudley in particular, and perhaps Sidney, were instrumental in decisions being taken contrary to Sussex's views.[41] There was more in this than the rivalry between English politicians. Cecil may very well have believed that the conclusions should have been more favourable to Sussex and it may have been due to him that negotiations with O'Neill were not concluded until the end of April. (O'Neill alleged subsequently that undue pressure had been put upon him, particularly in exacting pledges.)[42] On the other hand, the deterioration in the Ulster situation which followed from the killing by Turlough Luineach O'Neill of Brian, the eldest son of Matthew, baron of Dungannon, left the English without an effective alternative ruler of Tyrone. In a situation where the ecclesiastical question could be used against Protestant nominees and in favour of such papal provisors as Richard Creagh — recommended by David Wolfe for Armagh — the goodwill of O'Neill might make all the difference. With anxiety still existing about possible French interference the presence in the north of O'Neill, committed to an anti-Scottish policy, might in fact prove an advantage. Whether sufficient goodwill existed on both sides for Dublin and Tyrone to establish a more durable relationship remained to be seen.

The Earl of Desmond

Concurrently with the O'Neill negotiations the queen was involved in a more drastic arrangement with Gerald, 14th earl of Desmond, who secured little consideration when his public behaviour was as arrogant as that of O'Neill. In the process of imposing her rule upon the earls, in her determination to end a situation in which there could be an appeal to war between two of her own subjects, Elizabeth can have had little patience with the second over-mighty subject from Ireland swaggering in the streets of London. The Munster earl, of course, was in no position to secure such an agreement as had O'Neill. As a personality he had none of Shane's capacity to intimidate his enemies and overawe his friends. His main concern appeared to be connected with his fears of Thomas Butler, 10th earl of Ormond, with whom he was to become increasingly embroiled, despite his being married to Ormond's widowed mother, Joan Fitzgerald. In any rivalry between the southern earls it was almost inevitable that the queen should show her partiality towards her kinsman Ormond and against his rival. Accordingly, it was decided to prohibit Desmond from returning to Ireland. For a while he was actually held under restraint in London, whence he did not return until he had signed an accord with Ormond and undertaken to identify himself more amenably with the Dublin government.[43]

O'Neill's Allegations

Sussex's first reaction to the return of O'Neill was one of apparent good-will even to the extent of sounding tolerant about Shane's demand for an English wife and particularly for his sister, Lady Frances Radcliffe. Very soon, however, he commenced a series of complaints against O'Neill — alleging his failure to implement the conditions agreed upon and insisting that he was terrorizing his neighbours.[44] In both of these matters Sussex undoubtedly had justification for his statements. Neighbouring chiefs like Maguire who had been loyal to Dublin Castle against O'Neill were now made to realize that power had passed into the hands of their enemy. O'Neill set out to build up a substantial military force and they were compelled to assist him in becoming as formidable in Ulster as the Great Earl of Kildare had become throughout all Ireland half a century earlier.

Like the Great Earl of Kildare, after his return from England O'Neill identified his quarrels with the cause of his sovereign and insisted that it was to further his sovereign's interests that he made war upon the

Scots or on any other of his enemies. So far as the queen was concerned such a policy was unlikely to strengthen the Scots in north-east Ireland or bring their French allies into the picture. But she could not feel happy that O'Neill was using his position against her Dublin viceroy, whose prestige was becoming increasingly damaged in Ulster. When Sussex insisted that O'Neill had failed to provide the additional pledges promised or to bring the gentlemen of Tyrone into the Pale to express their allegiance to the queen, he was only doing what he felt was justifiable within the limits of the agreement between the queen and O'Neill. O'Neill, however, retorted that Sussex was not to be trusted, having previously attempted to have him assassinated, a statement which the queen knew to be correct. But O'Neill went on to draft an indictment of English governors in Ireland, who he alleged had used treachery and deceit to secure capture of independent Irishmen and sometimes to bring about their murder.[45] Again the queen was hardly in a position to gainsay this catalogue of untoward events in the preceding twenty years. Sussex was perhaps unfortunate in that he came up against other criticisms at the same time in which his conduct was not always fairly represented.[46] In the religious sphere, while he favoured the observance of the law, he was no fanatic and was not above pointing out to Cecil that 'the licentious professors of the law' were more dangerous than 'the superstitious and erroneous papists'.[47] As a result, Sussex encountered the hostility of devout Protestants like John Parker, the Master of the Rolls. When Sussex's regime came under fire from Irish law students in London and from some of the gentry of the Pale, Parker supported the allegation that the Lord Lieutenant had exceeded the law in imposing exactions on the Pale and in utilizing military sanctions. To the Lord Lieutenant, with limited financial resources from England, a policy of involving the loyalists in their own defence against the rebellious Irish appeared perfectly logical. To the Palesmen his actions were bankrupting them and they argued that the Lord Lieutenant and his supporters were becoming prosperous through their corruption.

These allegations, sponsored by a Palesman named Bermingham, led the queen, in October 1563, to establish a commission of investigation.[48] The commissioners, Sir Thomas Wrothe, Sir Nicholas Arnold, and a financial official named William Dixe, made a detailed investigation into the situation in Ireland. Both Wrothe and Arnold belonged to the more puritanical element of the English Protestants and they were appalled by the general state of laxity in Ireland and the lack of evidence of devotion to reform and the preaching of God's Word. Thus

Arnold pointed out that Parker was one of the few in office who really cared. Arnold of course had little favour for Shane O'Neill and fully corroborated Sussex's views on the sufferings of the loyal Ulster chiefs at his hands. But for the rest the commissioners, and Arnold in particular, were more prepared to listen to Sussex's critics than to favour him. And ultimately when Arnold temporarily replaced Sussex, as Lord Justice, on 25 May 1564, as head of the government and the Lord Lieutenant, who appears to have been seriously ill, secured permission to return to England, the investigations regarding military corruption in Ireland were carried into his own proceedings and the alleged defalcations of his brother, Sir Henry Radcliffe. It was in this atmosphere that, first in 1563 under Sussex and then in 1564 under Arnold, Sir Thomas Cusack, after visiting the queen and discussing matters with Dudley earl of Leicester in September 1564, was empowered to renegotiate an agreement with O'Neill.[49]

The Armagh Archbishopric

The Protestant position in the north of Ireland was now simply ludicrous. Since Goodacre's death it had been impossible to secure the temporalities for any royal nominee. Thus Sussex had had to report a failure to secure the election to Armagh of Adam Loftus, an able young chaplain regarded highly by the Protestant bishops of Meath and Kildare. Since the death of Primate Dowdall on 17 August 1558 ecclesiastical Armagh had been virtually controlled by Dean Terence Daniel (or Donnelly), a member of the family with which Shane O'Neill had been fostered.[50] Under the acts passed in 1560 the queen could have appointed Loftus, but evidently this procedure could not operate except where the temporalities at a vacancy did not come under the control of the queen's exchequer. Sussex reported that Daniel had told him the Armagh chapter was so much out of order that Loftus could not be elected. The viceroy was reduced to recommending that the proposed primate should be temporarily pensioned and that a commission for ecclesiastical causes should be set up to give him the necessary diocesan authority.[51]

Elizabeth's Religious Problems

The difficulties in the north of Ireland were rendered more complex by uncertainties in Scotland and in England. The queen's dissatisfaction with the more radical element among the Protestants (the puritans, as they came to be called) was largely due to their attempts to make the state's ecclesiastical usages more Protestant and more committed to a

Calvinistic viewpoint. She had not been prepared to welcome back to
England the future apostle of Scottish Presbyterianism — John Knox.
Knox's publication *First Blast of the Trumpet against the Monstrous
Regiment of Women* (1558) had been aimed at the Catholic sovereigns
Mary of England and Mary Stuart. Elizabeth was determined that she
would rule the churchmen and Knox's pamphlet provided an admirable
excuse to make an example of one whom she would not permit to
impose his concepts on the English Church. In the years after Knox
went north to Scotland, Elizabeth's treatment of puritanical clergy,
particularly at the universities, caused men like Adam Loftus in Ireland
to express to the queen's secretary, Cecil, their distress at such treatment of God's elect. And though the more puritanical Irish clergy
might rely upon Cecil to support their cause, as indeed he supported
the Scottish Protestants, his own situation was by no means satisfactory
when it came to attempting to control Elizabeth's policy. Thus in
August 1560 Cecil, having spent some time in the north negotiating an
understanding with the leading Scottish politicians committed to the
Reformation, found himself on returning to court virtually out of
favour. The queen's infatuation with Leicester led to rumours that a
change of religion was about to take place. The gossip ran that her
marriage to Leicester depended upon a renewed Catholic alliance
abroad and the jettisoning of the Protestant party at home. In the event,
Elizabeth did not marry Leicester and while Cecil breathed more freely
when she came to terms with her infatuation, he can never again have
felt as sure of his influence over her as he apparently had before the
Scottish episode. In a certain sense, particularly in dealing with Ireland
and Scotland, Cecil was obliged to adopt the pose of the courtier
rather than that of the statesman. And perhaps his acceptance from
time to time of substantial gifts from the king of Spain is an indication
that he learned to value his role. At least it saved him from the consequences of becoming too much a supporter of Protestant fanatical
elements whose political naivety could prove a serious liability. An
example of this is perhaps to be seen in the situation in the north of
Ireland when an attempt was made to link the invading Scots with the
Protestant cause. Through Sir William Fitzwilliam, Cecil had learned
of the difficulties in negotiating with the MacDonnells of Antrim. In
1561 Fitzwilliam had been negotiating with the Scots through William
Piers, the constable of Carrickfergus. Just at the point when James
and Sorley Bui MacDonnell seemed ready to co-operate with the
Dublin officials and to build up an Irish alliance in Clandeboy, the
Scots demonstrated hostility to the English in Ireland. On a public

occasion, Piers reported in a letter to Fitzwilliam,[52] MacDonnell had
declared that the young queen of England, having played the harlot,
had been beheaded together with the young lord of whom she was
enamoured. The MacDonnells simultaneously refused to support a
party among the O'Neills of Clandeboy unless they were prepared to
prove themselves by driving the English out of Carrickfergus. This was
an indication to both Fitzwilliam and Cecil, to whom he sent Piers's
letter, that the Scots were no more reliable than Shane O'Neill.

Loftus and the Argyll Letter

Nevertheless, Loftus and others among the more dedicated Protestants
in Ireland became concerned to link the Scots to the Protestant cause
and stigmatize Shane O'Neill as a papist and a traitor. A mysterious
document attributed to the earl of Argyll made reference to the
question of securing Protestant England's support for an attack on the
popish O'Neill.[53] Loftus, while questioning the origins of the
document, identified himself with Argyll as one devoted to the
Reformation and urged upon Elizabeth's advisers the necessity for a
break with Shane O'Neill. Unfortunately, at this point the elect of God
in Ireland began to be divided among themselves over the distribution
of benefices. Equally unfortunately for those like Sir Thomas Cusack,
who put their trust in O'Neill, evidence of his negotiations with foreign
Catholic powers proved decisive in eventually ranging the queen among
his enemies. It would be interesting to know the queen's reaction to
Piers's letter if Cecil had had the courage to show it to her.

Sussex and the North

Perhaps more damning for the MacDonnells than the rumours of her
flirtations were the reiterations of the queen's illegitimacy and the
insistence that Mary of Scotland was the rightful sovereign of England
and of Ireland. If the future of the Scots in Ulster still appeared in
doubt to Sussex, in 1563 the position of Shane became more and
more intolerable. The Lord Lieutenant found his proposals to protect
Dundalk and other northern towns ignominiously rejected. A force
of five hundred of the viceroy's army was apparently more of a
menace to the townspeople than any possible threat by O'Neill. They
were able to couch their objections in the assumption that in the
O'Neill peace a promise to respect the northern towns had been
agreed to by the Ulster chief. To Sussex it was no consolation that
Dundalk preferred to run the risk of being ravaged by Shane rather
than support the exactions of the force which Sussex has proposed to

quarter on them. Indeed, O'Neill was able to boast that the Pale, the so-
called land of peace, was so disturbed under Her Majesty's military
governors that a number of Palesmen took refuge in O'Neill's country
to escape the depredations.[54]

For some time after the O'Neill peace confusion over policy prevailed to such an extent that the queen was involved in the issuing of
contradictory orders. Thus the failure to secure the election of Loftus
in Armagh was followed by the establishment of his authority through
the appointment of a commission for ecclesiastical jurisdiction —
together with a specific direction to execute the anti-Catholic laws
against notorious infringers of the acts. Concurrently the queen was
committed to a compact with Shane which left no justification for an
anti-Catholic offensive. The queen's officials therefore were being asked
to enforce the law only against the loyalists of the Pale. It was a
situation in which the investigations into viceregal corruption inevitably
reacted against Sussex in Ireland, and led to his being virtually superseded by Arnold.

Sussex and Scotland

The prestige of the Lord Lieutenant was still as high with Elizabeth as
ever it had been. Sussex was immediately visualized as a reliable
commander when relations with Scotland deteriorated as a consequence
of anti-Protestant proceedings in France under the influence of the
House of Guise. To Elizabeth, just when she had been prepared to
negotiate directly with Mary queen of Scots, after the massacre of
Protestants at Vassy in March 1562, a meeting became unthinkable.
This French episode was effectively utilized by Cecil, reinforced no
doubt by the Spanish ambassador, to convince Elizabeth of the danger
of a Franco-Scottish conspiracy against her.[55] Accordingly, it was
necessary to fortify the Scottish border against possible northern
invaders, and Sussex was placed in a position of honour in command
over various local units.

Wrothe and Arnold

The decision to appoint Arnold as Lord Justice was therefore not
intended as a condemnation of Sussex. Changes of government in
Ireland were frequently followed by attacks on the Pale or demonstrations of force in defiance of English authority before a new regime
could be settled in. But while the reaction of the Irish to Sussex's
departure was not a particularly remarkable demonstration against an
exponent of the policy of sternness, Arnold in his own actions behaved

as if Sussex had been disgraced. During the commissioners' investigations into the complaints of the Pale against Sussex, Sir Thomas Wrothe, who was at one with Arnold in his devotion to the Protestant cause, was not prepared to accept that Sussex was necessarily at fault. However, when Arnold was elevated to the post of chief minister in Ireland, Wrothe was at once stronger and weaker than he had been before. On himself and the auditor, Dixe, devolved the work of the commission of inquiry, but in losing Arnold to the office of Lord Justice, the commission suffered in prestige. Ultimately, partly because of the critical international situation, the queen recalled Wrothe late in 1564, leaving it to Arnold to assume full responsibilities, except the particular auditing aspects which still devolved to Dixe. As an active Protestant Arnold felt fully justified in coercing the Catholic nobility and gentry of the Pale. Unfortunately, he felt equally justified in impugning the Sussex government by disgracing Sussex's brother, Sir Henry Radcliffe. The effect of these actions was ultimately to discredit Arnold. The renewed negotiations with O'Neill — undertaken through Sir Thomas Cusack and the earl of Kildare — resulted, in January 1565, in a substantial improvement of O'Neill's position, rendering him no longer liable to secure viceregal endorsement in his relations with his Ulster neighbours.[56] O'Neill, however, was still able to maintain a grievance, as the queen was not prepared to confirm his immunity when reporting to her chief governor, and it could be thus alleged that London had broken the treaty. It was a dispirited Dublin administration which accepted O'Neill's more powerful position; its only consolation was the minor one of giving immunity to the persons hired by Sussex to poison Shane, an immunity in which Shane acquiesced.

The Treaty of Troyes

Arnold's tenure of the office of Lord Justice coincided with the emergence of a new factor in the Irish situation. A few months earlier, on 13 January 1564, it was announced that Irish bishops who had attended the Council of Trent had presented themselves at the court of France.[57] In themselves they were few in number and relatively insignificant as well as extremely poverty-stricken, but they initiated the series of events which brought the question of Shane O'Neill into the international sphere and against Elizabeth. The English ambassador at Paris, Nicholas Throckmorton, like most diplomatic representatives of his day, used his position to act as an intelligence agent for his government. Few Irish intrigues or intriguers eluded his observation. At this moment he was concerned on behalf of his queen to strengthen the position of the Huguenots, who in order to secure Elizabeth's military support against the French Catholic League agreed to put her forces into possession of Le Havre until such time as Calais could again be transferred to England. However, Throckmorton and his queen were outmanouevred by Catherine de Medici, regent for her son Charles IX, who exploited the strong French national feeling to maintain French territory intact. In return for an invitation to leading Huguenots to be identified with her government the English force was abandoned, so that it was unable to hold out against Queen Catherine's assault. Ultimately, on 11 April 1564 by the Treaty of Troyes, Elizabeth was obliged to surrender Le Havre while gaining no admission of her continued claim to Calais. It was in this situation that a more Protestant policy for Ireland was adopted. This was strengthened by the discovery that on 13 July Pope Pius IV took steps to strengthen the ecclesiastical powers of Primate Richard Creagh (whom he had provided to Armagh), who was now recommended to Shane O'Neill with the legate David Wolfe.[58]

French Intrigues

At first perhaps, the queen was not particularly concerned, as it was known that King Philip of Spain had advised his ambassador to England to be wary of Irish intriguers.[59] Apparently Philip had accepted Elizabeth's assurances that her intervention in France was solely to secure the return of Calais. On 8 August, two days after the Spanish king had so expressed himself about the Irish, Sir Thomas Wrothe assured Cecil that he was satisfied that there were French links with O'Neill and with Desmond. It was about this time that Mary queen of Scots confided in an English Catholic named Christopher Rooksby, who passed the information to an Elizabethan diplomat, that she was contemplating stirring up trouble in Ireland and invading England with an army to secure its Crown and the restoration of Catholicism. For this, she boasted, she could depend upon promised foreign aid. Gradually it began to emerge that Mary of Scotland was looking beyond the Guise faction in France to Philip II.[60]

Primate Creagh

It was not until 1565 that the situation became really threatening. Primate Creagh, who had been captured, was examined in the Tower of London on 22 February and again on 17 March. He endeavoured to make light of his own role — insisting that he had left Ireland to join a reformed religious order, but as a graduate of Louvain, sworn to obey the pope, he had been obliged to obey when he had been ordered to accept provision to Armagh. He had intended, he said, to return to the continent and enter the Theatines, if his rejection should exonerate him from further efforts to implement the papal provision. On Shane O'Neill he expressed himself with some coldness — implying that he was not prepared to accept the Irishman's jurisdictional pretensions, but holding out the hope that through his influence the northern chief might be led to recognize the liberties of the Church. As a Limerick man, Creagh was probably genuine in his protestations of loyalty to Queen Elizabeth.[61]

Two months after these events the Dublin authorities made it clear to the queen that it was for her to decide on whether to proceed against notorious recusants in the Pale; she decided in favour of it; Sidney, designated as Sussex's successor, was instructed on 4 July to punish open contempt of the queen's ecclesiastical establishment.[62] In the same month Archbishop Loftus distinguished himself by deploring the decisions to deprive English puritans of their benefices. While this action at an earlier time might seriously have affected his ecclesiastical future in Ireland, the course of events so dramatically altered with the marriage on 29 July of Mary queen of Scots to her cousin Lord Darnley that the Protestant cause in both islands was materially strengthened.

For some time previously, in an effort to secure Elizabeth's good-will, Mary Stuart had been negotiating with her Tudor cousin about possible alternative choices of husband. Elizabeth had made it clear that she was opposed to possible Hapsburg candidates, preferring, she said, that Mary would consider an Englishman such as Lord Robert Dudley. Mary's decision to marry Darnley, heir presumptive to both queens, was regarded quite properly by Elizabeth as a defiance. Within a few weeks the Scottish queen, hitherto reluctant to appear in the role of Catholic champion, had appealed to the papacy and to Spain to secure financial and military aid to bring about the restoration of the former public splendour of Catholicism. It was in these circumstances that further reports from Loftus in Ireland, reinforced by Sir William Fitzwilliam, insisting on the existence of intrigues between O'Neill and the Scottish queen and against Protestantism, assumed credibility.[63]

O'Neill's Intrigues

On 20 January 1566 Sir Henry Sidney, having been formally appointed in October 1565, took office as Lord Deputy and very quickly became involved in a further change of royal policy towards Shane O'Neill.

Mary and Darnley had quarrelled and on 4 March the queen's Italian secretary, Rizzio, was murdered with the complicity of her husband. This destroyed all chances of implementing her new Catholic policy, to which, in any case, the Spanish king had not been prepared to commit himself. But Shane O'Neill persisted in his Catholic intrigues. By 25 April Throckmorton was aware that he had written to Charles IX for support for his Catholic war. O'Neill had apparently convinced himself that he was invincible in Ulster and was seeking allies elsewhere to contain the threatened English expansion. Thereafter it only required a few short steps to lead to the decision which brought about Shane's destruction. It became known soon after 31 March that Mary of Scotland had urged Argyll, a quasi-Protestant, to favour O'Neill. However, the Irish puritans, like Loftus, used all their influence to insist that Argyll would favour anti-O'Neill moves by the English because of his attitude to the Protestants. By 29 April Bishop Brady of Meath was denouncing O'Neill. By 4 May Desmond had become suspected as an ally of O'Neill. By 18 May Philip II was assured that O'Neill was an undoubted Catholic champion. On 23 May Elizabeth made a first move against Shane, directing that Scottish Protestants should be assured that O'Neill was hostile to their religion. Three months later Shane appealed to allies in Ireland, urging the necessity to combine against the English threat. In this he did not put emphasis on the religious factor in any particular way. Nor did Elizabeth, in the treaties made on her behalf towards the end of October with O'Donnell and other northern chiefs — whom she was primarily concerned to involve in a pincer movement against Shane. From this point onwards the religious issue became subordinated in the struggle between Shane and his opponents, though Primate Creagh, who had escaped from the Tower, implied in a communication to Sidney from Ulster that O'Neill might negotiate if Sidney was prepared to approve some tolerance for the old religious conventions, as Philip II had indicated indirectly in letters to Leicester.[64]

Defeat and Death

By June 1567 the northern menace to Sidney's viceroyalty had collapsed. Seemingly at the height of his powers, O'Neill had been defeated. The organization of opposition in the north-west had led to a surprise defeat of Shane by the O'Donnells, in which he lost a substantial part of his forces. So utterly was he discountenanced that he decided to seek an alliance with the MacDonnells of Antrim, whose leader, Sorley Bui, he had held in captivity. Then, in a drunken encounter, he was assassinated. Within a few days William Piers, the constable of

Carrickfergus, had secured his head, for which Sir Henry Sidney paid a substantial sum to enable him to exhibit it on Dublin Castle. The deputy had the additional satisfaction of recording his version of the last days of O'Neill in the preamble to the Act of Attainder of Shane, to be passed by the Irish parliament in 1569.[65]

Altogether, apart from the question of O'Neill, Sidney's outstanding problem was one of finance. Sussex had not been successful in maintaining an expansionist policy without getting into serious financial embarrassment. So far as his successors were concerned, an expansionist policy remained a desirable one, if only to maintain the prestige of England when her international standing was low. It might be said that the failure to recover a foothold in France necessitated the maintenance of a prestige policy elsewhere. There was, however, among many adventurous spirits in England an anxiety to participate in expansionist activities — which had secured substantial wealth for the Spanish and Portuguese in the New World.[66]

Stukely's Scheme

In these circumstances the English privy council came to regard with favour proposals to establish trading sites and perhaps even colonies off the coast of America as well as on the Irish coast. These proposals were often put forward with some financial backing from London merchants or from members of the nobility. Even the queen herself displayed an interest and was prepared to risk a contribution where the promise of profit appeared considerable. One such proposal under consideration by Cecil — to establish a colony in Florida — was put forward by a Devon adventurer named Thomas Stukely. It had seemed sufficiently attractive to secure the approval of the queen as well as that of several of her statesmen. Accordingly, Cecil had told the Spanish ambassador that he was not a subscriber to the doctrine that the pope was entitled to divide the nations of the New World among European powers. The result of Cecil's attitude was that projects such as that of Stukely, considered by Spain to be piratical, were sponsored at least informally by the English government. In Stukely's case it appears that his enterprise did not extend to Florida, but did involve unauthorized trading within Spanish territories — which led Philip II to denounce him as a pirate. Surprisingly, Shane O'Neill as well as Sidney had supported Stukely to the queen and urged his acceptance for military command in Ireland. The queen, however, apparently resentful of the failure of the Florida dividends, was not prepared to sanction this change of objectives and ultimately Stukely took the unexpected decision to transfer to Spain and involve himself in the Catholic enterprises against the infidel and the heretic. After the battle of Lepanto (1571), he participated in the defeat of the Ottoman Turks and was to be involved in the next decade in plans for a return to Ireland.[67] But these plans had been emerging in the years after the fall of Shane O'Neill as a reaction against the piratical activities in Ireland of Englishmen like Stukely's fellow countyman Sir Peter Carew.

Sidney and Ormond

Carew, of whose activities much more will have to be said, spearheaded a line of projects to establish colonies within the English sphere of influence in Ireland. So far as Sidney was concerned, they were at once an asset and a liability. They appeared to offer a means of extending the revenue, but were also likely to provoke troubles among the Anglo-Irish, already alienated by having to carry a substantial part of the military costs of the government's forward policy. The proposals already under consideration for provincial presidencies and councils seemed likely to add substantially to local liabilities, since the Crown was not prepared to underwrite the cost of its expanding administrative machine. Particularly aggravating to Sidney was the continued favour shown to Ormond and the fact that Ormond regularly received material testimonies of royal partiality. From the last days of Sussex, conflicts between the earls of Desmond and Ormond proved an embarrassment to the Dublin government because of its awareness that the queen would not permit any decision hostile to her favourite. Ormond's identification of himself with Sussex's critics for the undue exploitation of the Anglo-Irish gentry had therefore played a decisive part in bringing about the Wrothe-Arnold-Dixe commission of investigation, with its adverse consequences for Sussex's reputation in Ireland. A clash between Desmond and Ormond over feudal jurisdiction thus resulted in mutual conflict, the capture of Desmond, and Ormond's charge of high treason against his rival early in 1565.[68] Second only to the enormity of the northern problem was the difficulty imposed on the deputy as a result of Elizabeth's acceptance of the allegation that Desmond's actions had been treasonable. Following her usual policy of expecting her subordinates to grapple with the more difficult situations, Elizabeth put pressure on Sidney to investigate the issues in Ireland. And even if in this the queen was obliged to participate in the main decisions against Desmond, Sidney was almost involuntarily committed to accept that Desmond was not merely an accessory to the acts of traitors but was involved in the foreign conspiracies of O'Neill.

Desmond and Ormond

The situation between Desmond and Ormond was partly due to their temperamental differences. Ormond was an effective administrator and an acquisitive ruler capable of exploiting the main chance. Desmond was ineffective, irresolute, incapable of delegation or decision. As long as Ormond's mother — Desmond's wife — was alive, it was possible to resolve their difficulties, though the countess of Desmond knew she had to meet the challenge of being more partial to her son. After her death in 1564 the inevitable rival interests of the two lordships collided in the expansionist tendencies of the age, and it was here that Ormond's advantage with the queen helped to bring about Desmond's fall. To Sidney the situation was serious. Particularly when a commission for the assessment of damages found heavily for Ormond, he realized that the Desmond landowners might revolt against a situation where Ormond had become their lord in fact if not in deed.[69] To the Lord Deputy, as he confided to Cecil, it was a matter of some moment if the queen was prepared to give greater privileges to Ormond than she would to a great officer of state. Ironically, the favour for the Butlers came at the right moment to save the state from the imputation of partiality when England finally decided to approve the landed claims of adventurers like Peter Carew — a decision to which the collateral Butlers replied by resorting to violence.

Carew's Claims

Carew's claims were derived from his possession of documents allegedly inherited from substantial ancestors enjoying broad acres in Carlow, Cork, and Meath. Carew first took action through the antiquarian John Hooker, whose exposition of his employer's title to the barony of Idrone and the lands of Sir Christopher Cheevers secured an *ex parte* endorsement from the English Council and involved Sidney and his advisers in putting the records and resources of the Irish administration at the disposal of the claimant. The success of Carew's first action led to the commencement of proceedings involving lands occupied by Ormond's brothers Edmund, Edward, and Piers. This brought about their forcible resistance not merely to the claimant but their involvement in an alliance with the hereditary enemy of Desmond in a great land war which threatened to make Munster as devastated as was Ulster in the conflict with Shane O'Neill. The very issues which in the case of Shane O'Neill had finally led to the decision to destroy him after his appeal to the continental Catholic powers, seemed likely to become involved once more when the privy council followed its favour for

Carew with a tentative sanction for a plantation project by a number of English adventurers hungry to secure southern coastal rights and the possession of the main properties of Munster. The dilemma for Sidney was that the over-expenditure of revenue continued to create problems which could perhaps be resolved by successful plantations, but might also bring about a state of chronic war. It is perhaps in this context that we must view the Sidney preamble to the Attainder Act of Shane O'Neill as a preliminary to a vast plantation project in the most Gaelic province of Ireland.[70] The fact that the act was not to be promulgated until parliament met in 1569 and that even then its enactment was only of subordinate interest should in no way take from our realization that to Sidney it was the logical consequence of O'Neill's defeat. To the historian, then, the fall of O'Neill may be regarded as terminating the period in which the Elizabethan establishment was brought about.

Notes

1.   B. W. Beckingsale, *Burghley, Tudor statesman* (1967); F. Braudel, *La Méditerranée et le monde méditerranéen* (Paris, 1966); E. St J. Brooks, *Sir Christopher Hatton* (1946); Cyril Falls, *Elizabeth's Irish Wars* (1950); Cyril Falls, *Mountjoy, Elizabethan general* (1955); G. Mattingly, *The Defeat of the Spanish Armada* (1959); G. Mattingley, *Renaissance Diplomacy* (1955); D. B. Quinn, *Raleigh and the British Empire* (1947); F. Raab, *The English Face of Machiavelli* (1964); A. L. Rowse, *The Elizabethan Renaissance* (1971–72); L. Stone, *The Crisis of the Aristocracy* (1965); P. H. Williams, *The Council in the marches of Wales under Elizabeth I* (Cardiff, 1958).
2.   R. B. Wernham, *Before the Armada : the Growth of English Foreign Policy, 1485–1588* (1966), 239ff; W. MacCaffrey, *The Shaping of the Elizabethan Regime* (1969), chs. 3 and 4.
3.   Bagwell, *Ireland under the Tudors* II, ch. 19.
4.   See Neale quoted Paul Johnson, *Elizabeth : a Study in Power and Intellect* (1974), 90ff.
5.   F. C. Dietz, *English Public Finance 1558–1641*, 2 vols. (1921, 1932).
6.   Edwards, *Church and State*, ch. 12.
7.   2 Eliz. c.1. *Statutes*, 275.
8.   2 Eliz. c.2. *Statutes*, 284.
9.   2 Eliz. c.3. *Statutes*, 291.
10. 2 Eliz. c.4. *Statutes*, 300.
11. 2 Eliz. c.5. *Statutes*, 302.
12. 2 Eliz. c.6. *Statutes*, 304.
13. 2 Eliz. cc. 7–8. *Statutes*, 306ff, 358ff.
14. Edwards, *Church and State*, 180, n.2.
15. Bagwell, op.cit., II, 6ff.
16. Edwards, loc.cit. Also *Cal. Carew MSS*, I, 296–7, no. 224.
17. *Cal. S.P.Ire., 1509–73*, 160, n. 17.
18. Edwards, *Church and State*, 255.
19. Shirley, *Original Letters*, no. 35.
20. Edwards, *Church and State*, 223–4.

21. *Cal.S.P.Ire.*, I, 161, nos. 34–6.
22. *Cal.Carew MSS*, I, 300–4, no. 227.
23. Bagwell, op.cit., II, 7ff.
24. *Cal.Carew MSS*, I, 300–4.
25. *Cal.Carew MSS*, I, 312–14.
26. Shirley, *Original Letters*, no. 36.
27. *Cal.S.P. Sp.*, *1558–67*, 235.
28. *Cal.S.P.Ire.*, I, 193, nos. 99, 100.
29. Edmund Campion, *The Two Bokes of the Histories of Ireland*, ed. A. F. Vossen (Assen, 1963), 139.
30. *Cal.Carew MSS*, I, no. 232, 312–14.
31. ibid.
32. ibid.
33. ibid. *Coisire*, coign, livery: terms employed for various types of quartering of troops or retainers.
34. ibid.
35. ibid.
36. ibid.
37. ibid.
38. ibid.
39. ibid.
40. ibid.
41. *Cal.S.P.Ire.*, I, 191.
42. *Cal.S.P.Ire.*, I, 188.
43. Shirley, *Original Letters*, 116–17.
44. *Cal.Carew MSS*, I, 330–44, no. 236.
45. Bagwell, op.cit., II, 62ff.
46. *Cal.S.P.Ire.*, I, 198.
47. *Cal.S.P.Ire.*, I, 199.
48. *Cal.Carew MSS*, I, 240–41.
49. *Cal.S.P.Ire.*, I, 229.
50. *Cal.S.P.Ire.*, I, 203.
51. J. Morrin ed., *Cal.Pat.Rolls Ire.*, *Hen.VIII-Eliz.*, I (1861), 479.59.
52. *Cecil MSS* (HMC), I, 260 n. 830.
53. Shirley, *Original Letters*, 269 and note. Archibald Doun Campbell, 5th earl of Argyll, patron of the MacDonnells of Antrim, was an over-mighty subject of the queen of Scots who supported the English interest against the French.
54. Bagwell, op.cit., II, 59.
55. There was at this time evidence that Shane was in contact with the Scottish queen. See *Cal.S.P.Ire.*, I, 205.
56. *Cal.Carew MSS*, I, no. 242.
57. *Cal.S.P.Foreign, Eliz.*, VI, 647.
58. *Cal.S.P.Rome*, I, 168–9.
59. *Cal.S.P.Sp.*, *1558–67*, 370.
60. *Cecil MSS* (HMC), I, 338–9.
61. *Cal.S.P.Ire.*, I, 253.
62. *Cal.S.P.Ire.*, I, 267.
63. *Cal.S.P.Ire.*, I, 279.
64. *Cal.S.P.Ire.*, I, 325.
65. 11 Eliz. s.3.c.1. *Statutes*, 322.
66. D. B. Quinn, 'The Munster Plantation: problems and opportunities', *Cork Hist.Soc.Jn.* LXXI (1966).
67. J. Izon, *Sir Thomas Stucley* (1959), Pt I, 64–99.
68. See *Cal.S.P.Ire.*, I, 262.

69. For Sidney's attitude to Ormond see Bagwell, op.cit., II, 121.
70. 11 Eliz. s.3.c.1. *Statutes*, 322.

COLONIALISM AND PAPAL CRUSADE

A New Phase in English Policy

If the Elizabethan settlement appeared reasonably stable after the defeat
of Shane O'Neill, a new phase was emerging in English policy. Aggressive
colonialism immediately threatened Ireland's stability and provoked
protests in arms from the Anglo-Irish as well as the Irish, who in turn
attempted to stem the new English onslaught by appealing for a
Catholic sovereign who would maintain their traditions, temporal as
well as ecclesiastical. The first offer seriously entertained was to Philip
II of Spain, who wisely delegated such pretensions and duties to Mary
queen of Scots. As the Stuart queen was a prisoner in England, the
prospects of intervention in Ireland in her name were slight. What little
might be achieved in England was soon to be revealed by the Ridolfi
Plot and by the rebellion of the northern earls. One long-term consequence was to be the excommunication of Elizabeth in February
1570, which released Catholic subjects in Ireland, as in England, from
any obligations of allegiance to the Tudor queen. Thus the rebellious
Anglo-Irish and Irish felt strengthened in their quest for a Catholic
deliverer — pursued severally on the continent by James Fitzmaurice
Fitzgerald and by Archbishop Maurice MacGibbon of Cashel to whom,
somewhat unexpectedly, came reinforcement from Thomas Stukely. In
the decade which followed, however, it emerged that no foreign
temporal power was prepared to take on Elizabeth in Ireland and it was
left to Pope Gregory XIII to preach and endow a crusade. This expedition
successfully landed, but was quickly overwhelmed. Once again the long-
term consequences were to prove as significant as the disaster. Colonialism
had to be contained and Catholicism countenanced if England was to
preserve her hold on the kingdom of Ireland.

Attainder of Shane O'Neill

The parliament of 1569[1] provides a suitable curtain-raiser for the events
of this decade. The measures enacted and those defeated, the inter-
ludes brought about by opposition and by the protests in arms against
the new colonial policy, enable us to judge how a new situation arose to
threaten the Elizabethan settlement. From the summer of 1567 plans
for the parliament underwent strategic changes. Queen Elizabeth, no
lover of parliaments despite her occasional public pronouncement to

the contrary, had not favoured Sidney's proposal to hold one to activate
the main assault on Shane O'Neill. The deputy, however, persisted in his
plans, securing her grudging acquiescence. To Sidney, as Sir John Davies
was to appreciate in the next reign, parliament was to provide an
incomparable opportunity to assert England's right over Ireland and over
Ulster in particular; it was a fitting prelude for any grand plantation
scheme which the English privy council might be asked to approve and
which might succeed in finally quietening the realm by eradicating the
Scottish threat. The prelude to this plan was set out at length in the
great preamble to the Bill attainting O'Neill, in one of the longest statements of government propaganda in any Irish statute:[2]

Now thanks be unto Almightie God, thone well amended, and the
seates, signes, plattes, and places of thother recontinued to the quiet
possession of your most excellent Majesty, as well by the death
and final destruction of that caitife and miserable reble Shane Oneile,
as also by other godly and careful trade of government, used by
your Majesties deputie Sir Henry Sidney, which rebell, to the per-
petuall damage and infamy of his name and linage, refusing the
name of a subject, and taking upon him as it were the office of a
prince, hath proudly, arrogantly, and by high and perillous practices
enterprised great sturres, insurrections, rebellions, and horrible
treasons against your royall Majestie your crown and dignitie,
imagining and compassing thereby to deprive your Highnesse, your
heirs and successors, from the reall and actuall possession of this
your Majesties kingdom of Ireland, your true, just, and auncient
inheritance to you by sundrie discents, and authentike strong titles
rightfully and lawfully devoluted, as to the very indubitate and law-
ful heire thereof by pretext of keeping to him and his surname the
dominion and territories of Ulster, injustly claimed as their soile and
ancient inheritance, being the fift and one of the largest partes of
this your realm, and standing in the most perilous place of the same;
and forasmuch, most gracious soveraign lady, as for the manifold
heynous offences committed by the said traytour and his con-
federats, our intent and earnest desire is to intitle your Majestie,
your heires and successours, by Parliament, to the dominion and
territories of Ulster, as a foundation layd for your Highnesse to
plant and dispose the same for increasing your revenue, strengthening
of us, and confirmation of this your realm, wee think it not
unnecessarie first to open unto your Majestie and your nobilitie of
England, by this our humble supplication addressed unto your most

princely estate, the fall and trayterous attempt of that archrebell and arrant traytor, as an introduction to so great and good a purpose, to the intent that like as wee your people are replenished with incredible joy and gladness for being delivered from the perill of so great and cruell a tyrant, so your Majestie would vouchsafe to expresse your just deserved indignation by matter of record against the bloud, progeny and linage of so vile, abhominable, and seditious person.[3]

Clearly this introduction aimed at a reassertion of English royal pretensions in Ireland in the most solemn manner. It was followed by a recital of the events in Shane's iniquitous rebellion which tactfully ignored the royal and viceregal diplomatic negotiations with him, except to underscore his dissimulation and hypocrisy.[4] In identifying the Lord Deputy with Shane's defeat and destruction, it did not detract from his achievements by reference to Shane's defeat by the O'Donnells.

The preamble continued with a statement of the queen's several ancient titles to Ireland 'far beyond the Oneiles and all other of the Irishrie'. Six different justifications were advanced, beginning with mythological kings of Great Britain. In 'Biscan' in Spain, the Irish were ruled by King Gurmond, a son of a king of Great Britain. To their rulers Hiberus and Hermon, Gurmond granted Ireland. From these titles, which depended, no doubt, on Geoffrey of Monmouth, the preamble went on to the third title, citing Giraldus Cambrensis for Henry II's reception of Dermot MacMurrough and his claims by implication over all Ireland. But then the fourth title recited Henry's landing in Ireland, alleging the voluntary subjection of all the Irish kings, implying a justification of Henry's subsequent grant of Ireland to his son John. The remaining titles followed from an alleged decree of the clergy at Armagh and the voluntary submission of the Irish chiefs to Richard II.[5]

Thereafter particular attention was devoted to the queen's title to Ulster, stemming from Robert Fitzstephen, 'the first to open the way to Ireland'. John de Courcy, it was alleged, was sent by Henry II to conquer Ulster, which he held by the king's gift. Since that time 'stirpes of English blood' remained in Ulster. De Courcy's rights, transmitted through de Lacy, passed to de Burgo, from whom the queen was lineally descended. Under these ancestors the preamble declared the O'Neills had lived as vassals obedient to the Crown until the civil wars in England of York and Lancaster. By Henry VIII, O'Neill and other Irish chiefs who had submitted and surrendered their lands were rewarded with English names of honour and possessions to be held by

English tenure, and thus the queen succeeded indubitably to Ireland and to Ulster.[6]

After this overwhelming preamble the act's first clause concluded by declaring Shane attainted. By the second clause it was declared that the name of O'Neill was extinguished with the ceremonies of his creation, it being high treason for anyone to arrogate its titles to himself. The third clause exempted Ulster from the rule of O'Neill, declaring it dependent only upon, and yielding obedience and service to, the Crown of England. By the fourth clause the lands of Shane's adherents, declared forfeited and vested in the Crown, were stated to include the sept of the Neills in the country of Clandeboy, 'the countries of O'Cahan, MacGwylin, the inhabitants of the Glinnes, once known as Misset's lands, usurped by the Scots under James McConnell, McGynnes and his country, O'Hanlon, Hugh MacNeill More, four septs of MacMahounes, MacKyuon, MacCan'. Conveniently these comprised the territory covered by the six modern counties of Antrim, Down, Armagh, Londonderry, Tyrone, and Monaghan. By implication, the remaining Ulster counties of Donegal, Fermanagh, and Cavan were exempt. The clause continued with a recommendation to the queen to favour those alleged Irish allies of O'Neill who had submitted at early opportunities about the time of his death, expressing favour for their pardon and assignment to them of portions of their several countries where they might live on by English tenure and profitable reservation.[7]

The fifth clause preserved the rights and privileges of recited persons of English ancestry or name allegedly dating from before 1534 and including the archbishop of Armagh and the bishops of Down, Clogher, and Dromore, the earls of Kildare and Ormond, Lord Louth, and a number of landed gentry including Bagenal, Bellew, Darcy, Travers, Talbot, Dowdall, and White.[8]

Such was the basis upon which government plans to settle the Ulster question were drafted, including a secret scheme of the queen to reconstruct the Armagh ecclesiastical buildings as the centre and residence for a future governor of Ulster and his council.[9]

The Parliament of 1569

The rest of the legislative programme approved by parliament appears in the printed statutes. This parliament is somewhat better known than its predecessors from the fact that one of its participants, John Hooker, Carew's antiquarian adviser, recorded his own impressions in the *Chronicle of Ireland* which he continued for Holinshed. Hooker's version is naturally qualified by his own attitudes. His pride in his scholarship is represented by the inclusion in Holinshed of his *Treatise on Parliamentary Procedure*, which, he tells us, he presented to the members. His status as the agent for Carew in his attack on Irish land-holders like Sir Christopher Cheevers inevitably coloured his approach to the parliamentary opposition which involved Sidney in tortuous negotiations in order to secure approval for the greater part of his programme. Hooker would have it that after his intervention in the debate, he was jostled in the environs of the house. Much of what happened remains in doubt without independent evidence beyond the legislative measures as a check on the Hooker narrative.[10]

As in previous parliaments, Poynings's Law created procedural difficulties. The government's solution was to suspend the act for the duration of that parliament for all acts concerning the common weal, the reformation of abuses, the establishment of civil policy, or the augmentation of the revenue. The suspension act provided that such Bills as passed certified under the Great Seal to England for the queen's approval and subsequently returned, became of full force after proclamation in certain towns.[11]

As in Henry VIII's time this facilitating of the executive did not pass without a supplementary measure providing that future suspensions of Poynings's Law were not to be proposed until the terms had first been approved by the greater number of the lords and of the Commons.[12] It was specifically stated that while Sir Henry Sidney enjoyed their confidence, other governors had secured the passage of acts dishonour-able to the prince and obstructive to the subject. The complete omission of reference to the Poynings Amendment Act passed in Queen Mary's time is mystifying. It can only be conjectured that Elizabeth's govern-ment preferred a procedure which appeared to give more control to England.

In treating of the passage of the legislation, the sequence of measures passed is indicated by a dual system of numbering which existed on the parliamentary roll at the time these were listed by Shaw Mason. It appears that the acts were not fully numbered for the whole roll, but some certainty as to the sequence can be established as a second system of enumeration was carried out in relation to the successive parliamentary sessions. Thus we can tell the order of every measure passed and published, though we are not absolutely certain about the successive order of all of them on the roll and very little is known of the unpublished measures described as private acts.[13]

In the first session, beginning on 17 January 1569 and concluding on 17 February, Sidney succeeded in securing the enactment of a subsidy

Bill, the first to be passed by this parliament. This recited the fact that Mary's parliament had granted a subsidy of 13s. 4d. on every ploughland for ten years. As Sir Henry Sidney had suspended the imposition of coign and livery, the system of military quartering on the countryside, and as he had suppressed O'Neill's rebellion, parliament gratefully renewed the subsidy for a further ten years, extending its operation to the church lands, as these had been included in the 27th act passed in the parliament of 1536–37. The subsidy could be extended to those lands to be surveyed in future which had not previously come under contribution. Provision was also made for the same exemptions and exceptions which had operated previously.[14]

Six other Bills were passed in this first session. Chapter 2, obviously part of a plan for social and economic development, restricted the tanning of leather to specified towns to be determined by the Lord Deputy and Council.[15] By the fifth chapter certain statutes which had been passed in the 1541 parliament were revived after they had lapsed.[16] These related to grey merchants, a term used for those who operated outside the guilds and forestalled markets, and also to servants' wages and legal proceedings involving mispleading and other technical errors.

The land confiscation programme did not get beyond chapter 3, which found a queen's title for the lands of Christopher Eustace – executed in connection with the Geraldine rebellion of 1534–36.[17]

What might be described as administrative measures are represented by three acts of this session. By chapter 6 on the roll it was provided that the most senior five members of every nation among the Irishry were to bring in idle persons of their surname for judgement.[18] Chapter 3 prohibited Irish lords or captains from establishing fosterage relationships with any lord.[19] Chapter 4[20] exempted the governors of the realm from the act passed under Mary prohibiting the retaining of Scots. This was the sum total of the legislation of the first session, which was then certified by the Lord Deputy and Council and sent to the queen to be approved and returned or vetoed.

Disturbances in Munster

Five days earlier, on 12 February 1569, an offer for planting Munster was addressed by some English adventurers to Sir Henry Sidney. The matter had already been under consideration. Although it was not approved by the deputy before 30 June, Munster was already well aware of what was taking place. On 14 February Sir Warham St Leger reported from Cork to Sidney that the earl of Clancarty, James Fitzmaurice, and others of the south-west had agreed to send messages

to Spain by MacGibbon of Cashel and the bishop of Ross. St Leger
urged that the gentlemen who intended to plant the south-west should
be hastened over 'to adventure their lives and livings in these parts'.
We know from the Simancas archives of Philip II that the Irish
negotiators were to seek as an alternative to the heretical English a
Catholic sovereign of the king's blood to be approved by the pope.
We know from the voyages of Sir Humphrey Gilbert that concurrently
with these events he, Grenville, Wingfield, and St Leger, were concerned
to secure coastal privileges in Munster.[21]

Before parliament could reassemble for a second session, there were
further tales of troubles in Ireland. On 10 June, Nicholas White reported
to Sir William Cecil that Stukely had been accused at the Council
board of conspiracy to levy war against the queen: for this he had been
committed. A week later, trouble broke out in Cork. Kerrycurihy and
Tracton Abbey were attacked by Clancarty and Fitzmaurice, this being
an area in which Grenville was ultimately to plant. On 3 July 1569 the
municipal authorities at Kilmallock reported to the deputy that
Fitzmaurice had extracted an oath from them that 'they would use
none other divine service but the old divine service used by the Church
of Rome'.[22] Nine days later, Fitzmaurice directed the mayor of Cork
to abolish the old heresy of the Huguenots, whom he linked to
Grenville's family. The mayor was to set up Catholicism and see to it
that the clergy co-operated.[23]

Before the end of July disturbing news of the involvement of the
Butlers came to Sidney. Ormond's brother, Sir Edmund Butler, complained that Sir Peter Carew had attacked his castle and claimed his
lands with an approving order from the Dublin Council. This action
had followed Carew's suit against Cheevers, in which the Devon
adventurer's title deeds had been accepted and Cheevers had admitted
the claim, buying off Carew. Butler would have known that after the
Cheevers case he could not win. He went into rebellion along with his
younger brothers. A month later his elder brother, the earl, commenced
the difficult operation of trying to save the family. Sir Edmund, he
insisted, had on 24 August told Fitzmaurice he was prepared to fight
to the death against Carew to preserve his lands, but that he would not
be a party to the restoration of the Mass or to bringing the Spaniards.
Before the end of the year much of Munster had been devastated and
Desmond's new countess, Eleanor Butler, complained that in consequence she had no money to cover travel expenses to visit him.[24]

Second and Third Sessions

The second parliamentary session had been held for one day, 21 February. A solitary measure, that for the suspension of Poynings's Law, was attributed to this session on the roll, where it appeared as chapter 8.[25] The third session extended from 23 February to 11 March: ten Bills were passed in this, commencing with the attainder of Shane O'Neill.[26] Social and economic interests are represented in this group by the Bill to preserve the fry of salmon and eels,[27] and the prohibiting of the use of fresh-water rivers for soaking hemp and similar fibres.[28] A measure restricting the export of wool was also passed.[29]

Apart from O'Neill, a Bill to confiscate one Munster rebel, the Knight of Glin, was passed.[30]

Administrative measures of this session included one to restrict the number of days in the Trinity law term for legal business.[31] The viceroy was authorized for ten years to present to the ecclesiastical dignities of Munster and Connacht, subject to the presentees being in Orders, being capable of functioning in English, and undertaking to reside.[32] Ecclesiastical liberties were not overlooked in the measure providing for the transforming of countries into shires,[33] particular attention being paid to the franchises of the archbishops of Armagh and Dublin. Finally, a Bill was passed to abolish captainships in the Irish Pale.[34]

Fourth Session

Between the third and fourth sessions, an interval of nearly six months intervened. This was partly due to the slowness with which decisions about Ireland were made by the queen and her advisers and partly because of the Munster rebellion. When parliament reassembled on 10 October, two Bills were passed. The earl of Kildare, together with his brothers and sisters, was restored in blood, the attainder passed in the reign of Henry VIII being repealed so far as they were concerned.[35] The second measure, controlling the import of wines, aimed at cutting off the connection with France and with Spain, providing for a customs duty and for the restriction of the trade to English-bound vessels.[36] This measure had been adversely regarded by the vested interests, which feared they might lose substantially if the Spanish trade became illegal or because of the customs dues. The government regarded the measure as important if only because it was hoped that the independent Irish and Anglo-Irish territories would no longer be in a position to maintain direct trade links with the European continent. It has been argued that for Sidney this was the most important measure put before the Irish parliament, at least in the financial sense, as the existing revenue was

wholly inadequate to meet the expanding costs of government.
Indeed, about this time Sidney complained bitterly to Cecil that he
was the most unpopular man in Ireland, because of the lack of
sufficient money to pay the troops or meet the debts owing to the
merchants. The quartering of troops on the countryside made it
virtually impossible to secure the goodwill of the population. The
bankrupt merchants did not easily accept the government view that
the restriction of wine consumption was morally necessary and that
the exclusion of the continental trade would ultimately prove to the
mutual advantage of England and of Ireland. It is even possible that
the measure would never have been passed were it not for a rising
sense of panic at the possibility of a Spanish invasion.

Stukely and MacGibbon

The mission to Spain of Archbishop MacGibbon had nothing like the
same degree of interest for the public as the activities of Sir Thomas
Stukely. The latter's decision to go to Spain in April 1570 and organize
a force on behalf of the Irish Catholics was unexpected and, to some,
unwelcome. Archbishop MacGibbon in particular was extremely
resentful and took steps to dissociate himself from Stukely. He even
went to the length of interviewing Francis Walsingham, Queen
Elizabeth's ambassador in France, to indicate that if the queen was
prepared to restore him to Cashel and permit the use of the old
religious rites, he was prepared to use all his influence against Stukely.
Stukely, however, was a more formidable proposition, if only because
of his remarkable capacity to stimulate interest in his activities. The
rumour that he would return with a formidable force gathered
momentum and in the succeeding year was to become a matter of
major importance.[37]

The Parliament of 1570

In the meantime, in the fifth parliamentary session, five additional
statutes were passed, mostly concerned with administrative policy. By
12 Elizabeth chapter 1 it was provided that a system of free diocesan
schools be set up. The proposal had been linked to a measure to
provide for the more effective organization of parochial churches and
residences: this, however, was abandoned because of the difficulty
of agreement as to costs. Sidney, obliged to accept the queen's
penurious policy, was in no position to carry these church measures
without imposing the main financial liabilities on the bishops and
local clergy. The act for free schools only got through to the statute

book as the government undertook some responsibility. Even then in most of the dioceses it proved a dead letter, as the clergy were not prepared to shoulder the financial burden.

Other administrative measures included an act to give exemplifications (official copies of records) the authority of the originals; this was necessary because of the wholesale embezzlement of state documents which had become a main consequence of the tightening of royal control and the confiscating of landed property.[38] The act imposing standard measures on corn and other agricultural products is self-explanatory.[39] The measure empowering the executive to grant under letters patent to Irishmen and 'degenerate' Englishmen their lands or part of their lands, provided these were in accordance with English feudal tenure, is an indication that the policy of surrender and re-grant had not been abandoned.[40] In fact the measure was an attempt to control the panic that arose over Sir Peter Carew and because of the rumours about a Munster plantation. Finally, despite certain ferocious threats contained in it, the act for the attainder of those who went into rebellion after 1 April 1569 and who did not surrender themselves before 30 April 1571 was in fact a concealed measure of absolution for the Butlers.[41] This was not to be apparent at first and indeed some of those who surrendered seemed in danger of paying the supreme penalty. Sidney, however, must have known that the queen would never have been prepared to permit the Butlers to be treated like the Fitzgeralds, and the ultimate pardon of Ormond's rebellious brothers was made possible by this act.

In the second session of 1570 only one measure was adopted — that for the attainder of an isolated rebel, Thomas Queverford.[42]

Excommunication of Elizabeth

Before parliament concluded, a proposal supported by the Council in Ireland for the establishment of an Irish university was abandoned because, as Sidney assured the members, the government was in no position to finance it. The measure was of some interest to Edmund Campion, whose *History of Ireland* virtually concludes with Sidney's valedictory address before proroguing parliament. Campion had been interested in maintaining good relations with Leicester as well as with Sidney and may even have hoped that if a university were set up at this juncture in Ireland, he might be permitted to be associated with it.[43] However, the decision of the pope to excommunicate the queen on 25 February 1570 would have made such an arrangement impossible. The papal action not only released the queen's subjects from their allegiance but imposed upon them the obligation to refuse obedience under threat of being themselves excommunicated.

In contrast to what took place in the contemporary English parliament, where the papal action brought about positive affirmations of loyalty to the queen and denunciations of the pope, the political temperature in Ireland seems to have been kept reasonably cool. This was perhaps due to Ormond's diplomacy, concerned to preserve his brothers from any involvement over the religious issue or in the projected invasion. He was able to provide Cecil (Lord Burghley since February 1571) with a copy of the papal bull affixed to the gates of Limerick by the archrebel Fitzmaurice. But he was also able to point out that the failure to prevent Fitzmaurice from capturing Kilmallock need not have happened if more indulgence had been given to his contrite relatives, who might thus have been in a position to frustrate Fitzmaurice. The feared foreign intervention soon ceased to be of concern. Circumstances had led to a change of attitude on the continent.[44]

At one moment it seemed likely that Stukely would be provided with a force of 12,000 Spaniards to invade Ireland. Almost immediately afterwards the English government learned that this had been counter-manded.[45] While English agents in Spain conjectured that this was due to King Philip's becoming wearied by Stukely's pretentious extravagance, there can be little doubt that Spanish imperial interests would not have tolerated any plan for the invasion of Ireland. The duke of Alva in particular, concerned for good relations between England and the Netherlands, discouraged all such proposals. Moreover, the Anglo-French negotiations, culminating in 1572 in the Treaty of Blois, could very well have created insuperable difficulties for Spain. Stukely's with-drawal, his subsequent involvement in the Lepanto campaign, and his later negotiations with the pope for an Irish enterprise closed the chapter which had so greatly concerned Sidney.

Fitzwilliam replaces Sidney; Connacht

Before the Lord Deputy handed over authority to his successor, four further acts were passed, two of which were concerned with export trade.[46] The third authorized the Armagh archbishop to lease church lands;[47] and the fourth[48] attainted another Munster rebel, the White Knight, who had been killed. Thereafter Sidney could feel justified in withdrawing from Ireland. The queen had authorized this on the some-what unusual grounds that Sir Henry must be allowed to see his son Philip, who was too precious to permit him to risk the dangers of a voyage to Ireland; and so his father was to be permitted to return from exile (March 1571).

Sir William Fitzwilliam had been mainly concerned with financial matters during the previous twenty years in Ireland. The office of chief governor had become largely a military one and while Fitzwilliam was prepared to act and could act effectively in a military situation, he does not appear to have regarded himself pre-eminently as a soldier. Moreover, his appointment was as Lord Justice, always regarded as a temporary assignment between Lord Deputies or Lord Lieutenants. However, Fitzwilliam was destined to remain in office as Lord Deputy until 1575. Before his retirement, Sidney had succeeded in establishing active lord presidents with their councils in Connacht and in Munster. Sir Edward Fitton from Galway endeavoured to maintain order among the Burkes as well as among the native Irish. But on the whole he was not a success, except when he was provided with an adequate English army. Even then, with poor financial resources his quartering of his troops on the countryside created considerable dissatisfaction. This left the inhabitants with more grievances than they normally displayed while maintaining their customary chiefs and captains, whose exactions were not so considerable except in times of war.[49] Not until the 1580s would a later lord president, Sir Richard Bingham, bring Connacht more into the queen's sphere in Ireland.

Munster

Under Sir John Perrot as lord president, the position in Munster was different. Fitzmaurice continued his warfare in the hopes of a Catholic expedition from the continent. But apart from a few devoted followers and some enthusiastic ecclesiastics, he was unable to keep the field against Perrot. Thanks to Ormond, the Butlers were able to get out of the struggle and indeed, once the flag of religion was raised, they did service in the field against some of the rebels. Ultimately Fitzmaurice was reduced to a situation in which while he could not win, he could not be defeated, and Perrot, who rather prided himself on his martial prowess, attempted to resolve the issue by a duel with the Catholic leader. Fitzmaurice, however, was not prepared to hazard the religious issue like this and Perrot, who of course did not escape a royal reproof, was obliged early in 1572 to support Fitzmaurice's submission and pardon. Meanwhile, much to the president's disgust, Elizabeth had decided to restore Desmond, partly in the belief that this would terminate the war in the south and partly to indicate the abandonment of any government commitment to a massive plantation in Munster.[50]

The Earl of Desmond

During 1571 and 1572 English political rivalries had brought to the surface conspiracies against Burghley, as well as conspiracies to liberate Mary Stuart. Some who were involved in trying to liberate her had no intention of being disloyal to Elizabeth. Others, concerned to challenge Burghley's monopoly of power, had little desire to liberate Mary and none to dethrone Elizabeth. Among the latter was the earl of Leicester, usually hostile to the earl of Ormond and never particularly happy at Cecil's ascendancy over the queen. When Leicester was informed of the moves against Burghley, having already some inkling of the plot to release Mary, he apparently used the situation to strengthen himself with Elizabeth by revealing something of what he knew and securing a royal pardon. To Fitzwilliam, Leicester issued a mysterious warning that something was afoot which, in fact, may not have been any more than a warning about Ormond's opponent, Sir Warham St Leger. Desmond and his brother had been remanded in custody from the Tower to St Leger's London house, and it seems St Leger was conspiring with Martin Frobisher and others to smuggle Desmond out to Stukely in Spain. Some historians have regarded this as a piece of bluff on Cecil's part to secure Desmond's restoration to his estates against the advice of Ormond. But the coincidence of the massacre of St Bartholomew's Day in Paris inevitably confused the issue, as many English and Irish Protestants panicked — believing that they risked massacre at home. So far as Burghley was concerned, with more partiality for Spain than for France, the Paris event enabled him to strengthen the moves which would necessitate the French abandoning the Scots queen and allying with Elizabeth against any third party, even in the cause of religion. In such circumstances Elizabeth agreed to permit Desmond to return to Ireland early in 1573 on an undertaking to co-operate with the forces of reformation.[51]

To Perrot, of course, Desmond was more qualified to preside over Bedlam than his earldom. The earl, resentful at having been kept under restraint in Dublin on his way back and appalled at the devastation of his lordship during the rebellion, felt entitled to denounce the clauses of his agreement in London committing him to supporting Protestantism. Accordingly, he announced his intention of not being bound by such conditions. In fact Perrot was obliged to dissemble and prevaricate and turn the blind eye to Desmond's restoration of Catholicism in Munster which had the desired result of winning the province from Fitzmaurice, who early in 1575 withdrew to the continent.[52]

Ulster Plantation Schemes

With the death of Sir Peter Carew in November 1575[53] and the abandonment of the Munster plantation scheme it might be held that honours
were even in south Leinster and Munster. Whatever plantation would be
attempted, it was thereafter accepted that it would have to be in Ulster.

In the years 1571–75 three separate efforts were made to establish
colonies in the north-east of Ireland: the Smith scheme; the Chatterton-
Malby scheme; and the Essex scheme. None of them was successful. All
of them impaired England's reputation in Ireland; the first and last are
noteworthy landmarks in the development of the colonial idea of
England.[54]

On 5 October 1571 indentures were signed between the queen and one
Chatterton, Nicholas Malby, and Thomas Smith respectively. The
intention was to enable them to use their private resources, involving
the queen in no expense, to colonize the lands of the O'Hanrahans of
Armagh, the Macartans of Down, and the territory of the Ards peninsula.
Chatterton and Malby within five years had failed to make any substantial progress and on the recommendation of the Dublin executive
were withdrawn. More spectacular is the history of the Smith scheme.[55]

Sir Thomas Smith, one of the queen's secretaries, followed up the
agreement with a publication of the project by himself and his son
Thomas for the plantation of the Ards in Ireland, much to the annoy-
ance of the queen, whose sanction had not been obtained before
publication. Smith, who had reluctantly agreed to accept a temporary
diplomatic appointment to Paris, where he and Walsingham negotiated
the Treaty of Blois in April 1572, was obliged to use all his political
influence to save his grant. He appealed successfully to Burghley to
interest himself and he agreed to invest some capital in the enterprise.
On publication the plan gained widespread notice as the first full-scale
project for an English colony: it has been regarded by some American
historians as the prototype for English colonial schemes in America.
Young Smith believed that with a nucleus of 800 English volunteers, he
could establish a model settlement and ultimately get rid of the Scots
and the native Irish. Sir Brian MacPhelim O'Neill of Clandeboy
regarded himself as overlord of the Ards. Smith assured him he did not
intend to interfere with his rights. In reporting on this to Burghley,
Smith added 'as yet'. Within a short time Sir Brian MacPhelim, gauging
the weakness of Smith, only a hundred of whose volunteers had
materialized, devastated the Ards. Soon after Smith was killed, and
despite the efforts of his father, the project collapsed.[56]

Essex in Ireland

Walter Devereux, Viscount Hereford, had so distinguished himself in
the stamping-out of the rebellion of the English northern earls in 1569
that the queen made him a Knight of the Garter and created him earl of
Essex in 1572. The grateful Essex volunteered in May 1573 to conquer
Ulster and the queen and he took equal shares in the expedition to be
led by Essex. Each of them was to maintain 400 foot and 200 horse for
two years, the queen lending the earl £10,000 at 10 per cent interest on
the security of his English lands.[57]

The grant to Essex was of northern Clandeboy, the greater part of
the modern county of Antrim and part of the territory held by Smith,
which was duly surrendered on 8 July. Private adventurers were to be
encouraged by grants of 400 acres at 2 pence per acre per annum for
horsemen. Two hundred acres at the same rate were available for foot-
men. The project had the support, in addition to Smith's, of Burghley,
Sussex, and Leicester.[58]

Essex soon found himself in difficulties, both with the native Irish
and with the Scots. The queen favoured his being made governor of
Ulster with the powers of a lord president. Yet difficulties arose, as
Fitzwilliam was not prepared to interpret liberally the queen's
directions to reduce the army. He was not prepared to give military
support to Essex at the expense of denuding the Dublin defences. A
half-hearted appeal for volunteers to the lords of the Pale produced
only one favourable response. Essex was thus reduced to making a
truce with Turlough Luineach O'Neill, whose corn he could burn, but
whom even with the assistance of O'Donnell he was unable to capture.
Almost more humiliating was the position in Carrickfergus, where an
epidemic decimated the garrison: this was in any case too ineffective to
be employed in military activity, so that most of the soldiers were put to
work as labourers. Essex, like Sussex, was a man of high ideals. In the
Desmond dispute with Dublin after his escape, Essex had allowed himself to be used as a negotiator, secured Desmond's confidence and made
proposals for an honourable settlement with the southern earl — too
honourable for Fitzwilliam. In the north, however, his attitude to the
Irish and to the Scots was far from honourable. Treacherously, Essex
seized and executed Sir Brian MacPhelim O'Neill late in 1574, despite
his long record of loyalty to the queen. No official condemnation
followed. But when Essex proceeded similarly against the Scots and
massacred non-combatants on Rathlin Island, the queen could not ignore
the public reaction and Essex, once thought of as a possible successor
to Fitzwilliam, was deprived of his military powers. Under Sidney's

subsequent viceroyalty his failure was to be apparent. And as in the case of Malby, an exchange of territories was to be negotiated. Then, in September 1576, Essex fell sick and died, rumour attributing his death to poison, allegedly administered by Leicester, who could hardly escape malicious tongues when he subsequently married the widowed countess, Lettice Knollys. So ended the first projects of plantation in Ulster.[59]

Fitton in Connacht

Fitzwilliam, in contrast to Sidney, left less of a significant impression in Ireland. He tended to let matters go their own way as far as possible, rather than to direct them. To a large extent this was what he let happen in Ulster. However, as far as Connacht was concerned, he did not permit Sir Edward Fitton, the president, to keep matters entirely in his own control. In any case, Fitton soon demonstrated his inability to control Connacht. When the lord president early in 1572 accused Clanricarde of being an accessory to the illegalities of his sons, Fitzwilliam and the Dublin Council were furious that Fitton was not prepared to substantiate the allegations. He was therefore rebuked and ultimately humiliated when Clanricarde was pardoned and allowed to try to reconcile his sons to the government. In the early summer, feeling impotent in Galway, Fitton withdrew to Athlone and the Burkes burnt the Clanricarde castles and devastated as far east as Mullingar. So weak was Fitton's garrison at Galway that they were unable to defend the loyal O'Flahertys when they were attacked by the Burkes. Ultimately, it was necessary to transfer Fitton to Dublin, where he succeeded to the vice-treasurership, formerly held by Fitzwilliam. But the successive financial officials quarrelled over their retainers and in June 1573 Fitzwilliam imprisoned Fitton for illegally withholding the pardon of a follower of the Lord Deputy, accused of having murdered a Fitton supporter.[60]

Return of Sidney

In September 1575, Sidney returned to advise on the Ulster situation in particular. The acceptance of his advice almost inevitably led to the decision to restore him, which was, partly at least, dictated by the growing international anxiety which might have led to a foreign invasion. Pope Gregory XIII showed an interest in Fitzmaurice's cause and addressed letters to leading Irish lords exhorting them to adhere to the faith.[61] In issuing an interpretation of Elizabeth's excommunication the pope permitted temporary allegiance to the queen to be maintained, pending a crusade to bring about her deposition. In the hysteria of the

1570s and the aftermath of St Bartholomew, the papal construction of the excommunication led Elizabeth and Cecil to doubt the sincerity and trustworthiness of any Catholic, even though loyalists both in England and in Ireland felt entitled thereafter to distinguish between the claims of religion and politics. In these circumstances Sidney returned to the viceroyalty in Ireland.

A more active policy was resumed, Ormond having some fears that at least one of his brothers, Edward, might be brought to justice. Before Fitzwilliam had left, a direction to bring him in without protection was issued against Edward Butler: this was signed by Leicester, Sir Francis Knollys, Croft, Sir Thomas Smith, and Walsingham and dated 25 July 1575. As Burghley and Sussex did not sign it, these might be regarded as the anti-Ormond group at court who dominated political thinking about Ireland for the duration of Sidney's last viceroyalty. Perhaps Ormond in the ultimate resolve felt assured that he could rely on the queen, who consoled the earl when he expressed his fear that his enemies were trying to make his brother a traitor, by saying that she would believe nothing against him. Nevertheless, the price of liberty was eternal vigilance: ultimately Ormond was to survive the deputy's recall. In a series of tours Sidney surveyed the country as a whole. He seems to have been able to gain greater respect than had his predecessor. He established four counties in Connacht and arranged for new presidents to succeed Perrot and Fitton in the persons of Sir William Drury for Munster and Sir Nicholas Malby for Connacht. In each of these areas the president ruled through terror: Drury by extreme severity in Munster, Malby by consistent corn-burning in Connacht. In the north Sidney kept matters more particularly in his own hands, perhaps believing that he could yet supervise a more successful plantation scheme. Recent failures, however, convinced him that such projects should not be taken on so lightly. The phasing-out of the bankrupt planters of the north was followed in King's County and Queen's County by more realistic relations with the O'Connors and the O'Mores.[62]

Dispute over Cess

In his reports to England Sidney was struck by the poverty of the country and particularly by the miserable state of the Church. His plans for improvement were constructive, but were continually impeded by military exigencies. His own expenditure bordered on the extravagant and in the queen's view exceeded it. Ultimately it was for this alleged reason that he was to be recalled. More immediately, the deputy became involved in a serious quarrel in the English Pale over the cess.

To the queen the deputy defined cess as:

> a quantity of victual and a prisage set upon the same necessary for
> soldiers . . . . and so much for your Deputy's house, so far
> under the value, as it goeth between party and party, as the soldier
> may live of his wages and your Highness's officer of his entertainment,
> and this to be taxed by your Highness's Deputy and Council, calling
> to them the nobility adjoining.[63]

In March 1577 a Meath grand jury presented a bill against the cess.
The deputy took the view that this was to be regarded as a challenge to
the prerogative and was contrary to precedent, allegedly going back to
the early fifteenth century. The Palesmen insisted that cess had only
been imposed regularly for thirty years, that when initiated the fixed
prices had been reasonable, but that now they were ruinous. More
efficient and less costly troops, they declared, could be raised locally for
local work and to England they dispatched three lawyers, Barnaby
Scurlock, Richard Netterville, and Henry Burnell. Elizabeth supported
her deputy to the extent of imprisoning the Irish lawyers and approving
Sidney's dealing with those who had sent them. Accordingly, Lords
Baltinglass, Delvin, Trimleston, and Howth were imprisoned in Dublin
Castle for challenging a prerogative. Privately the queen deplored to
Sidney his action in choosing an inopportune time for publicizing this
grievance in view of the invasion danger, to which Sidney responded
that if Fitzmaurice did invade, then he 'had rather a good many of them
now in the Castle should still remain than be abroad'. The prisoners,
both in London and in Dublin, submitted formally, but they did not
abandon their case. Ormond let it be known that he was opposed to the
cess. Carew in Idrone had sought exemption from it, as had other
settlers. Ultimately a compromise was worked out, maintaining this
form of local subsidy, despite the lawyers' declaration that tax might
not be imposed except by parliament or Grand Council.[64]

The agreement affected the counties of Dublin, Meath, Westmeath,
Louth, Kildare, Carlow, Wexford, and Kilkenny. These were

> to victual as many of the thousand soldiers and officers as the Lord
> Deputy should appoint, and to pay 1*d.* a day for each man of that
> number, whether present or no, deducting that sum in the case of
> those men whom they were required to victual fully.

The same counties also agreed to supply 9,000 pecks of oats at 10 pence sterling to the horsemen and sell fresh provisions for cash at reasonable rates to the Lord Deputy. The Dublin officials held that Her Majesty had made a bad bargain.[65]

Gerrard's Report

In Sidney's last two years, 1577–78, the forces of repression became more accentuated. A new English Chancellor, Sir William Gerrard, with long administrative experience in Wales, reported adversely on the state of the Pale. As in Wales, a policy of severity by English judges and no pardons for important people would gradually extend the Pale. Most of the Irish could not be civilized and as these comprised the greater part of the lower classes in the Pale, they should be exterminated. English farmers should be brought in on good conditions to replace them.[66]

Drury in Munster

Drury's severe government in Munster, where he imposed the cess, caused increasing difficulties. Like Gerrard, he was dissatisfied with the habitual pardoning of great offenders. Anxious to keep Munster and Connacht apart, Drury arrested Sir John of Desmond on suspicion of abetting the Connacht rebels. In consequence Sir John's brother, the earl of Desmond, refused to pay taxes or to negotiate with Drury. Ultimately Sidney was obliged to interfere. Drury's face was saved after the earl submitted to Sidney at a ceremony where the earl and the lord president were reconciled. Like Leinster, the province of Munster was increasing in discontent in a time of growing international crisis. Perhaps Malby might feel he had been more successful in Connacht. The corn-burning and the harrying of the sons of Clanricarde were maintained until the earl's sons gave up the struggle and Malby allowed the corn to be sown. Thus Connacht was held down by force, although the earl's sons could not be captured.[67]

Sidney ceased to dominate the midlands in his later years, when a gifted guerilla leader, Rory Og O'More, devastated the plantation at every conceivable opportunity. Inevitably this war sank to the lowest depths of infamy, treachery being used remorselessly by both sides and more notoriously by the planters.[68]

Recall of Sidney

Ultimately Elizabeth, having intervened in the Netherlands, withdrew Sidney from Ireland on 12 September 1578. It remained to be seen whether more severe successors would prove more economical with resources than with lives. Soon Elizabeth was to be concerned to deny that she approved a war of extermination against the Irish.

Gregory XIII, Stukely and Fitzmaurice

About this time Pope Gregory XIII opened his new approaches to the question of Catholicism in England and in Ireland. To England he sent two members of the Society of Jesus, Edmund Campion and Robert Persons, with instructions to publish his *Explicatio* containing the decision to suspend the provision prohibiting Catholics from recognizing and obeying the queen pending the enforcement of the decree deposing her. Campion was captured, questioned, and in December 1581 executed after publicly asserting the purely spiritual nature of the work of the Jesuits, who were concerned for th salvation of souls and totally un-interested in the political issues. Persons withdrew to the continent, whence he concerned himself with every activity for the winning of England, whether spiritual or political. Whether Persons really confined himself to spiritual activities may be in doubt. What is indubitable is that to many English Catholics the pope's action in launching a Catholic crusade in Ireland proved a grave embarrassment.[69]

Pope Gregory's first efforts with regard to Ireland preceded the dispatch to England of the Jesuits. In consequence of Stukely's involvement with Don John of Austria against the Turks in one of the naval actions culminating in Lepanto the papacy decided that support for Stukely was more likely to be effective than supporting Archbishop MacGibbon or anyone else. Gregory XIII therefore recommended him to Philip of Spain, indicating that while the pope hoped that Philip would be ready to be directly involved, he was perfectly prepared to assume sole responsibility if the king preferred to be involved indirectly. Philip's thinking in the matter was not unlike that of Elizabeth, who intervened in support of Philip's rebellious subjects in the Netherlands indirectly — though everyone knew that prominent English nobles like Leicester would not dare involve themselves without her sanction.[70]

Papal enthusiasm for the campaign against Elizabeth even went to the lengths of condoning assassination. When the pope was asked whether it would be sinful to assassinate the queen, the written response made it clear that Gregory approved such a proposal. She had destroyed many Catholics and risked the immortal souls of many more by forcing them into heresy, and richly deserved to be put out of this world; no sin could be involved in such an action.[71] He can hardly have anticipated how fatal his decisions were to Catholicism in England.

On his return to the Iberian peninsula from Rome, Stukely soon

found himself dissatisfied with the dilatory measures and small contributions which Philip II was prepared to dispense. By contrast it
emerged that King Sebastian of Portugal was more crusade-minded.
Accordingly Stukely turned to negotiations with Lisbon, only to find
himself involved in a *quid pro quo* situation. If Stukely would first
assist Portugal in a campaign against the Moors of North Africa, he
would then be fully supported in his crusade in Ireland, assuming the
successful outcome of the expedition against the Moors. Unfortunately
for both Sebastian and Stukely their joint expedition ended disastrously
in 1578 on the field of Alcazar, from which neither of them returned.[72]
The pope thereafter was obliged to sanction another project for Ireland.
In the summer of 1579 there arrived at Dingle in County Kerry a
modest invading force led by James Fitzmaurice Fitzgerald. As papal
commissary there came the English secular priest Dr Nicholas Sander.
Gregory XIII, in appointing Fitzmaurice captain-general of the papal
army, provided him with the plenary indulgences customarily bestowed
upon crusaders. The crusade was to prove disastrous for those involved
in it; it failed to secure support outside of Munster save for one abortive
local uprising in Leinster by Lord Baltinglass. After Fitzmaurice's death
it was to involve the earl of Desmond in disaster too and bring about
the destruction of his earldom. It was also to lead to the capture, torture,
and execution of the papal archbishop of Cashel, Dermot O'Hurley. But
it may have contributed the essential life force to the survival of
Catholicism in Ireland at the very time it became almost extinguished
in England. While the reactions in Dublin under Drury and Sir William
Pelham, successive temporary governors after Sidney, were effective
through their very severity, the queen was soon apprised of the danger
that a general revolt might be provoked through what appeared to be
due to the counsels of panic. In particular she was anxious to avoid
actions against Desmond which would throw him into the arms of
Fitzmaurice. To contain the invaders due steps were taken, particularly
by naval actions. Off the coast of south-east Ireland, Perrot and Sir
William Winter functioned in close touch with government land forces.
More subtle methods were used against Fitzmaurice, against whom
Tibbot, son of Sir William Burke of Castleconnell, was successfully
employed.

The Catholic Crusade

If Fitzmaurice had really believed that Catholic Ireland would rise with
him, his own death was perhaps less of a loss than might have been
anticipated. One consequence of it was that Sander was able to press

the earl of Desmond into more and more participation. The reaction of
Desmond's brothers to the papal crusade was to involve themselves, even
to the point of assassinating English officials like Henry Davells, with
whom they had formerly been friendly. They were also able, more than
Fitzmaurice, to make use of the earl's resources for the crusade.
While the earl, like many other prominent Irish lords, endeavoured to
avoid a break with the queen, he was so provoked by Pelham that he
was driven into Sander's arms under threat of being proclaimed a traitor.
Pelham's action was afterwards adversely criticized by the queen and
indeed by Ormond, who believed that but for Pelham he could have
kept Desmond neutral.[73]

The Catholic crusade, surprisingly, managed to maintain the war for
some four years. During that period the Elizabethan forces experienced
several reverses, largely because of the totally inadequate means made
available by the queen, who despised the pope's forces. She rarely gave a
thought to Ireland while she concerned herself with the Netherlands
and her own projected marriage with the duc d'Alençon. Given that the
continental aid to the crusade was totally inadequate, it remains a
matter of astonishment that the Catholic crusade survived so long. A
possible explanation is the hope of more support from the Holy See
and from the Catholic powers which Sander and the few Counter-
Reformation clergy in the Irish Pale continued to insist would
inevitably arrive. The statement here restricting the area in which the
advocates of foreign intervention expressed themselves is deliberately
cautious. No evidence can be cited of Counter-Reformation advocates
of a policy of recognizing Elizabeth. It seems reasonable, however, to
assume that an attitude of political neutrality governed the actions of
men like Dermot O'Hurley. Provided by the pope to the archbishopric
of Cashel after MacGibbon's death, his activities in Ireland appear to
have been confined to the spiritual.[74]

A factor of decisive significance during this war resulted in part from
the military policy pursued by the queen's forces. Partly in order to
terrify their opponents, partly as a result of their own unexpected
defeats, the English forces resorted to a savage destructiveness against
non-combatants as well as against the crusaders, which on a short-term
basis proved successful, but in the long term added substantially to
Irish popular hatred for the English and for Protestantism. The panic
created among the English by even minor reverses provoked them not
only into excessive actions against opponents, but also led them to
wholesale destruction of objects of Catholic veneration — to the fury of
those venerating them. When, in 1580, the queen replaced Pelham by

Lord Grey de Wilton, this austere exponent of severity, having sustained an unexpected reverse in Glenmalure at the hands of Fiach MacHugh O'Byrne, successfully concerned himself with the destruction of the Smerwick garrison, mainly composed of Italians sent by the pope to reinforce the crusade. Their leader, Sebastiano San Guiseppe, having attempted to negotiate a surrender, appears to have been a party to its violation by the Lord Deputy in the false hope of saving his own life. Whether in fact Grey promised to spare them may never be absolutely established, but there is no doubt that to Catholic Europe the term *Greia fides* was considered as another manifestation of perfidious Albion. The Lord Deputy, patron and hero of Edmund Spenser, who immortalized him in *The Faerie Queene*, probably regarded himself as justly condemning the archangels of Antichrist to the extreme tortures meted out to them by chivalrous knights. Irish and English members of the expedition, like Oliver Plunkett and Laurence Moore, were hanged on the walls of Smerwick fort after their legs and arms had been broken with irons.[75]

To Spenser the destruction by death and starvation of 30,000 people in Munster was brought on themselves by their own wickedness. Elizabeth knew better, and while she first thanked her deputy for what he did at Smerwick, and indeed goaded him on to more, she quickly adjusted her attitude in the light of public opinion, reminding him that he had been cautioned against severity and had been warned to deny the allegation that her policy was one of extermination.[76] When, in January 1582, the queen proclaimed an amnesty, the exasperated Grey requested a recall and in August surrendered his office. The policy of frightfulness continued. It was used by Malby in Connacht to prevent the Munster war expanding, as it had been used by Grey in Leinster — even to the point of judicially murdering an ex-Chief Justice, Nicholas Nugent, whose relatives had been involved in the rising of Baltinglass. It was not so successful in the north, where the queen's parsimony reduced English influence to a minimum in the decade after Essex. In an effort to keep Ulster out of the Catholic war, English officials in the north were reduced to humiliating acquiescence at the hands of Turlough Luineach O'Neill. Obliged to treat this long-surviving successor of Shane as a loyal and trusted Irish lord with quasi-official military authority in central Ulster, they were reduced to intriguing against him with others, such as Hugh O'Neill, second son and successor of Matthew, baron of Dungannon. Hugh, indeed, was himself in no position to stand out against Turlough Luineach whose daughter, in 1579, he felt obliged to marry even at the risk of insulting O'Donnell, whose daughter, his first

wife, was sent home by Hugh on the plea that their matrimonial relationship was uncanonical. When, under pressure from Dublin, the baron of
Dungannon attempted to make himself independent of Turlough
Luineach, he was forced to realize that English authority in Ulster was
as impotent to maintain him as it had been to preserve the lives of his
brother Brian and of their father Matthew. Moreover, Turlough Luineach,
avowing himself the Catholic champion, secured the support of
virtually all Ulster. Successive Connacht presidents, Malby and Sir
Richard Bingham, might keep their province quiet and even intimidate
the border men, like O'Donnell and O'Rourke, so that in fact the war
did not spread to the north. The lesson was not lost on Hugh O'Neill
that his own political survival would depend upon his securing endorsement from the forces of the Counter-Reformation and perhaps also
from a Dublin government prepared to connive at this and support
him.[77]

The ultimate defeat of the Catholic crusade in Munster left a grave
legacy of destruction and hatred. Perhaps nowhere is this hatred more
clearly indicated than in the comments of Hooker in Holinshed's
Chronicle in describing the character of the Irishman.

And here may you see the nature and disposition of this wicked,
effrenated, barbarous, and unfaithfull nation, who (as Cambrensis
writeth of them) they are a wicked and perverse generation, constant
alwaies in that they be alwaies unconstant, faithfull in that they be
alwaies unfaithfull, and trustie in that they be alwaies trecherous and
untrustie. They doo nothing but imagin mischeefe, and have no
delite in anie good thing. They are alwaies working wickedness
against the good, and such as be quiet in the land. Their mouths are
full of unrighteousnesse, and their toongs speake nothing but cursed-
nesse. Their feet swift to shed blood, and their hands imbrued in the
blood of innocents. The waies of peace they know not, and in the
paths of righteousnesse they walke not. God is not knowne in their
land, niether is his name called rightlie upon among them. Their queen
and sovereigne they obeie not, and hir government they allow not:
but as much as in them lieth doo resist hir imperiall estate, crowne,
and dignitie.[78]

Understandably the murder of a fellow Devonshire man, Davells, by
Sir John of Desmond in summer 1579 was unforgivable treachery to
Hooker. Like Hooker, many officials confronted with the Catholic war
and the cold war saw the matter in terms of the reaction to the

colonizing projects and to some of them this, more than the question of religion, was the reason for the continuation of the conflict. Even Ormond knew this factor to be involved when Desmond announced his readiness to submit upon pardon and restoration to his estates. But Ormond well knew how much the queen's policy was responsible for the continuation of the terror and in a moment of utter exasperation declared he would never again undertake such service with such little support from his sovereign.

The end of the war revived plantation interest. The exceptions to the queen's amnesty, added to by Grey de Wilton, included a number of persons whose presence on the list was justified in Dublin as being due to the necessity to secure the forfeiture to the queen of their lands. This factor became increasingly important for adventurers and servitors against Desmond, for whom provision was to be made in the subsequent Munster plantation. In particular the new planters established themselves in Munster towns which thereafter maintained a microcosm of Protestantism. This was to play no small part in the civil war in the 1640s.[79]

Perrot Replaces Grey de Wilton

The departure of Lord Grey de Wilton probably eased the situation in the Pale, where his policy had tended to keep things fermenting. One of his final acts, for example, had been to urge the necessity for keeping the earl of Kildare in England under surveillance. Grey's argument was that Kildare's return would be the signal for the murder of Archbishop Adam Loftus, whom the deputy was keeping in protective custody.[80] Grey's fears were hardly shared by Loftus when it came to accepting office jointly with Sir Henry Wallop as temporary Lords Justices, pending the arrival of Sir John Perrot as Lord Deputy.

Archbishop O'Hurley

Nor did Loftus appear unduly fearful about the consequences of carrying out orders from England for the questioning under torture and execution of Archbishop O'Hurley. After a preliminary suggestion that the instruments of interrogation could be applied with more practice in the Tower of London, Loftus and Wallop accepted orders that it would be more convenient to execute O'Hurley by martial law in Ireland. O'Hurley was therefore questioned about accessories to the papal enterprise against Elizabeth, while his legs were being toasted in a fire, into which he was put in boots filled with combustibles. O'Hurley survived to be hanged with the customary barbarities at an early hour of

the morning on 19 June 1584 before the Dublin citizens could witness
the spectacle. He does not appear to have made any confession, nor was
any information allegedly extorted from him employed against the
few remaining suspects in the Pale whose trial took place about this
time. Loftus and his colleagues were not slow to realize that their
actions had made the religious issue a major factor for government in
the Dublin area. Sir John Perrot, a man with some inkling from his
Munster experience of the importance of religion, wisely postponed the
assumption of office until after the Lords Justices had hanged
O'Hurley.[81]

Perrot's viceroyalty may be regarded as the end of an era. Presumably
preoccupation with Munster activities played a major part in the
selection of Perrot, under whom as president the war of a decade earlier
had concluded without proceeding to extremities. Perrot, however,
was not destined to settle the future of Munster and most of his
activities as viceroy involved him elsewhere.[82]

At the same time Sir Richard Bingham went to Connacht as lord
president. He now had fuller authority than he had previously exercised
after Malby had moved to Munster. To the southern province a
commission under Wallop was sent to survey the escheated lands.[83]
Rumours of a Scottish invasion diverted Perrot to the north. He was
however, frustrated, as his hopes of military glory vanished with the
non-arrival of the Scots. Ultimately he was obliged to console himself
with reporting that Turlough Luineach O'Neill, the baron of
Dungannon, and O'Cahan had come in and that he had stabilized the
Antrim situation by approving a grant of the lands formerly held by the
Bissets to their alleged descendant Donal Gorm MacDonnell.

Perrot and Loftus

Returning to Dublin, Perrot endeavoured to carry out his instructions
for transforming St Patrick's Cathedral. Since Archbishop Browne's
time abortive plans for a collegiate institution had been under fire from
successive archbishops. Perrot soon found that Loftus was no exception
to this attitude. The archbishop based his objections on the usual
reason that the cathedral maintained benefices for the benefit of
preachers, the only preachers of the Word of God in the kingdom.
Perrot became enthusiastic over a scheme to combine the law courts
and two university colleges within the liberty of St Patrick's. The Lord
Deputy's determination, once he had decided on his plan, became upper-
most in his relations with Loftus and they quickly became involved in a
struggle which Loftus won at the cost of all future good relations with

Perrot — whom he never forgave. In fairness to Loftus it seems clear
that the extent of the deputy's self-control was about as remarkable as
that of Lord Leonard Grey or of Henry VIII.[84]

Perrot and Bingham

Perrot's manner so soon became a liability that the Council in Ireland
had to try to isolate him from confrontations. It seemed necessary to
advise the deputy to respect the jurisdiction of a comparable character,
Bingham, by not crossing the Shannon. Perrot, however, in September
1586 insisted on proceeding to Galway, solely, said Bingham, to secure
evidence against his government. Perrot could well hold that in his own
experience the observance of law and of agreements by the queen's
officials was essential to secure local confidence. That Bingham believed
in maintaining peace with the sword even to the extent of non-
observance of the law was undoubted. But Perrot's exhibitions of bad
temper and of bad judgement only alienated his contemporaries, who
ultimately secured a hearing at court against him. When the viceroy
argued for more expenditure for a short while, until the ports and
military installations could be put in order, the queen deflated him,
referring to the unnecessary expenses he had incurred through pointless
expedition to meet a non-existent invasion by the Scots.[85]

Perrot's Parliament

His meeting with parliament[86] was perhaps his most frustrating
experience as deputy. The usual precautions were taken to reduce the
incidence of opposition. The securing of a majority in the north seemed
likely, but the consecration of two new bishops was hastened to secure
this. Perrot appeared reasonably satisfied in having successfully excluded
some cranks from the Commons. In addition to the confiscation of the
lands of the rebels, the legislative programme was to include matters of
religion and taxation. For these a smooth passage was anticipated
through the securing of the repeal of Poynings's Law or, alternatively,
the suspension of its operation for the duration of the parliament.
Perrot was destined to be disappointed. Controversies over the election
of a Speaker for the Commons having been satisfactorily resolved,
proposals about Poynings's Law were defeated in both houses. Measures
to apply English laws to reform religion proved unacceptable, as also
was an attempt to give legislative force to a revived form of the cess.
Perrot was reduced to accepting the approval of a very restricted
programme, which reveals how little was achieved by this parliament.[87]
The eleven acts which were passed in two successive sessions may be

grouped into those concerning attainders, some administrative reforms, and a customs act. In the first group may be mentioned the attainders of Baltinglass,[88] of Desmond,[89] and of John Browne[90] of Knockmonhie, together with their aiders and abettors. Two acts repealed former attainders affecting Delahide[91] and Taaffe.[92] Five acts attempted administrative improvements by legislating against perjury,[93] forgery,[94] fraudulent conveyancing, and counterfeiting foreign coinage.[95] More mysterious was the act against witchcraft and sorcery, which appears to have originated in providing a satanic alibi for loyalists whose mis-demeanours and treasons were so uncharacteristic as to be otherwise inexplicable.[96] It has been said that Ormond secured the passage of this measure to reinforce his case for pardoning his brothers, whose revolt in 1570 was due to witchcraft, though it does not appear that any witches or sorcerers suffered exposure in the stocks as a consequence.

The act renewing the regulation of wine imports was the single remaining achievement of Perrot's parliament.[97]

The Lord Deputy was incensed. He urged the queen to punish the ringleaders of the opposition, some of whose names were known from the protest over the cess in the days of Sidney. Once more the Lord Deputy was left without satisfaction, while a modest tribute was paid to his ideas of honour and principle.[98] It was observed that persistence in the face of opposition was no longer to be countenanced as in the days of Henry VIII. The rebuke seems not to have been lost on Perrot, who reverted to more conciliatory methods in the toleration of Catholicism, in the restriction of Munster confiscations to known rebels, and in working out the composition of Connacht with the land-holders in an effort to give them security and win for the queen a substantially increased revenue. To his credit was also to be added the plan for the shiring of Ulster.

The Question of Toleration

On the question of toleration, there is no doubt that Elizabeth directed a change of policy. By ordering the Dublin executive to be moderate, the queen might not have appeared to be favouring religious toleration. In fact, officials failing to take the Oath of Supremacy were not to be punished. The further direction that the Protestant clergy were to moderate their sermons and cease to rail at their Romish rivals is much more significant. After some initial hesitation Perrot adopted the policy. Again, his public manner involved him in difficulties. Bishop Jones, who had succeeded Brady in Meath, openly denounced the deputy and other officials for their moderating counsels, seemingly unaware that they had emanated from England. He was reproved for his impertinence, as was Archbishop Loftus, who had agreed with him.[99] Subsequently the queen did her best to strengthen Perrot by endorsing his actions on the question, but when the opportunities arose, the ecclesiastics blamed Perrot for conniving at popery and thus for the failure of the Established Church. Nor did they fail after his recall in 1588 to contribute to the dossier of accusations which sent him to the Tower of London, where he was to die in September 1592 after a doubtful conviction for treason.

More immediately Elizabeth's new policy of toleration may have been linked with the decision to execute Mary queen of Scots, as she very well knew that a conflagration might break out, in Ireland as elsewhere, as an immediate reaction. Perhaps the failure of the Armada would justify her foresight.[100]

Munster Plantation

For the rest, Perrot, in the Munster plantation plan, was slow to come to conclusions. The general scheme, as Professor Quinn has pointed out, probably owes more to Burghley than to anyone else. The decision to restrict plantation to those directly involved with Desmond wisely avoided the involvement of neutral parties claiming to be freeholders, and probably made the first settlement possible without a further rebellion. The uncertainties which followed from the slowness in giving title to those put in possession certainly contributed to the violation of the principle restricting the new colony to English settlers. Perhaps Perrot, by taking time in decision-making, provided a safety valve which enabled the surviving Munster people to make their terms with the new settlers. It may be noted that Sir William Herbert, settled in north Kerry, reported favourably on his own success in winning the natives to the Protestant services. Herbert, whose plantation project was partly indebted to Machiavelli's views on state colonies, was perhaps justifying his own compromise with the Desmond people, though this, in his case as in that of the other settlers, would be regarded differently after the plantation collapsed in 1598.[101]

Connacht Settlement

Perrot's contribution to the land settlement in Connacht provided a detailed scheme involving indentures of agreement between the Crown and the landowners in each of the new counties set up in that province. Unfortunately, the inefficiency of the Dublin administration caused these instruments to remain without full legal sanction because of the failure to enrol them. However, they remained on record, being treated as legal until they were to be challenged by Wentworth half a century later. Again Perrot's policy here was valuable as a curb on a lord president who preferred to settle controversies with the sword and the halter rather than convince the people that the scales of justice were balanced and not tipped against them.[102]

Perrot and O'Neill

With regard to Ulster, after his ineffective first moves with the Scots, Perrot's success augured well for future stability. In particular he supported the proceedings leading to Dungannon's creation as earl of Tyrone in 1585.[103]

As an earl, Hugh O'Neill sat in Perrot's parliament, where he appears to have succeeded in staying out of the controversies between government and opposition. His elevation to the earldom of Tyrone followed an agreement whereby Turlough Luineach O'Neill leased him most of his lands. In return, the old chief's son Arthur O'Neill was provided for at Strabane, while Tyrone renounced any claims of overlordship in relation to the neighbouring chiefs and leased to the queen a sufficient area for a fort on the Blackwater near Armagh. Theoretically Perrot provided for the shiring of Ulster, though in practice little effort was made to introduce sheriffs and Perrot remained satisfied that through the arrangements with the O'Neills and the Scots, and the strengthening of modest English settlements under Marshal Sir Henry Bagenal at Newry and also at Carrickfergus, Ulster could be regarded as stable. The religious question, for the moment at any rate, was overlooked. Tyrone, apparently, was prepared to behave like a Protestant in the Pale, as appears when he came to ask the services of Thomas Jones, the state bishop of Meath, at his marriage to Mabel Bagenal in 1591.[104]

Recall of Perrot

Perrot's recall was probably due to the belief that Ireland was now sufficiently secure to justify an unspectacular viceroy, less likely to involve his colleagues in controversies and less committed to grandiose ideas calculated to involve unnecessary expenditure. Admittedly, since the death in 1587 of Mary queen of Scots, who had chosen Philip of Spain as successor to her rights in the three kingdoms of the British Isles, the possibility of Spanish intervention was under frequent consideration. Elizabeth, however, was more concerned about her own position at home and the building-up of the English national resistance to the

Armada. She considered Ireland would be satisfactorily guarded by Sir William Fitzwilliam, who as governor of Fotheringay Castle had presided over Mary's execution, and who on 17 February 1588 succeeded Perrot in Ireland. Perrot left Ireland after a ceremony attended by Turlough Luineach O'Neill and many of the less important people of the country, to whom he had become the romantic defender of their rights against the exploiter and the embezzler. It was the end of a chapter.

Notes

1. V. Treadwell, 'The Irish parliament of 1569–71', *R.I.A. Proc.* LXV (1966).
2. 11 Eliz. s.3.c.1. *Statutes*, 322ff.
3. ibid.
4. ibid.
5. ibid.
6. ibid.
7. ibid., clauses i–iv.
8. ibid., clause v.
9. *Cal.S.P.Ire.*, 1, 371 (87).
10. For Hooker see *Elizabethan Government and Society* ed. S.T. Bindoff, J. Hurstfield, and C. H. Williams (1961).
11. 11 Eliz. s.2.c.1. *Statutes*, 320.
12. 11 Eliz. s.3.c.8. *Statutes*, 346.
13. D. B. Quinn, 'Government printing and the publication of Irish statutes in the sixteenth century', *R.I.A. Proc.* XLIX (1943).
14. 11 Eliz. s.1.c.1. *Statutes*, 313.
15. 11 Eliz. s.1.c.2. *Statutes*, 316.
16. 11 Eliz. s.1.c.5. *Statutes*, 319.
17. 11 Eliz. s.1.c.3. *Statutes*, 316.
18. 11 Eliz. s.1.c.4. *Statutes*, 319.
19. 11 Eliz. s.1.c.6. *Statutes*, 359.
20. 11 Eliz. s.1.c.7. *Statutes*, 359.
21. D. B. Quinn, 'The Munster Plantation: problems and opportunities', *Cork Hist. Soc. Jn.* LXXI (1966).
22. *Cal.S.P.Ire.*, I, 412 (2).
23. *Cal.S.P.Ire.*, I, 413 (8).
24. Bagwell, op.cit., II, 156–7.
25. For the suspension of Poynings's Act see n.11. above.
26. 11 Eliz. s.3.c.1. *Statutes*, 322.
27. 11 Eliz. s.3.c.4. *Statutes*, 341.
28. 11 Eliz. s.3.c.5. *Statutes*, 343.
29. 11 Eliz. s.3.c.10. *Statutes*, 349.
30. 11 Eliz. s.3.c.3. *Statutes*, 340.
31. 11 Eliz. s.3.c.2. *Statutes*, 338.
32. 11 Eliz. s.3.c.6. *Statutes*, 344.
33. 11 Eliz. s.3.c.9. *Statutes*, 347.
34. 11 Eliz. s.3.c.7. *Statutes*, 345.
35. 11 Eliz. s.4.c.2. *Statutes*, 356.
36. 11 Eliz. s.4.c.1. *Statutes*, 353.

37. Edwards, *Church and State*, 231–9.
38. 12 Eliz. c.2. *Statutes*, 362.
39. 12 Eliz. c.3. *Statutes*, 363.
40. 12 Eliz. c.4. *Statutes*, 367.
41. 12 Eliz. c.5. *Statutes*, 369.
42. 12 Eliz. s.2.c.1. *Statutes*, 374.
43. On the university question see my article 'Ireland, Elizabeth I and the Counter-Reformation' in *Elizabethan Government and Society*, 323ff.
44. ibid.; also *Church and State*, ch. 18.
45. *Cal.S.P.Ire.*, I, 447.
46. 12 Eliz. c.1. *Statutes*, 376.
47. 13 Eliz. c.4. *Statutes*, 389.
48. 13 Eliz. c.3. *Statutes*, 387.
49. Bagwell, op.cit., II, 170–1.
50. ibid., 178–82.
51. J. B. Black, *The Reign of Elizabeth* (1936), 98ff.; also Paul Johnson, *Elizabeth: a Study in Power and Intellect* (1974), 169.
52. Bagwell, op.cit., II, 252–3.
53. ibid., 309–10.
54. R. Dunlop, 'Sixteenth century schemes for the plantation of Ulster', *Scot. Hist.Rev.* XXII (1924), 51–60, 115–26, 199–212.
55. ibid.
56. Mary Dewar, *Sir Thomas Smith* (1964), ch. 14. Essex took over all of Smith's lands and claims when he came to Ireland in 1575. In 1579, Smith tried unsuccessfully to recover these claims.
57. Bagwell, op.cit., II, 239–40.
58. ibid., 240–1.
59. ibid., chs. 31, 32.
60. ibid., 254–6.
61. *Cal.S.P.Rome*, II, 203.
62. Bagwell, op.cit., II, 304–6, 312–19.
63. ibid., 329–30, n.3. Letter dated 20 May 1577.
64. ibid., 327–33.
65. ibid.
66. 'Lord Chancellor's Gerrard's Notes of his Report on Ireland', ed. Charles MacNeill, *Anal.Hib.* II (1931).
67. Bagwell, op.cit., II, 337–40.
68. ibid., 340–44.
69. ibid.
70. J. Izon, *Sir Thomas Stucley* (1956), 146ff.
71. Black, op.cit., 144.
72. Izon, op.cit., 193ff.
73. Edwards, *Church and State*, ch.18.
74. ibid.
75. ibid.
76. ibid.
77. J. K. Graham, 'Hugh O'Neill, 2nd earl of Tyrone', M.A. thesis, Q.U.B. (1938).
78. *Holinshed's Chronicles of England, Scotland and Ireland* (1808), VI, 369.
79. Quinn, 'Munster Plantation'.
80. W. M. Brady, *State Papers concerning the Irish Church* (1868), 47–8.
81. Edwards, *Church and State*, 269ff.
82. ibid.
83. Bagwell, op.cit., III, 129–30.
84. ibid., 131–4.

85. ibid., 166ff.
86. For Perrot's parliament generally see ibid., III, 140ff.
87. 27 Eliz. c.1. *Statutes*, 391.
88. 28 Eliz. c.7. *Statutes*, 418.
89. 28 Eliz. c.8. *Statutes*, 422.
90. 27 Eliz. c.2. *Statutes*, 398.
91. 28 Eliz. c.9. *Statutes*, 429.
92. 28 Eliz. c.1. *Statutes*, 400.
93. 28 Eliz. c.3. *Statutes*, 405.
94. 28 Eliz. c.5. *Statutes*, 415.
95. 28 Eliz. c.6. *Statutes*, 417.
96. 28 Eliz. c.2. *Statutes*, 403.
97. 28 Eliz. c.4. *Statutes*, 410.
98. *Cal.S.P.Ire., 1574–85*, 568.
99. Edwards, *Church and State*, 270.
100. Black, op.cit., 331ff.; also Johnson, op.cit., 280–99.
101. Quinn, 'Munster Plantation'.
102. Bagwell, op.cit., III, 147–8.
103. ibid., 139–40.
104. Graham, op.cit.

7 CATHOLIC IRELAND'S WAR

The Armada

The Spanish Armada was launched against England in June 1588 in the name of the Infanta Isabella, to whom her father, Philip II, delegated his claims to the crowns of the three kingdoms as the legatee of Mary Stuart, and also his own hereditary pretensions from the Plantagenets. The expedition was intended to involve joint action with the governor of the Low Countries in a descent on south-east England. Its disastrous defeat in the English Channel and the subsequent catastrophic storms led to shipwreck and destruction around the coasts of Britain and Ireland, in which thousands of Spanish soldiers and sailors met their deaths. It has been calculated that few escaped from Ireland to return to Spain. Wherever the Dublin government was influential, the shipwrecked Spaniards were massacred in cold blood or semi-judicially executed by martial law. In the south and west, such actions were usual against the Armada survivors, but in the north and north-west they were protected and hidden by the independent Ulster chiefs and by the earl of Tyrone, subsequently being smuggled home through Scotland.[1]

English nationalist feeling gained a great stimulus from the Armada. Protestant prayers had apparently been heard and God had scattered England's enemies with a Protestant wind. The sense of solidarity around Elizabeth had been experienced even by Catholics, who felt the attack was as much on their country as on the queen. Hatred of Spain became the dominant unifying factor in the country, at least until peace was made some sixteen years later in the reign of James I. Hatred of Spain was identified more and more with hatred of the Inquisition, which became linked with the pope and with Catholicism. Not until after the Protestant hero, Henry of Navarre, became ruler of France — to win which he became a Catholic — and succeeded during the 1590s in bringing about the defeat of Spanish policy towards France, was a more tolerant attitude towards Catholicism to re-emerge in England.[2]

So far as Ireland was concerned, the general goodwill secured by Perrot lasted sufficiently long to secure acquiescence in the disposal of the Spaniards. Beyond this, the sense of Catholicism grew stronger, the Protestant officials and planters being more aware of their isolation and more uncertain, particularly as a result of divisions among themselves. Thus the atmosphere of war was accentuated.[3]

153

Fitzwilliam and the Dublin Officials

Perrot's successor, Sir William Fitzwilliam, had long experience in Ireland both as viceroy and as Treasurer. To a large extent he was committed to a moderate policy, quite as much opposed to a drastic military policy of expansion as Perrot had become, conscious of past criticisms of his financial integrity and efficiency, anxious to avoid involvement in the controversies that persisted after Perrot's recall, too weak to stand up to the hysteria which hounded Perrot to his death from natural causes in the Tower.[4]

Fitzwilliam, however, was in no way committed to Archbishop Loftus and the professional Protestant group who sensed a papist in every non-puritan. As in the past, the queen promoted ecclesiastics who would serve the state, taking her views sometimes from Burghley, less frequently from Canterbury, and quite usually from her Irish deputy. Loftus and Jones of Meath grew steadily more powerful in Dublin, but they can never have felt quite secure in influencing Elizabeth without the wholehearted support of the deputy. Thus the leading personalities of Church and state seemed in successive viceroyalties to be mutually antipathetic.[5]

Loftus

For his diligence the archbishop of Dublin had gained sufficient confidence to be allowed the major influence in a commission for ecclesiastical causes. The difficulty of securing a succession of Lord Chancellors, when Irish lawyers were not trusted and outstanding Englishmen would not migrate, resulted in the archbishop's attaining to both the Lord Keepership of the Great Seal in 1579 and from 1581 to the Lord Chancellorship in 1603. His obsession with personal preferment and money, if only for the advancement of his many children, continued to present problems to the Dublin administration, but Loftus was not without high qualities. He was courageous in supporting English puritans frowned upon by the queen. He was genuinely attached to his Protestantism, and his Calvinistic antipathy to popery led him to support theological scholarship, even when it appeared to threaten his family interests. His support for a university institution, which had weakened in the face of the Perrot scheme to liquidate St Patrick's Cathedral, revived in the days of Fitzwilliam. It led to the foundation of Trinity College and Dublin University with himself as first Provost. Dublin Corporation was induced in 1590 to donate the monastic estate of All Hallows, founded in the twelfth century by King Dermot MacMurrough, and Elizabeth, guaranteed against financial

commitment, agreed to sanction the venture. We need not take too
seriously the first justification for the college as a Protestant seminary
against the Counter-Reformation missionaries. Anglo-Irish anxiety for
a local university had a long history before 1590. Elizabeth was
prepared to acquiesce in a project which would be relatively less
expensive for the men of the Pale than education in Oxford, Cambridge,
or even the Low Countries.[6]

Although Fitzwilliam was one of the English party in the administration and therefore usually likely to support them, he was not totally
opposed to the Anglo-Irish officials. He was aware that they included
people more sensitive to changes in the political atmosphere. Less
positively than the English ecclesiastics in the country, he regarded the
question of religion as one in which it was necessary to be tolerant of
recusancy when this did not go beyond failure to conform over the oath
or attendance at church. He may even have connived at occasional
secret Masses. The Anglo-Irish element had few among them who wanted
to make difficulties about religion, which they sought to make a neutral
matter in the war between Elizabeth and her opponents. There were, of
course, exceptions to this even among the native Irish, for example the
questionable Meiler Magrath, archbishop of Cashel, who, since he had
become a Protestant, would yield to no one in his public condemnations
of popery.[7]

Fitzwilliam in Ulster

The Lord Deputy's decision after the defeat of the Armada to travel to
the north was probably partly dictated by his desire to make a brave
showing against the harbourers of Spaniards, in an area in which
hostility to popery was unlikely to have adverse consequences. In fact,
he did not particularly distinguish himself, as he achieved little more than
the arrest and subsequent imprisonment of an O'Doherty and an
O'Gallagher, nominally as hostages for the tax fixed by Perrot. He thus
supported a policy which tended to bring disrepute on Dublin Castle, as
it alienated people who regarded it as unjust.[8]

Similarly his behaviour in the MacMahon country of Monaghan did
more harm than good in the short term. Sir Ross MacMahon, the local
chief, had died heirless in June 1589; the Lord Deputy favoured his
brother, Hugh Roe MacMahon, against a kinsman, Brian MacHugh Og
MacMahon, in the succession dispute that followed. However, when his
favourite did not secure sufficient local support, Fitzwilliam abandoned
him by the questionable method of trying and executing him for what
the queen subsequently regarded as the normal Irish methods by which

a chief enforced his authority over those who withstood him. In the long term, Fitzwilliam probably pacified Monaghan by partitioning the country among a number of MacMahon septs and preserving the rights of a MacKenna as well as of the earl of Essex. More immediately these activities led to careful attention in the north towards the public behaviour of the viceroy, particularly on the part of Hugh O'Neill, earl of Tyrone.[9]

Bingham in Connacht

In the west Fitzwilliam, like Perrot, tried to exercise some authority over Bingham. More subtle than Perrot, in April 1589 he made use of a commission of inquiry into complaints against the lord president. In practice, however, he was no more successful, as Bishop Jones and other members of the commission only acted as a temporary brake on Bingham's activities. Jones in particular earned Walsingham's subsequent reproof for alleged hypocrisy, by upholding the view that the lord president's standard of honour should be higher than that of the subjects he chastised. Bingham's strength thereafter emerged in his dealings with Sir Brian O'Rourke, whom he drove out of his own country (approximately the modern Co. Leitrim) into Scotland after questionable allegations about his involvement with the Spaniards. Here, as in other cases, Bingham secured London's support. In this instance much has been made of O'Rourke's alleged public insults against the queen, which resulted in her pressing James VI to surrender O'Rourke for trial. This inevitably led in 1591 to his execution at Tyburn after he had refused to make the customary kneeling submission before the Council which, said O'Rourke, he refused, as he had always thought that a great distance separated the queen and her counsellors 'from God and the Saints, whose images alone' he was accustomed to venerate. Once again the independent rulers in the north registered their distrust of English governors in London as well as in Ireland.[10]

Munster

In the south a commission of inquiry into the Munster plantation increased the dissatisfaction with Dublin Castle as decisions were taken in favour of planters like Sir Walter Raleigh and adverse to alleged loyalists like Lord Roche, part of whose lands were allotted to Edmund Spenser. Inevitably resentment against the planters materially affected stability and rendered insecure their English tenants, some of whom returned home even before the mass migration in 1598.[11]

Fitzwilliam and O'Neill

In his later dealings with the north the Lord Deputy seems to have attempted to learn from his own mistakes. His personal courage was not in doubt. In May 1590 he dealt with mutineers in Dublin with the same fearlessness that he had shown when Jacques Wingfield panicked before Shane O'Neill in the north. In dealing with Hugh O'Neill he displayed a readiness to support him against rival O'Neills, perhaps in the belief that the northern earl was more likely to be sustained by London than would be his various cousins. He was careful not to oppose him in the row with Marshal Sir Henry Bagenal after O'Neill had eloped with and married his sister Mabel. Her brother tried to upset the marriage and never surrendered her dowry. When Hugh Roe O'Donnell, having escaped from Dublin Castle with other hostages, was inaugurated as O'Donnell in succession to his father, the Lord Deputy, on Tyrone's initiative, in 1592 accepted his submission, despite his actions in expelling the disreputable sheriff Willis from Donegal monastery and despite his devastation of Turlough Luineach's lands around Strabane. Thereafter, however, Fitzwilliam's attitude to Tyrone altered.[12]

Recall of Fitzwilliam

The circumstances in which Fitzwilliam was recalled early in 1594 are in no doubt on one fact: the queen disapproved of him. In the last decade of her reign Elizabeth was hard to please and disapproval of Irish viceroys almost invariably ended their Irish careers. Fitzwilliam had been the subject, not for the first time, of accusations reflecting upon his financial integrity. An adverse report about him by an English auditor certainly contributed to his recall. Tyrone declared that his own life was in danger if the Lord Deputy and Bagenal got their hands on him, and in the spring commissioners were appointed, in the persons of Lord Chancellor Archbishop Loftus and Chief Justice Sir Robert Gardiner, to negotiate with the northern earl. Their favourable report to the queen led her to declare to Tyrone in subsequent correspondence that Fitzwilliam had been recalled and Bagenal deprived of his offices as marshal in consequence.[13]

Bagenal

It seems unlikely that the Lord Deputy would have survived in office in any case. The Marshal's disgrace was another matter. In 1593 a concerted move from Dublin was made against Hugh Maguire, who harboured the papal primate Edmund MacGoran and who had taken part with him in an expedition into Connacht against Bingham. The Dublin

plan was to send Tyrone and Bagenal against Maguire. Tyrone subsequently complained that he had borne the brunt of the conflict and
had even been wounded while Bagenal had claimed the credit and used
his powers to displace O'Neill's officials in east Ulster by his own. In the
statement of his grievances to Loftus and Gardiner, it is clear that
O'Neill had come to the conclusion that he had been rejected in favour
of Bagenal for a quasi-presidential office in Ulster. Bingham's activity in
Connacht and against the north-west Ulster border, the disgraceful
behaviour of the disreputable officials appointed by the English
authorities as sheriffs in the north and west, the extent to which English
administration was being extended by harrying the countryside, making
the people pay for misgovernment and financially exploiting them whenever possible, were Tyrone's basic objections to how government had
developed since Perrot's time. There was also the vexed question of
religion, although it is not clear if the earl was committed to the
Catholic cause beyond a reluctance to deliver up any papal bishops to
the queen. On the other hand, the queen was obviously concerned to
mollify him. The combination of O'Donnell and Tyrone had assumed
such alarming proportions that she was desperately anxious to reassure
him, though she was perfectly prepared to have him arrested by any
underhand act if she got the opportunity.[14]

O'Neill and the Papal Bishops

It may very well be that Tyrone was impelled by events to involve himself on one side or the other, and by the possibility that in north-west
Ulster the Catholic war was about to break out. To ecclesiastics like
MacGoran, the disaster of the Armada was but an accident: it seemed
only a matter of time until a second Spanish expedition would successfully overwhelm the heretical Elizabeth. Their own particular contribution was that they were instrumental in linking Spain to an Irish
enterprise separate from one against England. Such a proposal involved
necessary papal approval for the establishment of Ireland as a state
independent of England. Perhaps it was not until he had allowed himself to be involved with Bagenal against Maguire that Tyrone came to
realize that the papal bishops of the north-west were sufficiently
influential with O'Donnell, Maguire, and young Brian Og O'Rourke to
keep them in armed resistance against the Protestant English expansion
until the Spanish conquerors came to their aid. As it was, Tyrone's
involvement could not be regarded with favour by a pro-Spanish group;
after all, he had been instrumental in the overthrow of some 600
Spanish survivors of the Armada, whom he subsequently dispatched to

Dublin. In the statement of his grievances to Loftus and Gardiner, Tyrone had objected that his service for the queen had involved him in considerable financial expense and that no part of the large ransom money ever came to him. His decision for the future thus appears to have been based on the belief that he would not be permitted to share in the glory with Bingham, Bagenal, Fitzwilliam, and Carew. In alliance with O'Donnell, particularly as the Great O'Neill in succession to Turlough Luineach, Tyrone would be accepted as the major ruler in Ulster, since O'Donnell's ambition lay rather in Connacht. A decision for the queen could in fact preclude him from ever being acceptable as the successor to Turlough Luineach, if he was not prepared to abandon the position in which, at her instance, he would fight the rebels, support anti-Catholic proceedings, and run the risk of arbitrarily incurring the displeasure of unscrupulous rulers like Bagenal, Fitzwilliam, and indeed Elizabeth herself. Thirty years after Shane O'Neill had complained of government plots to assassinate him, Tyrone could very well feel his own situation was no less dangerous.[15]

Russell Lord Deputy

In succession to Fitzwilliam, Sir William Russell arrived in Dublin in August 1594. After Fitzwilliam's departure Tyrone went to Dublin and submitted to the new deputy. On that occasion Sir Henry Bagenal drew up articles against Tyrone alleging his complicity with Maguire and that he was an accessory to the actions of his relatives including his brother, Cormac MacBaron, whose involvement with Maguire had been substantial. Bagenal's inference, that Tyrone would not have been defied by his brother had he been hostile to his involvement with Maguire, seems reasonable. The Lord Deputy and Council, however, decided to postpone any question of looking into Bagenal's allegations, which, they noted, were not accompanied by proofs. Their decision to put these on record and to permit Tyrone's return to his own country, after his submission on his knees to Russell before the whole Council, is understandable. Immediately after hearing of these events Elizabeth admonished the Dublin administration for letting Tyrone slip through their fingers. She realized, she said, that the decision to free Tyrone had been one in which the inexperience of the new Lord Deputy had been influenced by the Council; but she put it on record that their decision was displeasing and more than hinted that the Lord Deputy had been given contrary directions by her before leaving England. To Russell personally she directed a second missive (October 1594), taking him to task more severely than in the joint letter to him and the Council and stating that he could have been under no misapprehension about her views — expressed by her orally to him at court — as to the necessity to secure Tyrone on his arrival in Dublin. The queen did not deny the right of the Council to influence the deputy, but warned him that that body included irresponsible persons who could not be relied upon to uphold the English view of an Irish situation. Rather unfairly, she adverted to his instructions, which certainly did insist that an increased number of administrative posts, particularly among the judiciary, were in future not to be given to Irish natives, even of the Pale. But the instructions, beyond calling in question the propriety of some of the recommendations of commissioners Loftus and Gardiner with regard to the agreement with Tyrone, had not directed the deputy to question and detain him. So irate, however, was the queen that the deputy could be assured that his only means of recovering her goodwill would be by securing Tyrone in Dublin.[16]

Russell in Ulster

The Dublin reaction to the royal displeasure was to insist that Tyrone had to be set at liberty, if only to prevent all the forces of the O'Neills being employed by Cormac MacBaron in support of Maguire and the Roman Catholic bishops. It had not been forgotten that the Munster war had been brought on after the earl of Desmond was put under restraint, so that his influence was used as James Fitzmaurice decided. There was thus no reversion to a plan for entrapping Tyrone. Instead, the new Lord Deputy had proceeded to Ulster against Maguire, who was threatening Enniskillen Castle and who had already defeated one relieving force at what was known thereafter as the Ford of the Biscuits, after the loss of the intended English food supplies. Although Tyrone made excuses when Russell requested his support against Maguire, the deputy was strong enough to relieve Enniskillen — though that fort was obliged to capitulate to Maguire in May 1595.[17]

Russell in Wicklow

Early in 1595 the deputy next proceeded against the Wicklow rebels, Fiach MacHugh O'Byrne and Walter Reagh Fitzgerald, who had been in arms and threatening the Dublin suburbs. The latter was defeated and captured, and after rigorous questioning about O'Neill's involvement with the north-western papal bishops and with Maguire, was hanged with unusual barbarity.[18]

Sir John Norris

Much to Russell's disgust, the queen responded in April to his request for an able military subordinate by appointing Sir John Norris, a distinguished commander of Elizabeth's expeditionary forces to the continent. The queen had decided that Tyrone was bound to go the way of Shane O'Neill and determined accordingly to appoint a military commander independent of the viceroy, who would be reinforced from Brittany, from which she arranged to withdraw some of her troops. Unfortunately this proved to be no solution, as Russell and Norris were mutually antipathetic. Their rivalry guaranteed the failure of their individual efforts. By the end of the year, the castles of Enniskillen and Sligo were lost to the rebels.[19]

Beyond proclaiming Tyrone a traitor in the summer of 1595 no positive step had been taken. It is true that Norris became involved in a minor encounter with Tyrone, but its only consequence was that the English general sustained a wound which probably shortened his life.[20]

The Great O'Neill

In the autumn the Great O'Neill, Turlough Luineach, died, having held that office since he succeeded Shane in 1567. Immediately afterwards Tyrone disengaged himself from the English forces and had himself proclaimed as the Great O'Neill on the traditional inaugurating stone at Tullahoge. Tyrone's action was of course regarded as rank treason, if proof indeed was required of one who had already been proclaimed traitor. In the existing Ulster situation it is difficult to see whether Hugh had any option. If he had failed to take the initiative, it was almost inevitable that his brother Cormac MacBaron or even a distant cousin would have been inaugurated. The action, of course, put the seal on the alliance with the Catholic bishops, with O'Donnell and Maguire, and led to O'Neill's successful assertion of himself over all the minor Ulster chieftains. This he could probably never have achieved as earl of Tyrone.[21]

Failure of the Queen's Government

Elizabeth's Irish government had now to face the fact that in two provinces the queen's writ had virtually ceased to run. The Lord Deputy sought to maintain his diminished prestige with dignity and proceeded to Galway in demonstration of this. O'Donnell, however, was able to protect the Burkes from the English government and Russell realized his own impotence when a new MacWilliam Iochtar was inaugurated by O'Donnell outside the walls of Galway. The queen's writ was powerless

from the Shannon to the sea. As for Ulster, there was no alternative but
to negotiate a new peace with the rebels, for which purpose Wallop and
Gardiner were appointed commissioners and in January 1596 were
obliged to suffer the humiliation of admitting among O'Neill's demands
a claim for liberty of conscience.[22]

Negotiations with O'Neill

The reaction in Dublin was to displace the commissioners by Norris and
Sir Geoffrey Fenton. The new commissioners carried on for rather
longer than their predecessors. It seems clear enough that neither side
was anxious to undertake a major encounter. The queen, having decided
to destroy O'Neill, was now unprepared to meet the cost of pacifying at
least two provinces. O'Neill, by professing himself prepared to submit
on condition that he and his allies were restored to their estates, from
which all English officials were to be excluded, was quite prepared to
drop the liberty of conscience demand, as he had every expectation of
Spanish support.[23] Despite the fact that Dublin and London were
aware of O'Neill's letters to Spain and of Philip II's replies, the farce
went on. A truce which was virtually a pardoning of rebellion was
agreed upon.

In their turn, of course, Norris and Fenton were attacked at the
Dublin Council board. Nevertheless, their negotiations were allowed to
go on and they extended their activities to Connacht in an effort to
pacify the Burkes. Once again it was the rebels who scored. The Burkes
tried to convince the commissioners that they were not involved in the
Ulster Catholic crusade, that their only grievance stemmed from the
savagery of Bingham's rule. Almost inevitably the commissioners became
cast for the role of critics of the lord president, and a resentful Bingham
left Ireland in September without leave, only to be imprisoned in the
Fleet at London by the queen's order. Thereafter he was replaced in
Connacht by Sir Conyers Clifford, who soon showed himself unable to
make headway against the O'Donnell alliance.[24]

The commissioners were unhappily unaware that even in Munster
problems were again arising and that the northern rebels were securing
diplomatic supporters. They had but one success (in May 1597), the
defeat and death in Wicklow of Fiach MacHugh O'Byrne, eastern
Ireland's most outstanding rebel in the sixteenth century. By the
beginning of 1597, O'Neill, aware that the queen proposed to appoint
a new viceroy in Ireland, decided not to submit to a regime which
might have no authority with its successors.[25]

Burgh Lord Deputy

The appointment of Thomas, Lord Burgh as Lord Deputy in the spring of 1597 had virtually no effect on the Irish situation. The new deputy was not without military qualities and in fact for a short time played a distinguished part in the north. He succeeded in recapturing the Blackwater fort, from which O'Neill had previously expelled an English garrison. Beyond this, however, he effected little. A plan for a pincer movement against the northern rebels miscarried, when Clifford with the western forces was obliged in August to withdraw after he attacked Ballyshannon.[26]

Burgh returned to the north to relieve the Blackwater garrison, only to be seized with a serious illness necessitating his withdrawal to Newry: there in October he died. He had been involved in an abortive attempt to have O'Neill assassinated and it is ironical that rumour credited his death to poison administered at O'Neill's instigation. Whatever O'Neill's intentions, it is not impossible that in Burgh he might have found a more formidable opponent than any of his successors before Mountjoy. But the immediate result of the deputy's death was disastrous for the English in Ulster, who were weakened substantially by the Scots and in a short time were to lose Sir Henry Bagenal in battle.[27]

Thomas Norris Lord Justice; Battle of the Yellow Ford

On Burgh's death the Dublin government appointed Sir Thomas Norris as Lord Justice. In September Sir John Norris had died at Mallow and his brother seemed an obvious successor. Elizabeth, however, again changed the plan, appointing as Lords Justices Loftus and Gardiner, while reserving the control of military matters for Ormond. Again it seems that negotiations with the rebels were to be favoured. Again a truce was agreed upon after inconclusive negotiations. Again the Irish in the west and south responded to O'Neill's diplomacy by entering into an alliance based on the religious issue. Before the end of 1598 Munster, except for the fortified towns, was lost to the planters.[28] In the north, the English sustained a disastrous reverse after Dublin had sanctioned a renewal of operations against O'Neill. In August 1598 Bagenal was defeated at the battle of the Yellow Ford on the Blackwater, in which he lost his life.

Council Panic

The Dublin Council panicked, fearing O'Neill had sufficient supporters throughout Ireland to justify an attack on Dublin itself. A letter was dispatched to O'Neill in which the Council virtually grovelled at his feet.

O'Neill was reminded that the dead marshal was his personal enemy and an endeavour was made to convince him that with the death of his enemy, no hostility towards him existed among the queen's administrators.[29]

It is probable that O'Neill never got this letter, but Elizabeth certainly did and her stinging rebuke cannot easily have been forgotten by her abject Irish subjects.[30] The cautious O'Neill did not attempt anything against Dublin, preferring to hold off until the Spanish aid arrived.

Catholic Clergy

That common Catholicism was the cementing factor in the O'Neill alliance was generally agreed by English administrators in Ireland by 1598.[31] Even the London government was prepared to take a new view and ordered shortly afterwards that in the case of Henry Fitzsimon, a Jesuit priest imprisoned in Dublin, a distinction should be made between accusations against him for functioning as a priest and accusations of any alleged treasonable activities. The distinction was important, as Fitzsimon appears to have been wholly concerned with spiritual activities, unlike James Archer, one of the Jesuits supporting O'Neill's Catholic war. Unlike those in England, where it had been made treason by Act of Parliament for a priest ordained abroad to exercise his sacerdotal functions, the Irish statutes did not include any such provision. On more occasions than one, over-enthusiastic officials had advised the queen to permit the application of the English law to priests in Ireland, but the English government had come to realize that such measures were likely to prove very costly and in fact might lead to the loss of Ireland to Spain.

For more than a decade Irishmen educated in Catholic colleges on the continent had been returning in increasing numbers. Even where they were not involved in O'Neill's war, they so strengthened the feelings of the people that it was at last evident to the government that Anglo-Irish and Irish were united in their determination to reject Protestantism.[32] Nominal conformity was no longer conceded nor indeed expected if Elizabeth was to continue to be given the allegiance of the traditionally loyal Anglo-Irish.

Liberty of Conscience

When O'Neill had been asked to drop the demand for liberty of conscience, as a result of the queen's objection, it was implied that royal policy did not intend to enforce conformity and that Elizabeth merely expected that her Protestant ecclesiastics could be guaranteed peaceful

enjoyment of their temporal possessions. Perhaps when O'Neill agreed
to abandon this demand, he was already aware that Spanish aid would
not be available if he permitted liberty of conscience to heretics.
Accordingly his agents assured the Spanish king that the Irish war was for
the restoration of Catholicism and that no heretical ally existed among
the forces opposed to Elizabeth. O'Neill, then, must be regarded as
having fully adopted the Spanish alliance which would tolerate no
Protestants.[33]

Position of Catholics

In the last years of the century there were emerging in England some
few Catholic clergy — even among those incarcerated at Wisbech — who
were ready to swear political allegiance to Elizabeth while seeking the
right to maintain spiritual communion with Rome. Some tolerance for
such ideas existed among younger English politicians, especially after
Burghley's death in 1598. The success of Henry IV of France in
bringing the civil war to an end and conceding toleration to the
Protestants by the Edict of Nantes was watched with interest in England.
The decision of Pope Clement VIII to permit a distinction between
spiritual and temporal allegiance made it possible in Ireland for
Catholics to stay neutral in the war between   O'Neill and Elizabeth.[34]
O'Neill's interests and Spain's required compulsion against neutral
Catholics as well as against those involved actively on the queen's side.
While Clement VIII was prepared to give the privileges of crusaders to
O'Neill's army, he was not prepared to compel Catholics to support the
queen's opponents by threats of excommunication. It was probably for
this reason that while he appointed a Spaniard, Matthew of Oviedo, as
archibishop of Dublin, he would not approve him for legatine authority.
He preferred to reserve this for an Italian who was not a Spanish
subject, when Philip III, who succeeded his father in 1598, was not
prepared to allow him into Ireland.

When the war broke out once more in Munster, the Catholic
ecclesiastics supporting the crusade were alleged to have preached that
Catholics supporting Elizabeth incurred excommunication. There exists
among the Carew manuscripts in Lambeth Palace a forged papal bull to
this effect. It is not clear who perpetrated it. It may have been Owen
MacEgan, bishop-elect of Ross. Certainly allegations to this effect were
made against him at the time. On the other hand, the instrument may
have had its origin in the activities of a fanatical Protestant, anxious to
represent the Catholic position in its worst light. Certainly there were
many Catholics in Ireland, particularly in the towns, who remained

neutral and were strong enough to resist the pressures from either side as long as the war continued. In this way the O'Neill movement ceased to maintain its Catholic justification, becoming instead a war for the preservation of traditional interests against the expanding English colonial government. The failure of the Spaniards to reinforce O'Neill by more than moderate forces such as those which occupied Kinsale in 1601, made impossible the establishment of Ireland as a Catholic state independent of England, This, however, was not to be obvious for a long time to come.[35]

Essex Viceroy

After the English defeat in 1598, Elizabeth was aroused to the necessity of financing a major war against O'Neill. England's glorious reputation in the ten years after the repulse of the Armada seemed in danger of eclipse in Ireland. It was beginning to be realized in England that the queen's troops feared the invincibility of O'Neill and that this fear in the field had communicated itself to the Council in Dublin. Under the influence of Francis Bacon, Robert Devereux, earl of Essex, was interesting himself in Ireland. Essex enjoyed the prestige of 'having singed the king of Spain's beard' by raiding his naval forces at Cadiz in 1596. During discussions in London as to who should go to Ireland as viceroy, Essex had been critical about others, including Mountjoy, and ultimately secured the prize for himself. As one of Elizabeth's favourites he was in a position to secure maximum privileges, including the coveted title of Lord Lieutenant of Ireland, which had not been conceded to any viceroy in thirty years. His appointment greatly gratified popular opinion in London: it was anticipated that with the greatest army ever sent to Ireland, Essex would make short work of O'Neill and restore England's prestige.[36]

Essex and O'Neill

The arrival in Dublin of the new Lord Lieutenant in April 1599 did not bring about an alteration in the Irish Council's attitude. The sense of siege which had settled on the city since Bagenal's disastrous defeat at the Yellow Ford resulted in conflicting opinions on handling O'Neill. Most dominant with the councillors was the fear of his invincibility. It was considered essential that the new army should gain prestige by some success in the field before it faced O'Neill. Accordingly permission was sought and gained from the queen for the Lord Lieutenant to proceed first against O'Neill's allies in Leinster and in Munster. The result of this campaign was damaging, though this was not at first apparent, as Essex made much of a minor success against Cahir Castle, which resulted in the submission of Lords Mountgarret and Cahir. On his return to Dublin, however, Essex was mortified at the defeat of one of his subordinates in Wicklow at the hands of Felim MacHugh O'Byrne, son of Fiach. The cowardice of the queen's forces so stung the viceroy that on their return to Dublin he ordered the execution of every tenth soldier. Then there descended a lethargy on him, born of a reluctance to face O'Neill. To the queen he wrote of his loss of interest in life. Unexpectedly, however, he suddenly felt spurred to action at the news of the defeat and death in August of Sir Conyers Clifford at the hands of Brian Og O'Rourke in the battle of the Curlew Mountains. Proceeding north, Essex offered battle to O'Neill. O'Neill courteously refused, but invited negotiations. Essex consented and the two leaders met privately on 7 September, with the result that Essex returned to Dublin, where he announced that he must immediately communicate O'Neill's articles to the queen in person.[37]

The exact nature of O'Neill's proposals to Essex cannot really be determined. The succession to Elizabeth was almost certainly involved. O'Neill was definitely in communication with James VI of Scotland, whose anxiety over the succession predominated over all his other feelings. From O'Neill's standpoint, the choice lay between the Infanta Isabella and the Scottish king. From the standpoint of Henry IV of France, James VI was infinitely preferable to the Spanish candidate.[38] When many of the English courtiers were in communication with Edinburgh Essex's attitude could be important. O'Neill clearly succeeded in charming Essex into an agreement, but did this involve a private understanding about the succession? On the basis of Essex's subsequent conspiracy, for which he was to be tried and executed for treason in February 1601, there can be no question but that in Ireland he saw himself as the organizer of a heroic enterprise to win glory for England.

The story that O'Neill had influenced Essex to favour the Spanish candidate cannot be dismissed lightly. It was said that the earl doubted whether his conversion to the Spanish side could possibly be acceptable because of his former military successes against Spain. No doubt O'Neill would have been perfectly capable of resolving such anxieties for the quixotic Essex. Certainly he had few illusions about James VI, who had shown himself remarkably successful in keeping Scotland pacified, while quietly moderating its radical Presbyterianism to the point where he had been able to restore the bishops and connive at his queen's strong interest in Catholicism. O'Neill probably considered that it was due to James's connivance that he was able to recruit substantial mercenary forces from Scotland despite royal proclamations to the contrary. But he well knew that on the succession issue James dared not fall out with Elizabeth, but had to rely upon a party, and probably a Protestant one, at the London court. Whatever his personal prejudices, O'Neill's position depended upon foreign allies independent of Elizabeth. He cannot really have believed that the English queen would reverse her policy in Ireland at James's behest. The belief that a Spanish expedition would arrive soon was by no means confined to the Irish Catholic forces. At Elizabeth's court well-informed statesmen regarded it as certain that Philip III would renew his father's efforts — though they might disagree about his timing. Once again O'Neill resorted to diplomacy and through Essex (and after him through others) made it clear that his minimal demands involved the public restoration of Catholicism in Ireland and the establishment of a Dublin government under an Irish earl. Meanwhile he appealed to the pope.[39]

Clement VIII

From Clement VIII, O'Neill sought spiritual support for the Catholic war. He also appealed for spiritual sanctions against Elizabeth's Irish supporters, and against those Catholics not prepared to participate in the Catholic crusade. The pope was dilatory in reply.[40]

Clement was anxious to be on good terms with the converted Henry IV of France: this necessitated some detachment from Spain. So far as Ireland was concerned, he was not unaware that O'Neill was regarded in some quarters as having a hereditary claim to be king of Ireland. Clement was also aware that other Catholic crusaders preferred a Spanish ruler. Moreover, there was a third viewpoint, concerned primarily to maintain the connection between Britain and Ireland, particularly if this could be brought about by the succession of the Scottish king already secretly in negotiation with Rome.[41]

Anglo-Irish Jesuits let it be known at Rome that Catholic interests could be marred by giving O'Neill exclusive support. So the pope did not use sanctions against Catholics loyal to Elizabeth.[42]

Mountjoy Lord Deputy

On 21 January 1600, Charles Blount, Lord Mountjoy, was appointed Lord Deputy of Ireland. Mountjoy did not receive the same degree of support from the queen as had Essex; the title of Lord Lieutenant was not given to him. His military support was smaller, nor was it quite clear that he enjoyed the queen's full confidence. Sir Robert Cecil, no lover of Essex, was aware of Mountjoy's involvement with the Essex family. The appointment of Sir George Carew as lord president of Munster on 6 March gave the queen and Cecil an independent line on Ireland. Fortunately, Mountjoy and Carew were able to work together and avoid the rivalry which had frustrated the viceroyalty of Russell. The combination was strong enough to reduce Ormond, still nominally lieutenant of the military forces, to insignificance.[43]

Mountjoy, a very gifted and intelligent man, got down to a ruthless policy of reducing the rebels by a systematic destruction of crops and cattle-driving. Sir Henry Docwra was sent to Lough Foyle and established an effective fort at Derry from which it became possible to drive a wedge between the Ulster Irish. Very shortly afterwards a series of succession disputes arising among Ulster ruling families made it possible for Docwra to secure as supporters for the queen those prepared to desert O'Neill, provided they were permitted liberty of conscience.[44] In accepting the submissions of such deserters from O'Neill, Docwra was careful not to commit himself on the religious issue beyond a statement that, so far as he was aware, the queen had no more intention of interfering with their religious liberty than she had in the past, and that he undertook to respect their wishes in the matter until he was directed otherwise. Docwra was probably aware that Mountjoy had been instructed to operate a new religious policy. The queen had at last accepted that if her authority in Ireland was to be preserved, she must employ the methods of reason rather than compulsion. She may have been aware that the pope had come to a similar conclusion — at any rate, to the extent of abandoning the coercion of those who distinguished between spiritual and temporal allegiance. Elizabeth was of course not prepared to let the Dublin Council off lightly and, in the Lord Deputy's instructions, the Protestant ecclesiastical authorities were admonished in no uncertain terms for failing to win over the people.[45] Indeed, the queen's action did not deter the leading state bishops from maintaining their opposition to toleration. One phrase in the instructions could be construed to imply that the toleration policy was temporary, thus enabling Loftus and Jones to put pressure on Catholics in official positions whenever war did not appear to be imminent. Mountjoy, however, did not share the views of the churchmen and had no hesitation in making this clear when the occasion arose. A similar attitude was maintained in Munster by Carew and helped substantially in winning supporters from O'Neill. When Viscount Barry refused to support the Catholic crusaders, he made it his boast that thanks to the queen's indulgence he had both exercised

freedom of conscience and befriended Catholics in need of protection.
Cecil could assure Carew that Barry's son, who was being reared in
London, was in no way compelled to conform because of his father,
even though his views were aggressively popish.[46]

Mountjoy's military activities gradually succeeded in destroying
O'Neill's allies in the midlands, driving to the north the few who persisted. By degrees O'Neill was hemmed in by a series of forts which
could be relieved from the sea and, as he was deficient in artillery, he was
unable to take them.[47]

Defeat at Kinsale

The success of Mountjoy and his commanders led to wholesale desertions
from the Catholic crusade. By the middle of 1601 it seemed likely that
the O'Neill alliance, without Spanish support, would collapse. Then in
the autumn a substantial Spanish expedition reached Kinsale under
Don Juan de Aguila. For the moment the Catholic forces revived, but
the Spaniards were insufficient in number to make an effective sortie
against Mountjoy, who had laid siege to the town, and O'Neill and Hugh
Roe O'Donnell risked all on a night surprise attack in which the viceroy
disastrously defeated them.[48]

The Spanish commander's surrender was accepted on terms which
permitted the return of his forces to Spain, together with any Irish
soldiers who wished to go. O'Donnell, the Catholic allies agreed,
should take advantage of the opportunity to travel to Spain and urge
the king to further efforts to win victory for Catholic Ireland.[49]

The complaints of the Irish led to the disgracing of Aguila in Spain,
but no further expedition was sent to Ireland. Before the end of 1602,
O'Donnell was dead in Spain and Carew claimed credit for having had
him poisoned, though it is just possible that he died of natural causes.
The Irish were slower to credit the news that Spain and England were
taking the first steps to ending the war. In the meantime, under
pressure from France, Queen Elizabeth had changed her policy of
refusing to entertain any question of pardoning O'Neill. She saw the
wisdom of Henry IV's argument that by such a pardon Philip III could
be deprived of his excuse to intervene again in Ireland. As O'Neill
weakened, the Protestant ecclesiastics in Dublin, in Mountjoy's absence,
imprisoned Catholic aldermen for refusing to attend communion
services in the Protestant parish churches. Mountjoy's reproof of
Bishops Loftus and Jones for their action carried with it the stern
warning that their first concern must be with ending the war situation.[50]
Before the end of March 1603, O'Neill had submitted at Mellifont to

Mountjoy, had accepted his re-creation as earl of Tyrone on surrender of his title as O'Neill, and had signed at Dublin the viceregal proclamation of the new sovereign, James VI and I, on the death of Elizabeth.

Notes

1. R. Bagwell, *Ireland under the Tudors* (1885–90), III, 172ff.
2. J. B. Black, *The Reign of Elizabeth* (1936), 250ff.; Paul Johnson, *Elizabeth: a Study in Power and Intellect* (1974), ch. 9.
3. Bagwell, op.cit., III, 196ff.
4. ibid.
5. Edwards, *Church and State*, 274–7.
6. ibid., 214–17.
7. ibid., 274ff.
8. Bagwell, op.cit., III, ch. 43.
9. ibid., 201ff.
10. ibid., 203ff.
11. D. B. Quinn, 'The Munster Plantation: problems and opportunities', *Cork Hist. Soc. Jn.* LXXI (1966).
12. Bagwell, op.cit., III, 217ff.
13. ibid.
14. J. K. Graham, 'Hugh O'Neill, 2nd earl of Tyrone', M.A. thesis, Q.U.B. (1938).
15. ibid.
16. ibid.
17. ibid.
18. Bagwell, op.cit., III, 246ff.
19. ibid., 251ff.
20. ibid., 254ff.
21. P. Walsh, 'Historical criticism of the life of Hugh Roe O'Donnell', *IHS*, I (1938–39), 229.
22. Graham, op.cit.
23. *Cal.Carew MSS*, III, 172.
24. Bagwell, op.cit., III, 268ff, 282ff.
25. Graham, op.cit.
26. Bagwell, op.cit., III, 282ff.
27. ibid.
28. ibid., 291ff.; also ch. 47.
29. ibid., 300.
30. ibid.
31. *Cal.S.P. Ire.*, VII, 394.
32. *Cal.S.P. Ire.*, VII, 14–18.
33. *Cal. Carew MSS*, III, 122–3; also *Cal.S.P. Sp., 1587–1603*, 621.
34. Black, op.cit., 376–8.
35. Edwards, *Church and State*, 289 n.1.
36. Black, op.cit., 404–5.
37. L. W. Henry, 'Contemporary sources for Essex's lieutenancy in Ireland', *IHS*, XI, (1958), 8.
38. Edwards, *Church and State*, 294.
39. ibid.
40. F. M. Jones, 'The Counter-Reformation', in P. J. Corish ed., *The History of Irish Catholicism* (Dublin, 1967), III.
41. ibid.

42. ibid.
43. Bagwell, op.cit., III, 353ff.
44. For military campaign generally see ibid., chs. 49, 50.
45. *Cal. S.P. Ire.*, IX, 273–7.
46. *Cal. Carew MSS*, III, 419–20.
47. Bagwell, op.cit., III, 372ff.
48. ibid., 398ff.
49. ibid.
50. Edwards, *Church and State*, 295ff.

8 MELLIFONT COMPROMISE

Death of Elizabeth

With the death of Elizabeth, Ireland and England came into close
association with Scotland. As the ruler of the Three Kingdoms, King
James believed he had the opportunity to bring about a profound alteration in their mutual attitudes. The years after Elizabeth's death were
to indicate how little events were affected by his first thoughts after his
accession.[1]

Mellifont Settlement

What happened between Mountjoy and O'Neill at Mellifont in March
1603? From the English viewpoint, a rebel had submitted uncondition-
ally to his English sovereign, had been pardoned and restored to his
earldom. For the first time the king's writ ran throughout the length
and breadth of Ireland. A system of county administration under the
direction of the king's sheriffs and judges operated throughout every
province. There was an end to the independent Irish lordships, instead
society was organized under the Crown in a hierarchical system. The
safety of the realm was insured by the maintenance of substantial
armed forces in the fortresses and garrisons established by Mountjoy.
Ireland had been pacified. In 1604, James's representatives made peace
with Spain.[2]

From the standpoint of the restored earl of Tyrone, there were
certainly some achievements, although not as substantial as might have
been conceded had the Irish allies been able to stand firm until after
James's accession. O'Donnell's brother Rory, who had remained in
alliance with O'Neill until nearly the end, had also been received into
favour: he had been created earl of Tyrconnel. Mountjoy had used his
overriding authority in favour of those who had been last to surrender,
so they prevailed against the claims of their rivals who had submitted
previously, believing that they would be rewarded with earldoms in the
north-west. Docwra must at first have felt that his own prestige was
called in question when Mountjoy secured the earldoms for Hugh
O'Neill and Rory O'Donnell; but he was too good a courtier to quarrel
with his chief and the rejected Irish claimants were easily restrained,
having protested irregularly.[3] Perhaps the most mortifying experience
for Tyrone was to be pelted publicly on his passage through England on

his way to be received at London by James I. The protection accorded
to the pardoned rebels was a positive indication of the good faith of the
new English regime. The Tudors, with their ferocity and duplicity, had
gone. The Stuart regime, bringing in a dynasty descended from ancient
Irish kings, should react more sympathetically to the Irish outlook. Too
soon it would emerge that James had his own priorities and that the
first of these was to stand well with his new English subjects. So the
Scottish king became more English than the English themselves.[4]

Attitude of Dublin Administration

From the point of view of subordinate members of the Dublin administration it was vital that the pardoning of the former rebels should not be
allowed to bring back the reign of disorder and misrule, under a restored
Kildare or a restored Desmond. As the Protestant bishops saw it, an
army of malcontents attached to popery still existed throughout the
country in the persons of the Catholic priests.[5] Toleration might still
appear necessary as a public policy, but suspicion and distrust of ex-
Catholic crusaders must be maintained, especially as in the towns, east,
south, and west, the death of the old queen had been followed by the
restoration in varying degrees of Catholic religious rites. Mountjoy
himself had to take an army to Munster to coerce the towns into
restoring the Protestant services and maintaining the Elizabethan settlement of religion. Under him an increasingly discontented army of
occupation used every opportunity to erode the Mellifont arrangement.

To the bishops and the army can be added the English lawyers in
Ireland, like Sir John Davies,[6] concerned to use their professional
training to call in question ancient privilege in the interests of the new
Renaissance state. Until the death in 1606 of Mountjoy, whose standing
with the king was paramount in matters regarding Ireland, these new
forces were kept in check.

Position of Tyrone

The understanding between Mountjoy and Tyrone that followed from
Mellifont appears to have accorded to Tyrone something less than the
palatinate powers to which he had aspired in some of the peace
negotiations five years earlier. King's sheriffs there must be in the Ulster
counties and, so far as Tyrone was concerned, this involved the acceptance
of the earlier division of his jurisdiction into the two counties of Armagh
and Tyrone. But these sheriffs had to accept that the earl was accorded
more than an honorific position in these counties as *locum tenens* for
the king. There was, however, no likelihood that the understanding with

Mountjoy would have accorded Tyrone a lord presidency in Ulster. For such an office there was an English aspirant in the person of Sir Arthur Chichester, a military commander under Mountjoy who later succeeded him in the viceroyalty and who had hoped, but for the pardon of the Irish earl, to build up a predominant position for himself in the Lough Neagh area. While Mountjoy lived, and even for some time thereafter, the earl of Tyrone's good standing with the king was sufficiently strong to contain Chichester. In fact, while Mountjoy remained in Ireland, Tyrone was supported from Dublin in any disputes in which he was involved with former Irish colleagues and English officials.[7]

Position in Munster

How far beyond the interests of Tyrone did the Mellifont compromise extend? There is little doubt, apart from the religious question, that matters settled at Mellifont affected only the Ulster province. Thereafter in Munster the lord president's authority was paramount, allowing for the independent jurisdiction of Ormond in Tipperary and to a lesser extent of Donough O'Brien, 4th earl of Thomond, in Clare. After the defeat of Kinsale, the Munster planters were restored and the lord president made use of his powers to strengthen this new colonial element and prevail against the remnants of the Gaelic order by subjecting them to English feudal law.[8]

Position in Connacht

In the west, Richard Burke, 4th earl of Clanricarde, became sufficiently anglicized to exercise a considerable influence over Connacht, which to some extent kept in check the exactions of the new English officials.[9] However, both here and elsewhere, questions of church lands were increasingly to be decided in favour of the administration of the Protestant clergy and of English and Scottish land speculators. Outstanding military men, designated as English servitors, were concerned — usually successfully — to secure some landed position when properties came before the courts of Exchequer and Chancery. In this activity the office of escheator provided an administrative method of keeping open the opportunity for establishing title to lands under a system of law which presupposed that all lands were held directly or indirectly from the Crown.[10]

The Earl of Tyrconnel

Apart from Tyrone then, the other pardoned rebels — like those in the counties of Donegal and Fermanagh — were confronted with major difficulties, partly arising from the succession disputes which had enabled Mountjoy to break down the O'Neill alliance. Tyrone was a remarkable personality accustomed to a sophisticated organization of society. Tyrconnel's position was from the first handicapped by his limited experience of government and his weakness among the O'Donnells, who on the death of his brother Hugh Roe had accepted their cousin Niall Garbh as O'Donnell. As the latter had hoped to be accepted as earl of Tyrconnel, his securing of the chieftainship was a sufficient excuse for the English to abandon him and prefer Rory for the earldom. But this new earl was insufficiently strong to maintain himself against Niall Garbh and was obliged to reside in the Pale on a very limited income. Tyrconnel's position *vis-à-vis* English local officials was therefore much more circumscribed than that of Tyrone.[11]

Tyrone and O'Cahan

A similar weakness existed regarding Cuchonnacht Maguire, brother of Russell's old foe, in Fermanagh, with whom the English administration, including the official clergy and judiciary, were far more effective than they could possibly be against Tyrone. In southern Ulster, few obstacles now existed to resuming the system of native landed settlement which had been carried out in Monaghan under Fitzwilliam and which could now be introduced into the counties of Cavan and Fermanagh. In the north of Ulster, the county of Coleraine, so soon to be incorporated into the county of Londonderry, was for the moment left under the general protection of Tyrone. In this area, O'Cahan was traditionally subordinate to O'Neill and was obviously regarded by Mountjoy as still in such a relationship with the earl of Tyrone. However, the establishment of an enterprising Scot, George Montgomery, as bishop of three dioceses including Derry, brought about a situation in which, in the name of the Protestant Church, a series of legal and diplomatic battles were fought out, not only with the local lords but also with the Castle administration. After the death of Mountjoy, who had been made earl of Devonshire by James I, Montgomery in 1606 availed himself of a dispute between Tyrone and O'Cahan to persuade the latter to appeal against the overriding authority of the former, in circumstances which secured favour for O'Cahan with the Dublin administration.[12]

Tyrone and the Catholic Clergy

Tyrone's position was unexpectedly weakened by the rise of the conflict between the Dublin government and the Catholic clergy. As already mentioned, on the death of Elizabeth, Mountjoy had encountered difficulties in the towns, where it had been assumed that the restoration of Catholicism was permissible. The pacification of urban Ireland and re-establishment of official Protestantism did not come about without the Lord Deputy encountering disputatious Catholic clergy prepared to distinguish between spiritual and temporal obedience. Nevertheless, under Mountjoy's influence, as approved by the king, toleration for Catholicism was maintained in Ireland and apparently perpetuated after the peace with Spain.[13]

After Mountjoy's departure in June 1603, his successors in Ireland became increasingly susceptible to the Protestant episcopal objections to toleration, particularly against the Catholic clergy, whose intrigues, they insisted, were frustrating the Reformation and spreading disloyalty. Hence in 1605 the Gunpowder plot in England led to a proclamation in Ireland banishing the Roman Catholic clergy.[14]

Tyrone was obliged to tolerate the reading of the banishment proclamation[15] in his presence at Dungannon, though he did have the consolation that his authority was sufficiently superior to that of the county sheriffs of Armagh and Tyrone to enable him to act as a protector for some of the clergy concerned. More serious, however, was the fact that the proclamation re-established an atmosphere of military confrontation in which the Catholic powers abroad might be involved.

Henry O'Neill

While peace had been made with Spain, the latter was still at war with the Protestant Netherlands. The reports from the Low Countries to England provided ample evidence of the activities there of various Catholic exiles from England and Scotland as well as from Ireland.[16] Tyrone's son Henry held a commission there in the Irish regiment commanded by the Archduke Albert, husband of the Infanta Isabella. Proposals from Dublin that his father recall him had hitherto been ignored. But now the question of his involvement in intrigues to bring about a further Spanish enterprise against the British Isles was under consideration. In summer 1607 Maguire left Ireland for the Netherlands to take service with the Irish regiment. Tyrone was aware that there was a possibility of his returning to Ireland if he could secure for Tyrconnel a similar army commission. Tyrone's appeal in June 1606 to London to have the case between O'Cahan and himself adjudicated there was successful and the Irish earl had every reason to believe that the result would be as favourable as in the days of Mountjoy. Two events intervened, however, which radically altered his fortunes and led to the flight of the earls on 4 September 1607.

The Flight of the Earls

Information was conveyed to Dublin Castle that the northern earls and
Maguire were involved in a conspiracy to bring about a new invasion and
in particular to destroy the government in Dublin.[17] Unexpectedly,
Maguire arrived from the Netherlands much sooner than had been
expected and Tyrone was assured that Tyrconnel and his family were
fleeing from Ireland with Maguire. Tyrone, heartbroken, decided to go
with them. His leavetaking of his friends at Mellifont was never forgotten by them. Only after the news of the flight did they begin to
understand why he had appeared so mournful before returning home.

Undoubtedly Tyrone had come to the conclusion that if he were to
proceed with the plan of going to London on James's summons for the
hearing of his case against O'Cahan, he never would return to Ireland.
He would end his life in the Tower if Tyrconnel and other northern
chiefs joined his son on the continent, in what was arguably a project
for a renewal of the Catholic war in Ireland.[18] As if to confirm this,
proclamations were issued in London and in Dublin declaring that the
earls had been involved in a traitorous conspiracy before the flight. The
compliant solicitor-general, Sir John Davies, secured presentments from
grand juries in the northern counties corroborating the royal and viceregal proclamations. Thereafter government set out to plan a new
colonization in Ulster of British planters, from Scotland as well as from
England. The Mellifont compromise was ended. The northern Ireland
problem was about to begin.

Notes

1. R. Dunlop, *Ireland under the Commonwealth*, 2 vols. (Manchester, 1913), I,
    LXII ff.
2. R. Bagwell, *Ireland under the Tudors*, III, 438ff.
3. ibid.
4. R. Bagwell, *Ireland under the Stuarts* (1909), I, 30ff.
5. *Cal.S.P. Ire.*, James I, I (1603–06), 58–60, no. 70, 4 June 1603.
6. Davies was appointed solicitor-general in September 1603. He was the
    author of *A Discovery of the true causes why Ireland was never entirely
    subdued, nor brought under the obedience of the crowne of England, untill
    the beginning of his majesties happie raigne* (London, 1613).
7. F. M. Jones, *Mountjoy: the Last Elizabethan Deputy* (Dublin, 1958), 159ff.
8. Dunlop, *Ireland under the Commonwealth*, I, LXV–LXVI, LXVIIIff.
9. In November 1603 Clanricarde was appointed president of Connacht and a
    member of the Council. *Cal.S.P. Ire.*, James I, I (1603–06), 105–6, no. 164.
    In autumn 1602 he had married Frances Walsingham, countess of Essex, in

turn widow of Sir Philip Sidney and of the executed Lord Lieutenant.
10. See Sir John Davies, *Le primer report des cases et matters en ley resolues et adiuges en les courts de roy en Ireland* (1615; Edinburgh, 1907. The English Reports, vol. 80).
11. Bagwell, *Ireland under the Stuarts*, I, 33ff.
12. For this dispute see ibid., I, 30ff.
13. Jones, op.cit., ch. 19.
14. Dunlop, *Ireland under the Commonwealth*, I, LXVI.
15. *Cal.S.P. Ire.*, James I, I (1603–06), 301–3, no. 513, 4 July 1605.
16. *Cal.S.P. Ire.*, James I, I (1603–06), 229–30, no. 401.
17. *C.S.P. Ire.*, James I, I (1603–06), 254ff, no. 336.
18. Dunlop, *Ireland under the Commonwealth*, I, LXX ff.

9 EPILOGUE

Impact of the Counter-Reformation

The destruction of Hiberno-Norman civilization was partly the work of the Counter-Reformation, which also put limits to the success of the English conquest. Concurrently with the migration to Europe of Elizabeth's military opponents, there had departed those secular forces seeking education in a Catholic milieu. While many of these did not return, the strength of their devotion to their homeland provided a nucleus from which sprang resistance to the new British policy, Scottish as well as English, which began with the plantation in Ulster and culminated in the Protestant colonial ascendancy which ruled Ireland from the time of Oliver Cromwell to that of George III.

Even before Elizabeth's death, the Counter-Reformation forces had been strong enough in Ireland to dictate an aggressive attitude towards the Established Church in the towns. These forces were, thenceforward, divided; the Old English elements were seeking a compromise with England, while the Gaelic element, particularly in Ulster, under the shadow of plantation, continued to look for Spanish intervention.

Irish Writers Preserve the Records

More peaceful elements concerned themselves with the preservation of the records of the threatened civilization. Colgan[1] commenced his hagiographical collection which led to the annalistic work of O'Clery and the other Four Masters.[2] Franciscan and Jesuit martyrologists built up a record of the struggle for the faith. Archbishop Lombard,[3] who played a part in seeking a Catholic compromise with James I, had also contributed to the Catholic Irish national legend.

The distinction between history and propaganda is not always clearly discernible. Even O'Sullivan Beare[4] had his scholarly moments. Even James Ussher,[5] collateral descendant of the Stanihursts, sought a non-Roman origin in early Irish Christianity. Ware[6] and Keating[7] in their different ways preserved all they could of the Hiberno-Norman world of the past. Not everything written by those impugned by Keating was hostile. The translations into Irish of the New Testament and of the Old Testament and the part played by Bishop William Bedell,[8] whose name is associated with the Irish version of the Bible, contributed substantially to the preservation of the Gaelic literary tradition — even though the association with Protestantism made the translation suspect in the eyes of Catholics.

Destruction of St Patrick's Purgatory

The destruction of St Patrick's Purgatory as an object of superstitious veneration by the Protestant bishop of Clogher, James Spottiswood, while only a reindorsement of the condemnation of pilgrimages there by Pope Alexander VI more than a century and a half earlier was understandably resented and bitterly so — far beyond the confines of Catholic Ulster.

The Role of the Old English in the Cultural Tradition

After the flight of the earls the Old English in Ireland took over the initiative from the Old Irish in preserving the cultural tradition and setting limits to Protestant anglicization. Increasingly their hostility to Gaelicism weakened. Scholars like Sir James Ware, as well as Ussher, developed a sympathy as well as an anxiety to preserve the Gaelic treasures and established personal links with the learned men of the older tradition.

In parliament too under James I and Charles I, the Old English took the lead in bringing about an Irish consensus in legislative and administrative matters. While they accepted the necessity of passing acts attainting the earls of Tyrone and Tyrconnel and legalizing the Ulster plantation, they set limits to the extension of anti-Catholic laws and they participated in the establishment of the principle that every Irishman was a free-born citizen of the state. In the parliament held under Wentworth in 1634, however, this constitutional development was restricted in the face of his determination to establish more rigid uniformity in Ireland — bringing it into line with Archbishop Laud's policy for England and Scotland. At the same time the country experienced economic enrichment and the spread of an educated Catholic clergy, trained on the continent in the colleges of the Counter-Reformation. These latter were quick to seize the opportunity of the Bishops' War in Scotland and the parliamentary attack on royal absolutism. Thus they helped to destroy Hiberno-Norman civilization by countenancing the Ulster Irish rebels of October 1641. By the time the civil war of the three kingdoms was ended by Oliver Cromwell, little was left of Hiberno-Norman civilization but the spirit.

Hiberno-Norman Civilization After 1600

In the late seventeenth century, the spirit revived the Hiberno-Norman

concept. The Cromwellian conquest, confirmed by the Williamite confiscation, established the ascendancy in Ireland of the new planters,
who quickly responded in protest against the English parliament's
policy of treating them as colonists subordinate to England: in 1699
William Molyneux asserted the historic political claims of the Hiberno-
Normans to rule their own affairs. Slowly during the eighteenth
century there evolved a community sense among the Protestant landed
gentry with political rights, for the Catholics were excluded by the
Revolution from any political participation. But the Protestant
community became as independent-minded as their counterparts in the
New England colonies in North America. Thus, coincident with the
American War of Independence, there emerged the assertion by
Grattan, Flood, and Charlemont of the legislative independence of
the Irish Protestant nation. With the coming of revolution in Europe
and the conflicts at home precipitated by the politically subordinate
Presbyterians and Catholics, the Protestant nation became submerged
in the United Kingdom — created in 1800 by William Pitt to withstand
the revolution and Napoleonic imperialism. Once more, an individual
Irish culture proved unable to meet the challenge of changing political
situations. After the revolutionary wars, Anglo-Irish relations became
complicated by the uneven rates of development of the three kingdoms
in the British Isles.

The decisive factor in the failure of the United Kingdom to maintain
the confidence of the majority of the Irish people appears to have been
the false premises on which Pitt and Castlereagh erected the constitution
in the Act of Union. Fearful of the forces of revolution which had
infected the United Irishmen — challenging the ascendancy of the
ruling class — and which advocated an anti-English gospel of Irish
nationalism based upon the French revolutionary motto, the British
establishment shored up a settlement based upon the amalgamation of
parliaments and the political support of the three Irish Churches —
Protestant Episcopalian, Presbyterian, and Catholic. Within a generation,
it was clear that the Union settlement had perpetuated a political
tyranny in Ireland: this was destroyed by Daniel O'Connell. The
specific contribution of O'Connell to the political situation was to
revive the idea of an Irish nation theoretically based on English liberal
and reforming ideas in alliance with the Irish constitutional tradition
of the last quarter of the eighteenth century. His achievement was to
secure political equality for Catholics and Presbyterians in Ireland. But
in the very act of emancipating his fellow countrymen, his use of the
Catholic clergy as a counterbalance to the Protestant ascendancy created

permanent fear among the middle-class Presbyterians who allied with their old enemies the Protestant Episcopalians in the resistance to the new and terrifying Catholic menace — the nation created by O'Connell.

In the last phases of the O'Connell movement towards the end of the first half of the nineteenth century, a new gospel of Irish nationalism based upon O'Connell's nation was preached by a talented group — Duffy, Davis, and Mitchel, who came to be known as the Young Irelanders. Influenced and reacting against Mazzini's denial that Ireland deserved to be regarded as a nation as it was a mere negation of English nationalism, the Young Irelanders elaborated a concept of Irishness. This they based on the many surviving historical traditions including the pre-Norman Gaelic, the medieval Anglo-Irish, the Elizabethan O'Neills, the seventeenth- and eighteenth-century heroes like Owen Roe O'Neill and Sarsfield, and the writers and orators such as Swift and Flood and Grattan. In the calamity of the Great Famine, and influenced by the 1848 revolution in France, Young Irelanders attempted to affirm their renunciation of British allegiance in arms, only to destroy their political movement, except with those of the next generation stimulated by their spirit to reformulate their ideas of Irish self-government.

O'Connell's solution, the repeal of the Union, having failed to get support except from a predominantly Catholic group, provoked a reaction among independent Irish Protestants to preserve their interests by Home Rule, Isaac Butt's slogan for a federal Irish parliament. The immediate background to this movement was the Gladstonian policy of disestablishing the Protestant Church of Ireland, attempting to impose on the landlords a dual ownership with the tenantry of their lands, and conceding to Catholicism a greater influence in education than anti-liberal Irish tories were prepared to concede. Unfortunately for Butt, to maintain Home Rule he was obliged to ally with the growing Catholic powers, so that he was virtually abandoned by the gentry and the Protestants.

The Parnellite Home Rule movement was essentially within the framework of that of O'Connell, as the Fenian movement had been within the theoretical concept of the Young Irelanders. The Fenians formulated their republicanism as a logical development from the ideas of Davis and Mitchel — re-expressed in the Europe of anti-Imperialism and the America of the war between the states. Parnell employed the O'Connell device of being English to the English and Irish to the Irish by stressing to the former his convictions about constitutional rights and to the latter his sympathies with the boundless claims of Irish nationalism. Parnell's tragedy lay in his failure to secure endorsement by both great English political parties so that, in order to defeat him, Unionism was revived to shore up the declining forces of Protestantism and English capitalism. Parnell's achievement was ultimately to convince the latest believers in Irish revolution that its objects could be realized with the help of America and by paralysing English power. In the reaction against politics after his fall, there developed in a variety of ways a new interest in Irish culture and its preservation, which led directly to the divergent expressions of this in the Anglo-Irish literary movement, of which Yeats and Joyce remain the most interesting figures. From the Gaelic movement proper, as organized by Douglas Hyde, Eoin MacNeill, and Peter O'Leary, there evolved the gospel of Sinn Fein. In politics the reaction of Unionism just before World War I culminated in the armed defiance of the British government by the Ulster Protestant volunteers. When England became involved in the war against Germany, it was also predictable that Pearse and the revolutionary believers in the heroic Gaelic tradition should assert their convictions in arms, as they did at Easter in Dublin in 1916. Almost equally predictable was the British compromise of two federal parliaments, as expressed in the Lloyd George legislation in 1920–22. It remains for a subsequent generation to decide whether either or neither of the Irish states which emerged half a century ago has perpetuated the ideas of Hiberno-Norman civilization.

Notes

1. John Colgan, *Acta Sanctorum Hiberniae* (1645; IMC, 1948).
2. *Annala Rioghachta Eireann . . . ...* , ed. J. O'Donovan, 7 vols. (Dublin, 1848–51).
3. Peter Lombard, *De Regno Hiberniae, Sanctorum Insula Commentarius* (1632).
4. P. O'Sullivan Beare, *Zoilomastix*, selection ed. T. J. O'Donnell (IMC, 1964).
5. *The whole works of J. Usher*, ed. C. R. Elrington and J. M. Todd, 17 vols., (Dublin, 1847–64).
6. James Ware, *The Historie of Ireland, collected by M. Hanmer, E. Campion, and E. Spenser* (1633), 2 vols., (*Ancient Irish Histories*; 1809).
7. A. Cronin, 'The sources of Keating's Foras Feasa ar Eirinn', *Eigse*, IV, 235–79.
8. *Two Biographies of William Bedell*, ed. E. S. Shuckburgh (1902).

APPENDIX: HISTORIANS AND SIXTEENTH-CENTURY IRELAND

Historians like Edmund Campion[1] writing in the late sixteenth century have attempted to describe the situation of the country as well as giving their views about the people. To Campion, there were some four or five regions, these being the historic provinces, Ulster, Munster, Leinster, Connacht, and, for certain purposes, Meath. Leinster, he tells us, looks to England, Munster and Connacht to France and Spain, and Ulster to Scotland. He also points out that as English power began to decay, there emerged the English Pale and the Irish Pale, each concerned to maintain its own interest. Inevitably they tended to overlap. But at least the English Pale maintained contact with England and preserved the richer and more profitable lands, leaving the wilder and rougher parts to the Irish. Campion's sources are the chronicles and the collections of the family of Stanihurst in particular, whose association with municipal and viceregal Dublin went back to before the fall of the Fitzgeralds.

Writing a generation later, William Camden[2] refers to the richness of the vegetation. Ireland is predominantly a cattle country and there are also flocks of sheep. There are many small horses called 'hobbies' and the hawks and the hunting-dogs of Ireland are famous, as are the country's honey bees. The moisture of the climate rather taxes the stranger, who easily contracts the flux, for which the natural remedy is *uisce beatha* (usque bagh). Camden, who derives some of his information from the Anglo-Norman Giraldus Cambrensis, goes on to describe the inhabitants as warlike, ingenious, and comely. In between these writers come Edmund Spenser and Lord Mountjoy.

Spenser,[3] secretary of Viceroy Lord Grey de Wilton, whose harsh, puritanical policy he extols, became a planter after the Desmond confiscation in Munster and, as befitted a poet, was lyrical on the natural beauties of the country. Lord Deputy Mountjoy, whose own secretary, Fynes Moryson, was to make his own significant contribution to Irish historical writing, was a courtier with literary as well as military pretensions. Mountjoy assured his queen that Ireland was potentially almost as profitable to her as England, if only because of its former grandeur.[4]

Contemporary with Camden was John Barclay, the Scots satirist whose *Icon Animorum* appeared in 1614. His strictures on Irish home dwellings annoyed Geoffrey Keating.[5] Keating's criticisms of Barclay and other writers appeared in manuscript within a generation of Camden in his *Foras feasa ar Eirinn* (*Materials for the History of Ireland*).[6] Keating protested at the approach to Ireland of writers like Campion, Camden, and Moryson. He deplored what he regarded as an unequal contest in which these recent writers on Irish history laid the blame for the condition of Ireland on the old foreign settlers, from whom he himself claimed descent, and on the native Irish. One can sense that Keating, perhaps in the realization that his own work might not be published for generations to come, resented that the printed works of these recent historians would have it all their own way. He goes on to liken their habits in selecting the sources from which they draw to the way of a bee on the wing preferring to the flowers and to honey the noxiousness of the dung of the horse and the cow. The historians of whom he complains do not concern themselves with the noble and gentle people or with their valour and piety, their monastic foundations, their endowment of learning, and their reverence for the clergy. To Keating, they were unsurpassed in Europe in generosity and hospitality. He points out that there is no country without a rabble and on these no historian should concentrate. The writers he condemns have elected to dwell upon the ways of the contemptible people and the men of no station. In what he himself writes of the history of Ireland he writes without desire for favour. He devotes himself mainly to the history of the Gaelic Irish and, as one of the old foreigners, he cannot therefore be charged with partiality. Keating, not unnaturally perhaps, says little about himself as a Catholic priest in trouble, through over-zealousness with the authorities. Perhaps too, he is hardly aware that he is lauding the interests of faith, fatherland, and Irish Catholicism, though in no way denying the authority of King Charles I. His work, however, serves to enable us to take stock of the available sources for sixteenth-century Ireland and of its historians.

Fussner's English historical revolution[7] is associated with the concepts of the meaning of history of a small but significant group concerned with dramatic developments — Stow, Selden, Camden, Raleigh, and Bacon. These he connects with different aspects : Raleigh with universal history, Stow with local history, Camden with territorial history, Selden with problematic history, and Bacon with the idea of history. By paying particular attention to purpose, method, content, style, and significance, Fussner is able to come to some conclusions, offered tentatively. The antiquarian element in England was reinforced

with the common law tradition concerned to establish the supremacy
of law over the monarchy. The English revolution subordinated the
Church to the state, but did so by allying with the forces of the common
law, which in turn established the rule of that law over the constitution.
This was the revolution to which Fussner's historians made their modest
contribution.

In his *Englishman and His History*,[8] Sir Herbert Butterfield tells us
something of the prevailing obsessions of the English historians writing
in the sixteenth century; Fussner has summed these up as a concern
with antiquarianism and a hostility to popery. Viewing these attitudes,
one can regard the English chroniclers as identified with the glories of
the House of Tudor, much as were their contemporaries devoted to
describing the heroic deeds of the Hapsburgs and the valorous ways of
the Valois. In the rivalries between these dynastic states, it was natural
to make much of their cultural pretensions. As the sixteenth century
progressed, the wars between Protestantism and Catholicism tended
increasingly to divide these monarchies, which frequently found their
own centralizing policies substantially strengthened in securing international recognition for the claim of the prince to regulate the religion
of his subjects.

Almost inevitably, the more comprehensive forms of Protestantism,
as defined by Luther and by Calvin, tended to adopt the Catholic
medieval theory of the coinciding interests of Church and state. From
the great days of ecclesiastical reform some five centuries earlier, when
popes like Gregory VII and Innocent III laid down a system of public
morality, the Church had been associated with a policy of imposing an
almost monastic life upon Western Christendom. In sixteenth-century
Europe, as Protestantism identified itself with a movement for reform,
a more austere and intolerant attitude developed, ultimately emerging
as the Puritan movement, which even contaminated Catholicism and
led to deplorable excesses against artistic objects and revered centres of
popular piety. It was perhaps inevitable that those who were profoundly
influenced by the study of Holy Scripture, concurrently with their
renunciation of traditional authorities and teaching, should find in Holy
Writ and particularly in the Old Testament a justification for the
denunciation of idolatry and for the hatred of false gods, as they chose
to regard Catholicism.

It is in this atmosphere that we must attempt to assess the writings
on Ireland of English and Anglo-Irish chroniclers of the sixteenth
century. Inevitably they had become heirs to the medieval English
mission to justify intervention in Ireland as a necessary part in reclaiming

the natives from barbarisms in Christianity. Reference has already been made to the use of sixteenth-century chroniclers of the writings of the Anglo-Norman chronicler Giraldus Cambrensis.[9] It is not too much to say that this successful medieval writer had for long entertained or revolted audiences and readers with his varied selection of good stories about the Irish. Giraldus himself had been connected with the leading men among the second generation of Anglo-Norman conquerors in Ireland. An able and ambitious cleric, he courted successive Plantagenet rulers, beginning with Henry II, to secure advancement in the Church. If his ambitions were hardly realized, his literary efforts were highly successful at the court of the Angevin kings, and in the monastic academic centres of medieval England. So when there emerged in the sixteenth century a revived interest in travel and colonization, his writings, preserved in many manuscript versions, proved particularly adaptable and attractive to editors. In a certain sense, it may be said that the approach of Cambrensis had other appeals to English and Anglo-Irish writers on Ireland. In the still existing conflict with the Gaelic literary tradition, Cambrensis demonstrated an understanding of the issues confronting the English and Anglo-Irish in Ireland. He had identified himself with the ancestors of the Geraldines, his own relations. He was inclined to despise the native Irish ecclesiastics as being unfit for preferment to higher church offices, if only because they were not men of the world. His fund of Irish stories had a particular value to those who still advocated the superiority of the English way of life. Among the Anglo-Irish chroniclers, we can perceive this influence most clearly on Stanihurst.[10] It is also to be seen in Campion, who wrote his *History of Ireland* in the home of Richard Stanihurst's family. Perhaps all the more so, Campion earned the condemnation of Keating, who himself became a Catholic and broke away from the Protestant tradition. Both Campion and Keating were really involved in a new type of historical enterprise, the history of the country. In fairness to those criticized, the purpose for which they wrote must be ascertained. Just as Giraldus concerned himself with specific historical enterprises like the conquest of Ireland and with travel books like his *Topography of Ireland*, the Camdens, Spensers, and Barclays are confined to something more and something less than the interests of Campion and Keating.

The hibernicization of the Anglo-Normans emerges delightfully in a Fitzgerald of Kildare pietistic history which deals with the battle of Knockdoe. It records the vision of an angel who advised the spiritual petitioner for MacWilliam of Clanricarde that the contrary supplications of Kildare had already been granted. The hagiographical tradition of the Irish saints clearly still prevailed, as the political position of the patrons of the saints continued to be manifested in their proteges, accounts of the fortunes of their founders.[11]

To a large extent, the chronicles in the Anglo-Irish tradition were connected with a great monastic house, or some outstanding family, and even occasionally some town. In this they were not unlike the Irish annalistic writings which only gradually, and that in Keating's day, became associated with the country. It has been pointed out by James F. Kenney in his *Sources for the Early History of Ireland*[12] that the works of collection and historical writing particularly interested those conscious of the threatened destruction of a civilization. *The Annals of the Kingdom of Ireland*[13] by Michael O'Clery and his associates, usually known as the Four Masters, is a case in point. O'Clery had been commissioned by the Louvain professor John Colgan in connection with his projected *Acta Sanctorum Hiberniae*[14] to seek out in Ireland every locatable manuscript of the lives of the Irish saints. O'Clery, himself connected with a family of Gaelic historians in the north-west, also decided to collect the annals and concentrated mainly but not exclusively upon that area in the writing of the annals. It is therefore necessary to remember that the idea of writing the history of the country as a whole is still novel. The influence of a patron is to some extent apparent in the general work. Among the Anglo-Irish chroniclers the influence of the patron and of the tradition is also great.

In retrospect, Elizabethan Ireland was regarded with some concern under James I, so that the writing of its history seems to have been discouraged at court. Thus Fynes Moryson,[15] in publishing his historical account in 1617, is at pains to identify it with his journals of his travels and to deny any claim to be writing history. Similarly, Sir George Carew,[16] who, like Moryson, kept the archives of his office and copied extensively from the papers of officials, does not attempt to publish his narrative. Stafford's edition of his father's *Pacata Hibernia*[17] does not come to light until after Carew's death. About 1634, in a changing atmosphere, interest seems to have justified Sir James Ware in re-issuing Campion in his *History of Ireland*, together with Spenser and Hammer.[18] Ware's own antiquarian studies published over forty years added substantially to historical knowledge, based as they were upon an increasing body of source material to which he was privileged to have access, mainly because of his government office. Similarly, Stafford's *Pacata Hibernia*, based upon Sir George Carew's papers, widened the sixteenth-century horizons, even if, like Moryson, their main connection was with their heroes and patrons.

In attempting to present the history of sixteenth-century Ireland, the historian must be careful to disclaim any pretension to be definitive beyond the scope of contemporary material. Of necessity, this is a very serious restriction. The opening of the national archives by the government of the United Kingdom in the 1830s provided a sequence of documentation with the publication of the extant correspondence between the governments of London and Dublin in the reign of Henry VIII. A more far-reaching correspondence was revealed when there appeared after 1860 the volumes of the *Calendar of State Papers relating to Ireland*, ultimately extending into the late seventeenth century. However, the documents in this *Calendar*, unlike the earlier publications noted above, did not reproduce complete transcripts of the originals; instead, a brief summary usually not exceeding a few lines was as much as was provided for successive numbered entries.[19] While later volumes improved in quality and enlarged the entries, for the ordinary reader dependent upon published works, it had a very limited amount of information on which to judge the individual documents. Moreover, the uniformity of the entries and their laconic nature tended to bring about an uncritical attitude to this body of material. At the same time, while in no way absolving the professional historian from studying the originals — often more accessible today through isolated publications and through microfilms — it is to be remembered that the availability of these volumes has transformed our understanding of sixteenth-century Irish history. It should also be possible to present historical findings from the viewpoint of the archivist rather than that of the historian. With the establishment in the reign of James I of officials responsible for the custody of State Papers, a body of archival material was assembled, which, as it turned out, extended back to the beginning of the preceding century. Understandably, the sixteenth-century material is in no way as comprehensive as that for the seventeenth. The sixteenth-century material, particularly when it was very limited in documentation, tempted historians to come to conclusions with insufficient evidence and to involve themselves with hypotheses going beyond what the evidence obliged them to believe. It is is in these circumstances that the myths and the legends enshrined in the chronicles came to be adopted, frequently because modern historians have themselves allowed their preconceptions to dominate their thinking. It must be here remembered that since the sixteenth century successive political fashions have dictated to historians prepared to accept such patronage the viewpoint of the Protestant imperialist, the Catholic liberal, or the Gaelic separatist, to refer to but a few such fashions.

In the present century, the conflict with England, culminating in the establishment in the early 1920s of a new state claiming self-government, almost inevitably involved a new political attitude. The movement was part of the western European nationalist movement which followed the great French Revolution. However, it must be seen in succession to the dynastic nationalism which emerged in many places in the sixteenth century. As that movement in the British Isles had been a Protestant one, it must be seen as part of the efforts to unify the three kingdoms in these islands under a Protestant monarch. The emergence in Keating's generation of a different national theory identified with Catholicism, with the papacy, with some variation regarding dynastic allegiance between English rulers and foreign patrons, inevitably influenced Irish exiles such as the banished Catholic clergy who, like Rothe,[20] produced their books of martyrs. In Ireland, however, it is not going to be possible to see the reality of the political situation if either of these theories is regarded as having governed the ordinary political affairs of the Gaelic and Anglo-Irish lordships. The traditions of medieval Europe continued to prevail over a great part of Ireland; while pope and king were trying to compel every individual to pay absolute obedience, each to the exclusion of the other, medieval traditions continued and many people successfully avoided taking up exclusive attachment to one view or another. The writers were usually more up to date.

Historiographically, it is possible to classify the writers according to whether they were dominated by one assumption or another. Thus the sixteenth-century conquest dominates the works of Davies,[21] Farmer,[22] Perrott,[23] Spenser, and Stafford. The progress of the seventeenth century accentuated the conflicts along the lines indicated by Keating. After the outbreak of the civil war in the three kingdoms, the myth of the popish massacre dominated the works of Cox,[24] Loftus,[25] and Leland.[26] Thereafter, the respective Protestant and Catholic traditions were coloured by the mutual animosities of these bloody myths.

The exiled Catholic viewpoint is to be found in O'Sullivan Beare[27] and in Carve.[28] The standpoint of the Counter-Reformation papacy comes through in the writing by O'Ferrall and O'Connell of the *Commentarius Rinuccinianus*,[29] and to a certain extent in that of the Jesuits, in Edmund Ignatius Hogan's *Distinguished Irishmen*.[30] C. P. Meehan's studies present a Victorian reassessment from the standpoint of Roman Catholic nationalism in the same tradition.

The annalistic tradition which had produced in the early sixteenth century, usually under family patronage, such works as the *Annals of*

Connacht,[31] the *Annals of Loch Cé*,[32] the *Annals of Ulster*,[33] and the O'Clery biography of Hugh Roe O'Donnell,[34] also dominated the thinking of MagCarthaigh.[35] The antiquarian scholarship of Sir James Ware maintained on a high level the best English tradition, distinguished by a new concern with the Gaelic sources, which were, however, presented descriptively. By contrast, in their *Annals of the kingdom of Ireland*, the Four Masters were associated with a patronage assuming loyalty to Charles I, which implied acceptance of the particular claims of the English Protestant state since Elizabeth I.

Oliver Cromwell's designation of the main protagonists in the Commonwealth conquest as being either British Protestants or Irish papists dominated the political thinking of succeeding generations. Robert Ware, son of the antiquarian, subordinated scholarship to the frenzy of anti-popery, even to the extent of fabricating material.[36] Cox appealed for the rescue of Ireland from papists by William of Orange. After the defeat of James II by William III, the imposition of the Penal Laws seemed to confirm Cromwell's distinction.

In these circumstances the Protestant colonists gradually evolved a theory of political liberty which first they claimed for themselves as Englishmen and later, in the context of the fashionable republicanism of America and France, as the Irish nation. The winning of legislative independence in 1782 created for eighteen years a romantic attachment to the Irish parliament. After the Union with Great Britain in 1800, the growing number of its opponents convinced themselves that political independence could be secured by a reversion to the situation immediately before that Union.

With the nineteenth century, however, there emerged once more a complicated situation in which a common political policy was never adopted by the country as a whole. The failure to give equality to Catholics and Presbyterians until towards the end of the first generation after the Union left a permanent mark on the body politic. To secure Catholic Emancipation, it was necessary to build up an effective organization to intimidate a complacent and apathetic Protestant parliament. A political genius, Daniel O'Connell, created such a terrifyingly successful machine that not merely was Catholic Emancipation conceded, but Protestant fears were roused, particularly in the north-east, that Catholics were attempting to establish independence with every intention of eradicating the Protestant interest. Thus it came about in the days of romantic nationalism in Europe that an Irish nationalist movement was also elaborated, a political atmosphere already reflected in the post-Union writings of

Francis Plowden.[37] Unionists, not unnaturally, questioned the new nationalism.

The nationalist movement is particularly associated with Mitchel[38] and others of the Young Ireland movement, which grew out of O'Connell's attempt to repeal the Union. If, however, Young Ireland was theoretically republican, it had few supporters who were not Catholics. And even when a more positive republican doctrine was elaborated by the Fenians, it still commanded few Protestant disciples. Almost inevitably, the Catholic republicans identified themselves with the opposition to the English conquest of the sixteenth and seventeenth centuries. Equally, every transient opponent of the centralization of government in that same period was credited in the nineteenth century with the altruistic motives of patriotic Victorian republicans. Perhaps nowhere is this more clearly realized than in the writings of two twentieth-century historians whose own associations with Catholicism were minimal. In her *Irish Nationality*,[39] Alice Stopford Green produced the classic exposition for democratic Irish independence which she fondly regarded as logically following the writings of her husband, the English historian John Richard Green, in his *Short History of the English People*.[40] Mrs Green's influence is to be seen in Constantia Maxwell's *Irish History from Contemporary Sources*,[41] in which the disciple showed a laudably objective approach to the conflict of civilizations.

The predominance of politics in Irish historical thinking is reflected in Patrick Sarsfield O'Hegarty's *The Indestructible Nation*,[42] wherein he presents Hugh O'Neill, 2nd earl of Tyrone, as the representative of the Fenian republican Irish nation, conceived by John Mitchel in hatred of British rule. O'Hegarty's O'Neill is contrasted with the older, more moderate, and even imperialist nationalism which distinguished the writings of fair-minded historians like Wilson,[43] O'Connor,[44] Hayden,[45] and Stephen Gwynn.[46] The moderate tradition continued after 1922 in the works of MacNeill[47] and Curtis,[48] in those of MacNeill's disciples Hogan[49] and Hayes-McCoy,[50] and in those of Curtis's pupils Bryan[51] and Otway-Ruthven.[52]

Among contemporary historians, J. C. Beckett,[53] Aubrey Gwynn,[54] G. A. Hayes-McCoy,[55] F. X. Martin,[56] T. W. Moody,[57] Tomás Ó Fiaich,[58] and D. B. Quinn[59] may be singled out for their illuminating utilization of original sources in London and Rome.[60] Horizons have been widened by the pioneer work of Nicholas Canny,[61] D. F. Cregan,[62] F. M. Jones,[63] K. W. Nicholls,[64] Victor Treadwell,[65] and Art Cosgrove.[66] In this connection particular reference must be made to Fr Brendan Bradshaw,[67] whose study of the Henrician monastic dissolutions uses fully for the first time the unpublished sources in the Public Record Office in London. Their achievements will be appreciated more fully when the multi-volume *New History of Ireland* sponsored by the Royal Irish Academy begins to appear.

Historians are starting to accept the fact that the archival appraisal of material provides an additional dimension to historical thinking. When such material is available and can be exploited, the ultimate historical achievement will be all the greater. Thus future research workers will have enviable opportunities which it is hoped they will exploit.

Notes

1. Edmund Campion, *A History of Ireland* [1571] by James Ware in *Ancient Irish Histories*, 2 vols. (Dublin, 1809 : repr. New York 1940).
2. William Camden, *Britannia, sive florentissimorum regnorum Angliae, Scotiae, Hiberniae chorographica descriptio* (1586; 6th ed. 1606; English tr. 1610; enl. by Richard Gough, 3 vols., 1789).
3. Edmund Spenser, *A View of the State of Ireland . . . . in 1596*, Best edition by W. L. Renwick, *Complete Works of Spenser*, IV (1934).
4. C. Maxwell, *Irish History from Contemporary Sources* (1923), 314.
5. A. Cronin, 'The sources of Keating's Foras Feasa ar Éirinn', *Éigse*, IV, 235–79.
6. ibid.
7. F. S. Fussner, *The Historical Revolution, 1580–1640* (1962).
8. Herbert Butterfield, *The Englishman and His History* (1944).
9. *The Irish Historie composed and written by Giraldus Cambrensis and translated into English . . . . by Iohn Hooker* in Holinshed's *Chronicles of England, Scotland and Ireland*, VI (1808).
    For Cambrensis generally see P. W. A. Asplin, *Medieval Ireland, c. 1170–1495, a bibliography of secondary works* (RIA, 1971). As has been pointed out by Robin Flower in 'Histories and Annals. Manuscripts in the British Museum', *Anal.Hib.*, II (1931), the manuscript tradition of Cambrensis was well known to the literati of medieval Europe. Holinshed, Hooker, Campion, and Stanihurst in their published writings simply provided him with canonical sanctions by diffusing him more widely.
10. Richard Stanihurst, *De rebus in Hibernia gestis*, libri quattuor (Antwerp, 1584).
11. Flower, art.cit., 310–29.
12. J. F. Kenney, *The Sources for the Early History of Ireland* (New York, 1929), I.
13. *Annala Ríoghachta Éireann, Annals of the Kingdom of Ireland by the Four Masters . . . to 1616*, ed. J. O'Donovan, 7 vols. (Dublin, 1848–51).
14. John Colgan, *Acta Sanctorum Hiberniae* (1645; IMC, 1948), introd. B. Jennings.
15. Fynes Moryson, *An Itinerary . . . containing his ten yeeres travell through the twelve dominions of Germany, Bohmerland, Sweitzerland, Netherland, Denmarke, Poland, Italy, Turkey, France, England, Scotland and Ireland* (1617; repr. 4 vols., Glasgow, 1907–08).
16. Carew collected chiefly copies and notes rather than original documents. They

are a miscellaneous collection relating to affairs of state and the history of Ireland. On the history of the Carew MSS see *EHR*, XLII (1927), 261–7.

17. Thomas Stafford, *Pacata Hibernia* (1633), ed. S. J. O'Grady, 2 vols. (1896).
18. James Ware, *The Historie of Ireland, collected by . . . M. Hanmer, E. Campion, and E. Spenser.* (1633), 2 vols. (*Ancient Irish Histories*; 1809).
19. The quality of editing distinctly and impressively improved with the appointment of C. W. Russell and J. P. Prendergast as editors. Their first volume, that for 1603–06, appeared in 1872.
20. David Rothe, *Analecta sacra nova et mira de rebus Catholicorum in Hibernia gestis* (Pt I, Cologne, 1616; Pts I, II, Cologne, 1617; Pt III entitled *De Processu martyrali*, Cologne, 1619). Ed. P. F. Moran (1884).
21. Sir John Davies, *A Discovery of the true causes why Ireland was never . . . . brought under obedience of the crowne of England, untill the beginning of his majesties happie raigne* (1613).
22. William Farmer, *Chronicles of Ireland 1594–1613*, by C. L. Falkiner, *EHR* XXII (1907), 104–30, 527–52.
23. Sir James Perrott, *The Chronicle of Ireland 1584–1608*, ed. Herbert Wood (IMC, 1933).
24. Sir Richard Cox, *Hibernia Anglicana*, 2 vols. (1689).
25. Dudley Loftus, *Annals, 1180–1625*. Report by N. B. White in *Anal.Hib.* X (1941).
26. Thomas Leland, *A History of Ireland from the Invasion of Henry II*, 3 vols. (2nd. ed., Dublin, 1814).
27. P. O'Sullivan Beare, *Zoilomastix*, selection ed. T. J. O'Donnell (IMC, 1964).
28. Thomas Carve de Mobernon, *Lyra seu anacephalaeosis Hibernica, in qua de exordio seu origine, nomine, moribus, ritibusque gentis Hibernicae succincte tractatur; cui quoque accessere annales ejusdem Hiberniae . . . ab anno 1148 usque ad annum 1650* (Vienna, 1651; 2nd ed. with many alterations, Sulzbach, 1666). It is also to be found in the works of Bruodin, see T. Wall, 'Bards and Bruodins', in *Father Luke Wadding* (Dublin, 1957), and D. Mooney, see B. Jennings in *Anal.Hib.* VI (1934), 12–131.
29. G. B. Rinuccini, *Commentarius Rinuccinianus* by R. B. O'Ferrall and R. D. O'Connell, ed. S. J. Kavanagh, 6 vols. (IMC, 1932–49).
30. Edmund Hogan, *Distinguished Irishmen of the Sixteenth Century*, 1st ser. (1894).
31. *Annála Connacht, The Annals of Connacht* (A.D. 1224–1544), ed. A. M. Freeman (Dublin, 1944).
32. *Annals of Loch Cé* (1014–1590), ed. W. M. Hennessy, Rolls Series, 2 vols. (1871). Reprinted, 2 vols. (1940).
33. *Annals of Ulster* (431–1541), ed. W. M. Hennessy and B. MacCarthy, 4 vols. (Dublin 1887–1901).
34. Lughaidh O'Clery, *Life of Hugh Roe O'Donnell*, ed. Paul Walsh, *Arch.Hib.* VII (1908–22); Irish Texts Society, XLII (1948).
35. Daniel MacCarthy, *The Life and Letters of Florence MacCarthy Reagh* (Dublin, 1867).
36. Robert Ware, *Historical Collections of the Church in Ireland . . . set forth in the life and death of Geo. Browne* (1681, repr. in his father's *The Antiquities and History of Ireland*, 1704). For the forgeries interpolated by his son in Ware's works see *Bull.Inst.Hist.Res.* XI (1933), 54–6.
37. Francis Plowden, *Historical Review of the State of Ireland, from the invasion of Henry II*, 2 vols. (1803).
38. John Mitchel, *Life and Times of Aodh O'Neill . . . with some account of Con, Shane, and Tirlough* (1845; repr. New York, 1868).
39. Alice Stopford Green, *Irish Nationality* (1911).

40. John Richard Green, *A Short History of the English People* (1874).
41. Maxwell, op.cit.
42. P. S. O'Hegarty, *The Indestructible Nation* (Dublin, 1918).
43. P. Wilson, *The Beginnings of Modern Ireland* (Dublin 1912).
44. G. B. O'Connor, *Elizabethan Ireland* (Dublin, 1906).
45. M. T. Hayden, *A Short History of the Irish People* (1920).
46. Stephen Gwynn, *The History of Ireland* (1923).
47. Eoin MacNeill, *Early Irish Laws and Institutions* (Dublin 1935). A more complete list of MacNeill's works and those of the following authors can be got from Conyers Read, *A Bibliography of British History: Tudor Period 1485–1603* (2nd ed., 1959) and from the annual Writings on Irish History published in *Irish Historical Studies*.
48. Edmund Curtis, *A History of Medieval Ireland* (rev. ed., 1968); also *A History of Ireland* (6th ed., 1950; repr. 1964).
49. James Hogan, *Ireland in the European System* (1920).
50. G. A. Hayes-McCoy, *Scots Mercenary Forces in Ireland 1563–1603* (1937); also *Irish Battles* (1969).
51. Donough Bryan, *Gerald Fitzgerald, the Great Earl of Kildare* (Dublin, 1933).
52. A. J. Otway-Ruthven, *A History of Medieval Ireland* (1968).
53. J. C. Beckett, *A Short History of Ireland* (rev. ed., 1971); also *The Making of Modern Ireland 1603–1923* (1966).
54. Aubrey Gwynn, *The Medieval Province of Armagh* (Dundalk, 1946).
55. Hayes-McCoy, op.cit.
56. F. X. Martin, 'The Irish Augustinian reform movement of the fifteenth century', in *Medieval Studies presented to Aubrey Gwynn*, ed. J. Watt (Dublin, 1961).
57. T. W. Moody, 'The Irish parliament under Elizabeth and James I', *R.I.A. Proc.* XLV (1939), 41–81.
58. Tomás Ó Fiaich, 'The O'Neills of the Fews', *Seanchas Ardmhacha* VII (1973).
59. D. B. Quinn, *The Elizabethans and the Irish* (Ithaca, 1966).
60. Reference may be made here to the pioneering work of Fr. Paul Walsh, *Irish Men of Learning* (Dublin, 1947) and *Irish Chiefs and Leaders* (Dublin, 1960).
61. Nicholas Canny, 'Changing views on Gaelic Ireland', *Topic* 24, 19–28.
62. D. F. Cregan, 'Irish recusant lawyers in politics in the reign of James I', *Irish Jurist* V (1970), 306–20.
63. F. M. Jones, 'The Counter-Reformation', in P. J. Corish ed., *The History of Irish Catholicism*, III, pt III (Dublin, 1967).
64. K. W. Nicholls, *Gaelic and Gaelicised Ireland in the Middle Ages* (Dublin, 1972).
65. V. Treadwell, 'The Irish parliament of 1569–71', *R.I.A. Proc.* LXV (1966).
66. Art Cosgrove, 'The Gaelic Resurgence and the Geraldine Supremacy', in T. W. Moody and F. X. Martin edd., *The Course of Irish History* (Cork, 1967).
67. Brendan Bradshaw, *The Dissolution of the Religious Orders in Ireland under Henry VIII* (Cambridge, 1974).

ANALYSIS OF SOURCES

The source material for the study of sixteenth-century Ireland may be approached conveniently through a simple classification distinguishing (i) introductory works, (ii) finding aids, (iii) presentations of material, and (iv) bibliography. By numbering the entries, alphabetically, it is possible to locate relevant entries readily.

Entries which are introductory to the sources can be conveniently subdivided into (ia) bibliographies of bibliographies, (ib) bibliographies and bibliographical guides, and (ic) auxiliary and reference works. Finding aids to source content and location are divided into (iia) guides, (iib) select lists of documents, and (iic) catalogues and descriptive lists. Presentation and analysis of the sources fall conveniently into (iiia) calendars, and (iiib) select edited documents, transcripts, translations, and facsimiles, and (iiic) detailed commentaries. There are 313 numbered entries in (iv), the bibliography.

Of the introductory works, bibliographies of bibliographies (ia) are represented by but two items, Besterman and Eager (the first for general material, the second for Irish); they are numbered 15 and 92 respectively in the bibliography (iv) appended below.

Bibliographies and bibliographical guides (ib) are represented by nineteen items (5, 6, 7, 16, 97, 98, 104, 136, 151, 155, 162, 164, 167, 203, 214, 232, 256, 295, and 312). Of the bibliographical guides, four are specialized Irish (97, 164, 214 and 232) and two are British (104 and 167). Two of the thirteen bibliographies are general (5 and 6). Specialized bibliographies are represented by six Irish entries (7, 98, 151, 155, 295, 312) and five more general, British and European, ones (16, 136, 162, 203, and 256). Additional reference to such material previously put forward by the author can be located in 97 and 98 and also in his contributions to 6, 162 and 256. It is expected that a bibliographical study for this period will be published at an early date as part of the Royal Irish Academy's New History of Ireland (cf. no. 7 below).

With regard to (ic), while it is not always possible to differentiate, sixteen auxiliary aids and eighteen reference works are listed. The classification adopted here would accord to the former, four entries for authorship and historiography (71, 111, 114, 144), and six for structure and maps (99, 122, 183, 184, 189, 219) and six for government

(103, 146, 237, 238, 243, 263). With regard to reference works, chronology is represented by one entry (127), biography by five (10, 60, 137, 297, 298), law and institutions by five (17, 126, 139, 140, 211), military history by two (74, 220), finance by two (87, 228), while diplomatic history has three entries (88, 128, 194). It may be added that works like the *Encyclopaedia Britannica* and the *New Catholic Encyclopaedia*, to which the present author has contributed, and also the *Dictionary of National Biography* with addenda and corrigenda published in the *Bulletin of the Institute of Historical Research* of the University of London, sometimes repay consultation.

The presence of few entries among finding aids to source content and location (ii) is a reminder that sixteenth-century Irish history is still imperfectly served. Among guides (iia), four works are singled out, of which the first two (66, 116) are concerned to direct attention to the Roman material, the third (120) to the English, and the fourth (132) presents under dates, persons, places, subjects, the manuscript material for the history of Irish civilization located by the National Library of Ireland.

Again, select lists of documents (iib) are few and are here represented only by the *Account of the Facsimiles of the National Manuscripts* (117) (i) and the *Lists and Indexes* of the Public Record Office, London, (233).

Catalogues and descriptive lists (iic) are here confined to two, the *Catalogue of Irish Manuscripts*, published by the British Museum (29), and the brief study of the Carew MSS by M. R. James (153). There are other possible entries to be located mainly through the NLI *MS Sources* (132) cited above, which with its supplement and the multi-volume work of the same editor dealing with periodical literature was published in 1966 and 1970. These works have to a great extent superseded other catalogues and descriptive lists.

The first category in the Presentation of Source Material (iiia) is concerned with *Calendars* providing abstracts of documents in the chronological sequence of the calendar year. Fourteen entries in the bibliography are numbered respectively 37–44, 57, 89, 168, 201, 271, 278. On the whole, these may be regarded as providing an adequate impression of surviving archival collections, though the volumes first published require the most cautious approach.

The seventy-eight entries in the second category (iiib) are concerned with documentation usually presented with a minimum of attention to their archival provenance. For the convenience of the student, they are tentatively subdivided into select edited documents (iiib 1), transcripts (iiib 2), translations (iiib 3), and facsimiles (iiib 4). Among select edited documents, a distinction is here made between treatises (iiib 1a), of which seventeen are noted, and non-treatises (iiib 1b) which extend to thirty-eight entries. Of the treatises, three are Gaelic (215, 216, 225), five others are by English commentators (45, 47, 48, 83, 200), five are by English chroniclers (46, 109, 179, 229, 246), two are by an Irish Catholic in exile (226, 227), and two by Irish-based supporters of the English establishment who were probably Protestants (250, 251).

The term 'non-treatise' is here employed to cover three types of select documents concerned respectively with persons, subjects, and events. The nineteen collections formed around persons are nos. 19, 36, 61, 62, 100, 110, 129, 130, 169, 171, 178, 187, 234, 262, 269, 270, 279, 287, 313. The eleven collections based on subjects are nos. 25, 26, 70, 80, 84, 105, 195, 212, 213, 235, 286. Editions concerned with eight particular events, in what are here regarded as single or closely associated documents, are nos. 78, 79, 115, 135, 172, 186, 261, 305.

Of those twenty-one here classed as transcripts, five are from Gaelic Scriptoria (1, 2–4, 28), six are from English commentators (8, 275, 276, 293, 299, 310), six may be described as of official origin (64, 141, 280, 281, 285, 291), three are by Irish Roman Catholic commentators (173, 265, 266), and one is that of an Anglo-Irish Protestant (292). Their classification here as transcripts in the case of those of them which have been edited may direct attention to their palaeographical significance.

Only one item is noted for each of the remaining categories, translations, (82) and facsimiles (117). In the case of the former, the existence of an English draft from which the law reporter's 'law French' was derived must continue to concern the critical student. As for the latter, it is to be hoped that reprographical facilities will lead to substantial increases in the future. It is here that early substantial developments could bring about significant increases in the depth of our understanding of the sixteenth century.

The final section concerned with source presentation (iiic) is allocated to commentaries. By including 160 items, rather more than half of the total number of entries (313) in the bibliography (iv), the present author has attempted to ensure that sufficient allowance would be made for the progression with which a professional approach has developed. Nearly 60 per cent of these items are primarily commentaries on Irish history, though less than half of these are exclusively concerned with the sixteenth century. The presence of nearly seventy European, mainly British, studies may help to emphasize our close historical associations.

The fact that about 70 per cent of all these commentaries are the work of persons accustomed to the historical discipline represents a notable advance in the last half-century, even allowing for the fact that the present author in making this estimate was careful to include among the professionals those persons whose formal training commenced with their being involved in historical operations as their normal full-time activity. To exclude from the category of professional, for lack of formal training, the pioneers like Bagwell (9) and MacNeill (188) would be a little unreal. In this way a mere handful of non-professional works remains (e.g., 81, 197, 217, 223, 309), some of which might well merit more consideration than some slighter productions technically entitled to be regarded as professional. The author is only too conscious that his selection may seem arbitrary. He would feel more justified if it was certain that no seminal work omitted had failed to be recorded in his previous publications.

It would also be more satisfactory if such a large proportion of sixteenth-century publications were not the work of persons who first entered this field over a generation ago (such as the authors of nos. 31, 54, 69, 90, 107, 121, 138, 174, 182, 198, 236). Among the few specialized historians whose more recent advent must be welcomed (e.g., the authors of nos. 23, 49, 56, 67, 125, 156, 222, 255, 272, 288), 304 it is to be hoped that most of them will not be content with only one appearance in future lists.

Sixteenth-century sources could still prove adequate to monopolize the research-time of more than a score of gifted scholars.

The select list of printed works appended to the bibliography (iv) is presented, usually, in the alphabetical sequence of the authors. Where this has not been possible, the titles of the works or of the organizations sponsoring their appearance have been followed. Publication, as this term has been employed in relation to printed works, assumes a less exclusive significance in bibliographies with the multiplication of reprographical methods in recent times. So far as Ireland is concerned, the case for including the 'copy' has been established dramatically with the emergence of the *Manuscript Sources of Irish Civilisation*, edited by Dr R. J. Hayes.

At the same time, the historian's concern with the establishment of the facts must, if anything, become more demanding. The Hayes work, while providing reference to the provenance of his sources, is not systematically involved in the historian's tasks. On the latter there still devolves the duty of making that sustained analysis of his documentation necessary to enable him to ascertain the circumstances in which it originated and, if possible, to ascertain the archival arrangements through which the papers were processed and preserved. It must always remain a main preoccupation for historians to find out the reasons for the construction of the documents. If these can be traced to their archival beginnings, the historian will be in the best position to appraise the static as well as the dynamic society in which the sources were written down.

As the internal sources for much of sixteenth-century Ireland no longer exist, it becomes important to distinguish between the various external organizations where the archives were originally assembled for specific purposes. In this connection the State Papers relating to Ireland for the sixteenth century must be used with caution as the material only came into official custody in the reign of James I. When the *Calendars* were edited in the mid-nineteenth century the distinctions between the archives of the State Paper Office, of the Exchequer, of the Chancery, and of other departments of government were not of such concern as they have become in the present century.

BIBLIOGRAPHY

1. *The Annals of Connacht (Annála Connacht)* (A.D. 1224–1544), ed. A. M. Freeman (Dublin, 1944).
2. *Annals of Loch Cé* (1014–1590), ed. W. M. Hennessy, 2 vols. (Dublin, 1871). Reprinted, 2 vols. (Dublin, 1940).
3. *Annals of the Kingdom of Ireland (Annála Ríoghachta Éireann) by the Four Masters . . . . to 1616*, ed. J. O'Donovan, 7 vols. (Dublin, 1848–51).
4. *Annals of Ulster* (431–1541), ed. W. M. Hennessy and B. MacCarthy, 4 vols. (Dublin, 1887–1901).
5. *Annual Bulletin of Historical Literature* (London, 1911–).
6. *International Bibliography of Historical Sciences* (Paris, 1926–).
7. P. W. A. Asplin, *Medieval Ireland, c.1170–1495, a bibliography of secondary works* (RIA, Dublin, 1971).
8. *The Works of Francis Bacon*, ed. J. Spedding, R. C. Ellis, D. D. Heath, 14 vols. (1857–74).
9. R. Bagwell, *Ireland under the Tudors*, 3 vols. (1885–90; repr. 1962).
10. F. E. Ball, *The Judges in Ireland 1221–1921*, 2 vols. (New York, 1927).
11. J. C. Beckett, *A Short History of Ireland* (rev. ed., 1971).
12. ————, *The Making of Modern Ireland* (1966).
13. B. W. Beckingsale, *Burghley, Tudor Statesman* (1967).
14. *Two Biographies of William Bedell*, ed. E. S. Shuckburgh (1902).
15. T. Besterman, *A World Bibliography of Bibliographies*, 5 vols. (4th ed., Geneva, 1965–66).
16. *Bibliographie de la réforme, 1451–1648, ouvrages parus de 1941 à 1955*, 2me fasc.: *Irlande*, ed. A. Gwynn (Leiden, 1960).
17. D. A. Binchy, 'The Passing of the old order', in *Proc. International Congress of Celtic Studies, Dublin 1959*, ed. B. Ó Cuív (1962).
18. S. T. Bindoff, *Tudor England* (repr. 1969).
19. *Memoirs of the Reign of Queen Elizabeth*, ed. T. Birch, 2 vols. (1754).
20. J. B. Black, *The Reign of Elizabeth* (1936; 2nd ed., 1959).
21. John Bossy, 'The Character of Elizabethan Catholicism', *Past and Present* 21 (1962).
22. ————, 'The Counter-Reformation and the people of Catholic Ireland', *Historical Studies* VIII (1972), 155–69.

23. B. Bradshaw, *The Dissolution of the Religious Orders in Ireland under Henry VIII* (Cambridge, 1974).

24. ———, 'George Browne, the first Reformation archbishop', *Jour. Eccles.Hist.* XXI, 301–26.

25. W. M. Brady, *The Episcopal Succession in England, Scotland and Ireland A.D. 1400–1875* (new ed., A. F. Allison, 1971).

26. ———, *State Papers concerning the Irish Church* (1868).

27. F. Braudel, *La Méditerranée et le monde méditerranéen* (Paris, 1966; Eng. tr., 1973).

28. P. Breathnach, 'Marbhna Aodha Ruaidh Ui Dhomhnaill', *Éigse* XV, 31–50.

29. British Museum, *Catalogue of Irish MSS*, 3 vols. (1926–53).

30. E. St. J. Brooks, *Sir Christopher Hatton* (1946).

31. D. Bryan, *Gerald Fitzgerald, the Great Earl of Kildare (1456–1513)*, Dublin (1933).

32. H. Butterfield, *The Englishman and His History* (1944).

33. F. J. Bryne, *Irish Kings and High-Kings* (1973).

34. ———, 'Senchas : the nature of Gaelic historical tradition', *Historical Studies* IX (1974).

35. ———, *The Ui Neill and the High Kingship* (Dublin, 1970).

36. *Cabala sive scrinia sacra*, 2 parts (1691).

37. *Calendar of the Carew MSS*, ed. J. S. Brewer and W. Bullen, 6 vols., Rolls Series (1867–73).

38. *Calendar of Ormond Deeds*, ed. E. Curtis, 6 vols. (IMC, 1932–43).

39. *Calendar of State Papers, Domestic*, 8 vols. (1856–72).

40. *Calendar of State Papers, Foreign*, 25 vols. (1863–1950).

41. *Calendar of State Papers, Ireland*, 11 vols. (1860–1912).

42. *Calendar of State Papers, Rome*, 2 vols. (1916–26).

43. *Calendar of State Papers, Scotland*, 13 vols. (1898–1952).

44. *Calendar of State Papers, Spanish*, 4 vols. (1892–99).

45. *The Irish Historie composed and written by Giraldus Cambrensis and translated into English by Iohn Hooker* in Holinshed's *Chronicles of England, Scotland and Ireland*, VI (1808).

46. William Camden, *Britannia, sive florentissimorum regnorum Angliae, Scotiae, Hiberniae chorographica descriptio* (1586; tr. R. Gough, 3 vols., 1789).

47. Edmund Campion, *The Two Bokes of the Histories of Ireland*, ed. A. F. Vossen (Assen, 1963).

48. ———, *A History of Ireland* [1571], ed. James Ware in *Ancient Irish Histories*, 2 vols. (Dublin, 1809; repr. New York, 1940).

49. Nicholas Canny, 'Changing views on Gaelic Ireland', *Topic* 24,

19–28.

50. ———, 'The flight of the earls', *IHS* XVII (1971).

51. ———, 'Hugh O'Neill, earl of Tyrone, and the changing face of Gaelic Ulster', *Studia Hib.* X (1970), 7–35.

52. ———, 'The ideology of English colonisation from England to America', *William and Mary Quarterly* ser. 3, XXX (1973).

53. ———, 'The Treaty of Mellifont and the re-organisation of Ulster', *Irish Sword* IX, 249–62.

54. James Carney, 'Society and the Bardic Poet', *Studies* LXII, 233–50.

55. Thomas Carve de Mobernon, *Lyra seu anacephalaeosis Hibernica, in qua de exordio seu origine, nomine, moribus, ritibusque gentis Hibernicae succincte tractatur; cui quoque accessere annales ejusdem Hiberniae . . . ab anno 1148 usque ad annum 1650* (Vienna, 1651; 2nd ed. with many alterations, Sulzbach, 1666).

56. Jerrold Casway, 'Henry O'Neill and the formation of the Irish regiment in the Netherlands, 1605', *IHS* XVIII (1973).

57. *Cecil MSS*, 14 vols. HMC, 1883–1923.

58. E. P. Cheyney, *History of England from the Armada to the Death of Elizabeth*, 2 vols. (New York, 1914–26).

59. S. B. Chrimes, *Henry VII* (1972).

60. John Colgan, *Acta Sanctorum Hiberniae* (1645; IMC, 1948), introd. B. Jennings.

61. *Collection of State Papers relating to Burghley*, ed. S. Haynes and W. Murdin, 2 vols. (1740–59).

62. J. P. Collier ed., *Egerton Papers* (Camden Society, 1840).

63. P. Collinson, *The Elizabethan Puritan Movement* (1967).

64. *The Compossicion Booke of Conought*, ed. A. M. Freeman (Dublin, 1936).

65. Agnes Conway, *Henry VII's Relations with Ireland and Scotland* (Cambridge, 1932).

66. D. Conway, 'Guide to documents of Irish and British interest in Fondo Borghese', *Arch.Hib.* XXIII (1960), 1–147.

67. Art Cosgrove, 'The Gaelic Resurgence and the Geraldine Supremacy', in T. W. Moody and F. X. Martin edd., *The Course of Irish History* (Cork, 1967).

68. Sir Richard Cox, *Hibernia Anglicana*, 2 vols. (1689).

69. D. F. Cregan, 'Irish recusant lawyers in politics in the reign of James I', *Irish Jurist* V (1970), 306–20.

70. ———, 'Irish Catholic admissions to the English Inns of Court 1558–1625', *Irish Jurist* V, 94–114.

71. A. Cronin, 'The sources of Keating's Foras Feasa ar Éirinn', *Éigse* IV, 235–79.

72. Claire Cross, *The Puritan Earl: the Life of Henry Hastings 3rd Earl of Huntingdon* (1967).

73. ————, *The Royal Supremacy in the Elizabethan Church* (1969).

74. C. G. Cruikshank, *Elizabeth's Army* (2nd ed., 1966).

75. L. M. Cullen, *Life in Ireland* (1968).

76. E. Curtis, *A History of Ireland* (6th ed., 1950; reprint 1964).

77. ————, *A History of Medieval Ireland* (rev. ed., 1968).

78. ————, 'Rental of the manor of Lisronagh, 1333, and notes on "betagh" tenure in medieval Ireland', *R.I.A. Proc.* XLIII (1935–37).

79. ————, *Richard II in Ireland, 1394–95, and Submissions of the Irish Chiefs* (Oxford, 1927).

80. E. Curtis and R. B. McDowell, *Irish Historical Documents 1172–1922* (1943; 2nd ed., 1968).

81. Sir John Davies, *A Discovery of the true causes why Ireland was never . . . brought under obedience of the crowne of England, untill the beginning of his majesties happie raigne* (1613).

82. ————, *Le primer report des cases et matters en ley resolues et adiuges en les courts de roy en Ireland* (1615; Edinburgh, 1907).

83. J. Derricke, *The Image of Irelande* (1581; Edinburgh, 1883).

84. *Desiderata Curiosa*, ed. F. Peck, 2 vols. (1732–35).

85. M. Dewar, *Sir Thomas Smith* (1964).

86. A. G. Dickens, *The English Reformation* (1970).

87. F. C. Dietz, *English Public Finance 1558–1641*, 2 vols. (1921, 1932; repr. 1964).

88. Dudley Digges, *The Compleat Ambassador* (1655).

89. R. Dunlop, *Ireland under the Commonwealth*, 2 vols. (Manchester, 1913).

90. ————, 'The plantation of Leix and Offaly', *EHR* VI (1891), 61–96.

91. ————, 'Sixteenth century schemes for the plantation of Ulster', *Scot.Hist.Rev.* XXII (1924), 51–60, 115–26, 199–212.

92. A. R. Eager, *A Guide to Irish Bibliographical Material* (1964).

93. R. D. Edwards, 'The kings of England and papal provisions in fifteenth century Ireland', *Medieval Studies presented to Aubrey Gwynn S. J.* (Dublin, 1961).

94. ————, 'The Irish Reformation Parliament of Henry VIII 1536–37', *Historical Studies* VI (1968), 59–84. Cites W. Shaw Mason, *Collation of the Irish Statutes*, TCD Add. MSS W8.

95.   R. D. Edwards, *A New History of Ireland* (Dublin, 1972).

96.   ———, 'Venerable John Travers and the rebellion of Silken Thomas', *Studies* XXIII (1934).

97.   R. D. Edwards and D. B. Quinn, 'Sixteenth century Ireland', in *Irish Historiography 1936–70*, ed. T. W. Moody (Irish Comm. Hist. Sci., 1971), 23–42.

98.   R. D. Edwards, *Church and State in Tudor Ireland* (Dublin, 1935; repr. 1971).

99.   Ruth Dudley Edwards, *An Atlas of Irish History* (1973).

100. H. Ellis, *Original Letters*, 11 vols. in 3 series (1824–46).

101. *Elizabethan Government and Society* ed. S. T. Bindoff, J. Hurstfield, and C. H. Williams (1961).

102. G. R. Elton, *England under the Tudors* (new ed., 1969).

103. ———, *England 1200–1640* (Sources of History series; 1969).

104. ———, *Modern Historians on British History 1485–1945* (1970).

105. ———, *The Tudor Constitution* (Cambridge, 1961).

106. C. L. Falkiner, *Essays relating to Ireland* (Dublin, 1909).

107. Cyril Falls, *Elizabeth's Irish Wars* (1950).

108. ———, *Mountjoy, Elizabethan General* (1955).

109. William Farmer, *Chronicles of Ireland 1594–1613*, by C. L. Falkiner, *EHR* XXII (1907), 104–30, 527–52.

110. Fitzwilliam Papers in Carte Manuscripts (transcripts in PRO, PROI, PRONI).

111. Robin Flower, 'Histories and Annals. Manuscripts in the British Museum', *Anal.Hib.* II (1931), 310–29.

112. R. Frame, 'The Justiciar and the murder of the MacMurroughs in 1282', *IHS* XVIII (1972), 223–30.

113. J. A. Froude, *History of England from the Fall of Wolsey to the Defeat of the Spanish Armada*, 12 vols. (1856–70).

114. F. S. Fussner, *The Historical Revolution, 1580–1640* (1962).

115. 'Lord Chancellor Gerrard's Notes of his Report on Ireland', ed. Charles MacNeill, *Anal.Hib.* II (1931).

116. Cathaldus Giblin, 'Vatican Library, Barberini MSS : a guide to the material of Irish interest in microfilm in the National Library, Dublin', *Arch.Hib.* XVIII, 67–144.

117. J. T. Gilbert ed., *Facsimiles of the National MSS of Ireland, Account of* (I–IV, 1879–84).

118. Alice Stopford Green, *Irish Nationality* (1911).

119. J. R. Green, *A Short History of the English People* (1874).

120. *Guide to the Contents of the PRO*, 3 vols. (1963–69).

121. A. Gwynn, *The Medieval Province of Armagh* (Dundalk, 1946).

122. A. Gwynn and N. Hadcock, *Ireland: Medieval Religious Houses* (1970).

123. Stephen Gwynn, *The History of Ireland* (1923).

124. W. Haller, *Foxe's Book of Martyrs and the Elect Nation* (1963).

125. Helga Robinson-Hammerstein, 'Aspects of the continental education of Irish students in the reign of Elizabeth I', *Historical Studies* VIII (1972), 137–52.

126. G. J. Hand, *English Law in Ireland, 1290–1324* (Cambridge, 1967).

127. *Handbook of British Chronology* (rev. ed., Royal Hist. Soc., 1962).

128. E. H. Harbison, *Rival Ambassadors at the Court of Queen Mary* (Princeton, 1940).

129. Sir John Harington ed., *Nugae Antiquae*, 2 vols. (1779).

130. G. B. Harrison, *Letters of Queen Elizabeth I* (1968).

131. Mary T. Hayden, *A Short History of the Irish People* (1920).

132. R. J. Hayes, *Manuscript Sources for the History of Irish Civilization,* II vols. (Boston, Mass., 1966).

133. C. Hill, *The Economic Problems of the Church* (1956).

134. ———, *Society and Puritanism in Pre-revolutionary England* (1964).

135. G. Hill, *An Historical Account of the MacDonnells of Antrim* (Belfast, 1873).

136. HMC, *Guide to the Reports:* I (Topographical, 1914–74); II (Persons, 1935–60).

137. Edmund Ignatius Hogan, *Distinguished Irishmen of the Sixteenth Century*, 1st ser. (1894).

138. James Hogan, *Ireland in the European System* (1920).

139. ———, 'Law of Kingship', *R.I.A. Proc.* XI (1932).

140. ———, 'The tricha cét and related land measures', *R.I.A. Proc.* XXXVIII (1928–29).

141. James Hogan and N. MacN. O'Farrell, *The Walsingham Letter Book 1578–9* (IMC, 1959).

142. James Hogan, 'Shane O'Neill comes to the court of Queen Elizabeth', *Essays presented to Torna*, ed. S. Pender (Cork, 1947).

143. *Holinshed's Chronicles of England, Scotland and Ireland*, 6 vols. (1808).

144. Kathleen Hughes, *Early Christian Ireland; an introduction to the sources* (1972).

145. P. Hughes, *The Reformation in England*, 3 vols. (1951–54).

146. P. Hughes and J. F. Larkin edd., *Tudor Royal Proclamations*, 3

vols. (New Haven, 1964–69).

147. E. Hull, *History of Ireland*, 2 vols. (1926–31).

148. J. Hurstfield, *Elizabeth I and the Unity of England* (1960).

149. J. Hurstfield, 'The Succession struggle in late Elizabethan England', in *Elizabethan Government and Society* (1961).

150. J. Hurstfield and A. G. R. Smith edd., *Elizabethan People; State and Society* (1972).

151. IMC, *Catalogue of Publications, 1928–66* (Dublin, 1966).

152. J. Izon, *Sir Thomas Stucley* (1956).

153. M. R. James, 'The Carew MSS', *EHR* XLII (1927).

154. Paul Johnson, *Elizabeth : a Study in Power and Intellect* (1974).

155. E. M. Johnston, *Irish History, a Select Bibliography* (2nd rev. ed., Historical Assoc., 1972).

156. F. M. Jones, 'The Counter-Reformation', in P. J. Corish ed., *The History of Irish Catholicism,* III, pt III (Dublin, 1967).

157. ————, *Mountjoy : the Last Elizabethan Deputy* (Dublin, 1958).

158. W. K. Jordan, *The Development of Religious Toleration in England* (Cambridge, Mass., 1932).

159. W. K. Jordan, *Edward VI : the Young King* (1968).

160. ————, *Edward VI:: the Threshold of Power* (1970).

161. ————, *Philanthropy in England 1480–1660* (New York, 1959).

162. M. F. Keeler, *Bibliography of British History : Stuart period* (2nd rev. ed., 1970). (1st ed. by Godfrey Davies).

163. M. H. Keen, *England in the Later Middle Ages* (1973).

164. J. F. Kenney, *The Sources for the Early History of Ireland* (New York, 1929).

165. Robert Lacey, *Robert Earl of Essex: an Elizabethan Icarus* (1971).

166. Thomas Leland, *A History of Ireland from the Invasion of Henry II,* 3 vols. (2nd ed., Dublin, 1814).

167. M. Levine, *Tudor England 1485–1603*, Bibliographical Handbooks (Cambridge, 1968).

168. *Letters and Papers, foreign and domestic, of the reign of Henry VIII*, 23 vols. in 38 (1862–1932).

169. D. M. Loades, 'Papers of George Wyatt', Camden Society, 4th series, V (1968).

170. ————, *Two Tudor Conspiracies: Wyatt and Dudley, against Queen Mary* (Cambridge, 1965).

171. E. Lodge, *Illustrations of British History*, 3 vols. (1838).

172. Dudley Loftus, *Annals, 1180–1625.* Report by N. B. White, *Anal. Hib.* X (1941).

173. Peter Lombard, *De Regno Hiberniae, Sanctorum Insula Commentarius* (1632).

174. A. K. Longfield, *Anglo-Irish Trade in the Sixteenth Century* (1929).

175. J. F. Lydon, *The Lordship of Ireland in the Middle Ages* (Dublin, 1972).

176. T. B. Macaulay, *The History of England*, ed. C. H. Firth, 6 vols. (1913–15).

177. W. T. MacCaffrey, *The Shaping of the Elizabethan Regime* (1969).

178. Daniel MacCarthy, *The Life and Letters of Florence MacCarthy Reagh* (Dublin, 1867).

179. Millar Maclure, *The Paul's Cross sermons 1534–1632* (Toronto, 1958).

180. J. McConica, *English Humanists and Reformation Politics under Henry VIII and Edward VI* (1965).

181. G. A. Hayes-McCoy, *Irish Battles* (1969).

182. ———, *Scots Mercenary Forces in Ireland* (1937).

183. ———, *Ulster and Other Irish Maps* (IMC, 1964).

184. Eileen McCracken, 'The Woodlands of Ireland c.1600', *IHS* XI (1959), 271–96.

185. P. McGrath, *Papists and Puritans under Elizabeth I* (1967).

186. C. MacNeill and N. B. White edd., *Calendar of Archbishop Alen's Register* (RSAI, 1950).

187. C. MacNeill, 'Rawlinson MSS', *Anal.Hib.* I, II (1930–31).

188. E. MacNeill, *Early Irish Laws and Institutions* (Dublin, 1935).

189. N. MacNeill ed., *Map of Monastic Ireland* (1st ed., Dublin, 1959; 2nd ed., 1964).

190. J. P. Mahaffy, *An Epoch in Irish History* (1913).

191. F. X. Martin, 'The Irish Augustinian reform movement of the fifteenth century', *Medieval Studies presented to Aubrey Gwynn S.J.* (Dublin, 1961).

192. ———, 'The Observant movement in Ireland', *Proc.Ir.Cath. Hist.Comm.* (1960).

193. G. Mattingly, *The Defeat of the Spanish Armada* (1959).

194. ———, *Renaissance Diplomacy* (1955; 2nd ed., 1973).

195. C. Maxwell, *Irish History from Contemporary Sources* (1923).

196. C. S. Meyer, *Elizabeth I and the Religious settlement of 1559* (St Louis, 1960).

197. John Mitchel, *Life and Times of Aodh O'Neill . . . with some account of Con, Shane, and Tirlough* (1845; repr. New York, 1868).

198. T. W. Moody, 'The Irish parliament under Elizabeth and James I',

R.I.A. Proc. XLV (1939).

199. T. W. Moody, *The Londonderry Plantation 1609–41* (Belfast, 1939).

200. H. Morley ed., *Ireland under Elizabeth and James I* (1890).

201. J. Morrin ed., *Calendar of Patent and Close Rolls: Henry VIII– Elizabeth; 1–8 Charles I*, 2 vols. (1861–63).

202. Fynes Moryson, *An Itinerary . . . containing his ten yeeres travell through the twelve dominions of Germany, Bohmerland, Sweitzerland, Netherland, Denmarke, Poland, Italy, Turkey, France, England, Scotland and Ireland* (1617; repr. 4 vols., Glasgow, 1907–08).

203. National Register of Archives, *Bulletin* (1948–).

204. J. E. Neale, *Elizabeth I and her Parliaments*, 2 vols. (1949–57).

205. ———, *The Elizabethan House of Commons* (1949).

206. ———, *Essays in Elizabethan History* (1959).

207. ———, *Queen Elizabeth* (1934).

208. J. F. H. New, *Anglican and Puritan, 1558–1640* (Stanford, 1964).

209. *New Cambridge Modern History*, vols. I and II.

210. K. W. Nicholls, *Gaelic and Gaelicised Ireland in the Middle Ages* (Dublin, 1972).

211. ———, 'Rectory, vicarage and parish in the western Irish dioceses', *Journ. R.S.A.I.* CI (1971), 53–84.

212. ———, 'Some documents on Irish law and custom in the sixteenth century', *Anal.Hib.* XXVI (1970).

213. J. Nichols, *Progresses and Public Processions*, 3 vols. (1823).

214. F. O'Briain, 'The Expansion of Irish Christianity to 1200 : an historiographical survey', *IHS* III (1943), 241, IV (1944), 131.

215. T. Ó Cianáin, *The Flight of the Earls*, ed. Paul Walsh (Dublin, 1916); ed. P. de Barra and T. O'Fiaich (Dublin, 1972).

216. Lughaidh O'Clery, *Life of Hugh Roe O'Donnell*, ed. Paul Walsh, *Arch.Hib.* VII (1908–22); Irish Texts Society, XLII (1948).

217. G. B. O'Connor, *Elizabethan Ireland* (Dublin, 1906).

218. J. F. O'Doherty, 'The Anglo-Norman invasion, 1167–71', *IHS* I (1938–39), 154–7.

219. Eamon Ó'Doibhlin, 'O'Neill's own country and its families', *Seanchas Ardmhacha*, VI (1971).

220. S. Ó'Domhnaill, 'Warfare in sixteenth century Ireland', *IHS* V (1946), 29–54.

221. Patrick O'Farrell, *Ireland's English Question* (1971).

222. T. Ó Fiaich, 'The O'Neills of the Fews', *Seanchas Ardmhacha*, VII (1973).

223. Sean O'Faolain, *The Great O'Neill* (New ed., Dublin, 1970).

224. P. S. O'Hegarty, *The Indestructible Nation* (Dublin, 1918).

225. *The Bardic Poetry of Tadhg Dall O h-Uiginn*, ed. Eleanor Knott (Irish Texts Society, 1920).

226. Philip O'Sullivan Beare, *Ireland under Elizabeth*, tr. M. J. Byrne (Dublin, 1903).

227. Philip O'Sullivan Beare, *Zoilomastix*, selection ed. T. J. O'Donnell, (IMC, 1964).

228. R. B. Outhwaite, *Inflation in Tudor and Early Stuart England* (1969).

229. Sir James Perrott, *The Chronicle of Ireland 1584–1608*, ed. Herbert Wood (IMC, 1933).

230. Francis Plowden, *Historical Review of the State of Ireland, from the invasion of Henry II*, 2 vols. (1803).

231. A. F. Pollard, *The Political History of England, 1547–1603* (1910).

232. K. Povey, 'The Sources for a bibliography of Irish history', *IHS*, I (1938–39), 393–403.

233. PRO, *Lists and Indexes.* See HMSO Books, sectional list 24. *British National Archives* (1976).

234. D. B. Quinn, 'Additional Sidney State Papers, 1566–70', *Anal. Hib.* XXVI (1970), 91–102.

235. ————, 'Bills and statutes of Irish parliaments of Henry VII and Henry VIII', *Anal.Hib.* X (1941).

236. ————, *The Elizabethans and the Irish* (Ithaca, 1966).

237. ————, 'Government printing and the publication of Irish statutes in the sixteenth century', *R.I.A. Proc.* XLIX (1943).

238. ————, 'Guide to English financial records for Irish history, 1461–1558, with illustrative extracts, 1461–1509', *Anal.Hib.* X (1941), 39–40.

239. ————, 'Anglo-Irish Ulster in the early sixteenth century', Proc. Belfast Nat. Hist. and Phil. Soc. (1933–34), 56–78.

240. ————, 'Henry VIII and Ireland 1509–34', *IHS* XII (1960–61), 318–44.

241. ————, 'Henry Fitzroy, Duke of Richmond and his connexion with Ireland 1529–30', *Bull.Inst.Hist.Res.* XII (1935), 175–7.

242. ————, 'The Munster Plantation : problems and opportunities', *Cork Hist.Soc.Jn.* LXXI (1966).

243. ————, 'Parliaments and Great Councils in Ireland, 1461–1586', *IHS* III (1942), 60–77.

244. ————, 'The early interpretation of Poynings' Law, 1494–

1534', *IHS* II (1941), 241; III (1942), 106.

245. ————, *Raleigh and the British Empire* (1947; repr., 1970).

246. ————, *The Roanoke Voyages* (Hakluyt Society, 2 vols., 1955).

247. ————, 'Sir Thomas Smith and the beginnings of English colonial policy', *Amer.Phil.Soc.Proc.* LXXXIX, 543–60.

248. ————, 'Tudor Rule in Ireland 1485–1547', Summary of Univ. of London Ph.D. thesis (1934).

249. ————, *The Voyages and Colonizing Enterprises of Sir Humphrey Gilbert* (Hakluyt Society, 2 vols., 1940).

250. ————, 'Edward Walsh's "Conjectures" concerning the state of Ireland (1552)', *IHS* V (1947), 303–22.

251. ————, ' "A discourse of Ireland" c.1599', *R.I.A. Proc.* XLVII (1942), 151–6.

252. ————, 'Ireland in sixteenth century European expansion', *Historical Studies* I (1958).

253. F. Raab, *The English Face of Machiavelli* (1964).

254. P. H. Ramsey, *Tudor Economic Problems* (1963).

255. T. O. Ranger, 'Richard Boyle and the making of an Irish fortune 1588–1614', *IHS* X (1957), 257–97.

256. Conyers Read, *A Bibliography of British History : Tudor Period 1485–1603*, (2nd ed., 1959).

257. ————, *Lord Burghley and Queen Elizabeth* (1960; 2nd ed., 1965).

258. ————, *Mr. Secretary Cecil and Queen Elizabeth* (1955; 2nd ed., 1965).

259. ————, *Mr. Secretary Walsingham and the Policy of Queen Elizabeth*, 3 vols. (1925).

260. E. P. Read and Conyers Read edd., *John Clapham's Elizabeth of England* (Philadelphia, 1951).

261. *Registrum diocesis Dublinensis*, ed. N. B. White and J. A. Watt (IMC, 1958).

262. *Relations politiques des Pays-Bas et de l'Angleterre sous le règne de Philippe II*, ed. K. de Lettenhove, 11 vols. (Brussels, 1882–1900).

263. H. G. Richardson and G. O. Sayles, *The Administration of Ireland 1172–1377* (IMC, 1963).

264. ————, *The Irish Parliament in the Middle Ages* (Philadelphia, 1952).

265. G. B. Rinuccini, *Commentarius Rinuccinianus*, by R. B. O'Ferrall and R. D. O'Connell, ed. S. J. Kavanagh, 6 vols. (IMC, 1932–49).

266. David Rothe, *Analecta sacra nova et mira de rebus Catholicorum*

in Hibernia gestis (Pt I, Cologne, 1616; Pts I, II, Cologne, 1617; Pt III entitled *De Processu martyrali*, Cologne, 1619). Ed. P. F. Moran (Dublin, 1884).

267. A. L. Rowse, *The Elizabethan Renaissance*, 2 vols. (1971–72).

268. A. J. Otway-Ruthven, *A History of Medieval Ireland* (1968).

269. M. P. Sheehy, *Pontificia Hibernica : medieval papal chancery documents concerning Ireland 640–1261*, 2 vols. (Dublin, 1962–65).

270. E.P. Shirley ed., *Original Letters and Papers in illustration of the history of the church in Ireland during the reigns of Edward VI, Mary and Elizabeth* (1851).

271. *Sidney State Papers 1565–70*, ed. T. Ó. Laidhin (IMC, 1961).

272. J. J. Silke, *Kinsale : the Spanish Intervention in Ireland at the End of the Elizabethan Wars* (Liverpool, 1970).

273. A. G. R. Smith, *The Government of Elizabethan England* (1967).

274. ————, 'The Secretariates of the Cecils', *EHR* LXXXIII (1968).

275. Edmund Spenser, *A View of the State of Ireland in 1596*. Best edition by W. L. Renwick, *Complete Works of Spenser*, IV (1934).

276. Thomas Stafford, *Pacata Hibernia* (1633), ed. S. J. O'Grady, 2 vols. (1896).

277. Richard Stanihurst, *De rebus in Hibernia gestis*, libri quattuor (Antwerp, 1584).

278. *State Papers, Foreign series 1589–90*, ed. R. B. Wernham (1964).

279. *State Papers, Henry VIII*, 11 vols. (1830–52).

280. *Statute Rolls of the Parliament of Ireland, 12th and 13th to the 21st and 22nd years of the Reign of King Edward IV*, ed. J. F. Morrissey (Dublin, 1939).

281. *The Statues at large, passed in the parliaments held in Ireland : from the third year of Edward the second, A.D. 1310, to the fortieth year of George the third, A.D. 1800*, 20 vols. (1786–1801).

282. *Statutes 10 Henry VI to 14 Elizabeth established in Ireland* (1572).

283. L. Stone, *The Crisis of the Aristocracy 1558–1641* (1965).

284. ————, *Family and Fortune : Studies in Aristocratic Finance in the Sixteenth and Seventeenth Centuries* (1973).

285. J. Strype, *Annals of the Reformation*, 4 vols. (1820–40).

286. R. H. Tawney and E. Power edd., *Tudor Economic Documents* (1924).

287. Augustin Theiner, *Vetera monumenta Hibernorum et Scotorum historiam illustrantia quae ex Vaticani, Neapolis ac Florentiae*

deprompsit et ordine chronologio disposuit A. Theiner ab Honorio III usque ad Paulum III, 1216–1547 (Osnabruck, 1969).

288. V. Treadwell, 'The Irish parliament of 1569–71', *R.I.A. Proc.* LXV (1966).

289. W. R. Trimble, *The Catholic Laity in Elizabethan England* (Cambridge, Mass., 1964).

290. A. Tuck, 'Anglo-Irish relations, 1382–1393', *R.I.A. Proc.* LXIX (1970).

291. H. F. Twiss, *Statute Rolls of the Parliament of Ireland. 1st to the 12th years of the Reign of King Edward IV* (Dublin, 1914).

292. *The Whole Works of J. Usher*, ed. C. R. Elrington and J. M. Todd, 17 vols. (Dublin, 1847–64).

293. A. F. Vossen ed., *The Two Bokes of the Histories of Ireland* by Edmund Campion (Assen, 1963).

294. T. Wall, 'Bards and Bruodins', in *Father Luke Wadding* (Dublin, 1957).

295. M. O'N. Walsh, 'Check list of Irish books printed abroad 1470–1700', *Irish Book*, II, 1–36.

296. P. Walsh, 'Historical criticism of the life of Hugh Roe O'Donnell', *IHS* I (1938–39), 229.

297. Paul Walsh, *Irish Men of Learning*, ed. C. Ó Lochlainn (Dublin, 1947).

298. ———, *Irish Chiefs and Leaders*, ed. C. Ó Lochlainn (Dublin, 1960).

299. James Ware, *The Historie of Ireland, collected by . . . M. Hanmer, E. Campion, and E. Spenser* (1633). 2 vols. (*Ancient Irish Histories*; 1809).

300. Robert Ware, *Historical Collections of the Church in Ireland . . . set forth in the life and death of Geo. Browne* (1681).

301. W. L. Warren, 'The Interpretation of twelfth century Irish history', *Historical Studies* VII (1969).

302. R. B. Wernham, 'Elizabethan War Aims', in *Elizabethan Government and Society* (1961).

303. ———, *Before the Armada : the Growth of English Foreign Policy 1485–1588* (1966).

304. D. G. White, 'The reign of Edward VI in Ireland', *IHS* XIV (1965), 197–211.

305. N. B. White, *The Extent of Irish Monastic Possessions, 1540–41* (Dublin, 1943).

306. Neville Williams, *Elizabeth, Queen of England* (1967).

307. P. H. Williams, *The Council in the Marches of Wales under*

Elizabeth I (Cardiff, 1958).
308. C. Wilson, *Queen Elizabeth and the revolt in the Netherlands* (1970).
309. P. Wilson, *The Beginnings of Modern Ireland* (Dublin, 1912).
310. T. Wilson, *The State of England, Anno Domini 1600*, ed. F. J. Fisher (Camden Miscellany, 1936).
311. T. Wright, *Queen Elizabeth and her times*, 2 vols. (1838).
312. 'Writings in Irish history', annually in *Irish Historical Studies* (1938–).
313. P. Yorke ed., *Miscellaneous State Papers* (Hardwicke), 2 vols. (1778).